# Lisa M. Orban

*Okay, Picture this...*
## BOOK ONE

# It'll Feel Better when it Quits Hurting

Copyright © 2015 by Lisa M. Orban

Second Edition published March 2019

Published by Indies United Publishing House, LLC
All rights reserved worldwide. No part of this publication may be replicated, redistributed, or given away in any form without the prior written consent of the author/publisher or the terms relayed to you herein.

First Print Edition November 2015

Interior illustrations by Alexander Mann Copyright © 2015
All rights reserved worldwide. No artwork in this book may be copied, reproduced or redistributed in any form without prior written consent of the illustrator.

This book contains an excerpt from Wine Comes in Six-Packs by Lisa M. Orban, the second book in the Okay, Picture this... series.

ISBN-13: 978-1-64456-028-0

*In other words, be nice to the book and to the people who spent so much time, energy, and sanity in its creation.* ☺

www.indiesunited.net

The sale of this book without a cover is unauthorized.
If you purchased this book without a cover, the poor author who slaved over a hot computer to bring you this fine book did not receive any compensation for all of her hard work and dedication. And just so you know, every authorized book sale results in a happy dance by the author. So please, be kind, and don't deprive the author of her happy dance just to save a few pennies.

**Sorry Mom**

## ACKNOWLEDGMENTS

A special thanks to Alexander Mann who is responsible for all of the artwork contained within this book.

Many thanks to Charles Wm. (Bill) Anderson who believed in my words enough to volunteer his time to do the final editing of my book.

To Squirrel Boy a.k.a. Cory Grigsby, without his ADHD style of attention to detail while reading endless rough drafts, and his ability to make me laugh, even when I wanted to cry, this book would not have been possible.

# Fall into the LIFE of author LISA ORBAN

## and her highly acclaimed book series
## OKAY, PICTURE THIS...

IT'LL FEEL BETTER WHEN IT QUITS HURTING
WINE COMES IN SIX-PACKS

**COOKBOOK**
I'D RATHER STARVE THAN COOK!
A cookbook for people who hate to cook

**VISUAL VERTIGO:**
**OPTICAL ILLUSION COLORING BOOKS**
VOLUME ONE
VOLUME TWO
VOLUME THREE
VOLUME FOUR

**POLITICAL SATIRE**
IF I WERE DICTATOR
A tongue-in-cheek guide to saving our democracy

# Handy Guide to Finding the Stories

*Foreword by Charles Wm. (Bill) Anderson* — 11

*Dear Reader* — 13

**Prologue**
**And then it got bad...** — **17**

    I want to be the Madame of a House of Ill-Repute — 19

    Twiddling Thumbs & Peanut Butter Cookies — 21

    Earning Sainthood — 24

**Chapter One**
**I'm all the remains of my bizarre childhood** — **27**

    Sister for Sale — 28

    Illustration by Alexander Mann — 31

    Song to Soothe the Savage Beast — 32

    I could read the Mayo on the wall — 34

**Chapter Two**
**The Descent** — **37**

    A new daddy for Lisa — 38

    We don't clean, we move — 41

    Marcus O'Realious — 43

    How to get an Atari — 50

    Your Mother sent me to you — 53

    Illustration by Alexander Mann — 58

    What a Riot — 59

    Ante Up — 63

**Chapter Three**
**The Rebellion** — **67**

    Freedom — 69

    Illustration by Alexander Mann — 74

    You can lead a horse to water... — 75

    I do believe it's time for you to go — 79

    A Wet Rat — 83

| | |
|---|---|
| I didn't have any plans anyway | 87 |
| Illustration by Alexander Mann | 92 |
| Vaseline in a Police Station | 93 |

## Interlude One: Stuck in the System — 105

## Chapter Four
## Life with Eula — 107

| | |
|---|---|
| A Life Resumed | 109 |
| An Extra Ticket | 114 |
| Lisa's a girl! | 121 |
| Meeting by Accident | 124 |
| Free Pizza | 128 |
| Illustration by Alexander Mann | 131 |
| A Living Canvas | 132 |
| Pick me! Pick me! | 137 |
| Another Sad Ending | 143 |

## Chapter Five
## And now, for what's behind family #3 — 145

| | |
|---|---|
| My Kingdom for a Story | 147 |
| Weekend at Laura's | 151 |

## Chapter Six
## The Final Home — 157

| | |
|---|---|
| Ghost in the House | 159 |
| The Left Side of the Menu | 164 |
| Never say Never | 170 |
| Stuck on a Bridge | 173 |
| Graduation | 180 |

## Chapter Seven
## The Great Escape — 185

| | |
|---|---|
| Two Kittens and a Toyota Truck | 193 |
| Looking for a Living | 199 |
| My Guardian Angel | 203 |

| | |
|---|---:|
| Sliding down a Mountain | 208 |
| Illustration by Alexander Mann | 211 |
| Drugs in the Oven | 212 |
| The Leaning Tent | 215 |
| The Boys are Back | 219 |

**Interlude Two: Here there be Monsters** — 223

**Chapter Eight**
**Moving On** — 225

| | |
|---|---:|
| The Married Life | 229 |
| Look! I have boobs now!!! | 235 |
| An Inconvenient Baby | 237 |
| Locking Myself In | 243 |
| A Shot in the Ass | 249 |
| Right Name, Wrong Number | 255 |
| Selling Death over the Phone | 258 |
| The Second is Coming | 261 |

**Chapter Nine**
**Until Death do We Part... Sorta** — 271

| | |
|---|---:|
| A Broken Vase | 272 |
| The Event Horizon | 279 |
| Ten Boxes | 282 |
| Illustration by Alexander Mann | 290 |
| An Infomercial Changed my Life | 291 |

**Epilogue** — 297

**You are Not Alone** — 301
**\*Author's Note about the Title** — 303
**Excerpt from Wine Comes in Six-Packs** — 305
**About the Author** — 321

# It'll Feel Better when it Quits Hurting

# Book One

Indies United Publishing House, LLC

## *Foreword by*
## *Charles Wm. (Bill) Anderson*

When I first learned of It'll Feel Better When It Quits Hurting, I thought, "No kidding. It always feels better after it quits hurting." Still, the title reminded me instantly of something my father always said.

So when the author contacted me seeking a review, I agreed to read this as a free borrow through my Kindle Unlimited account. Within 50 or so pages, though, I was so overtaken by the trials and travesties within this story, finding myself laughing at some of the author's statements and shenanigans, and in stunned disbelief at others enough to purchase her touching memoir. It is a hard book to put down and forget about.

The author's life is much that of a character in a Stephen King masterpiece. She is almost Carrie in the flesh. Yet, despite failed parenting and failures by most of those caring for her in her years as a foster child, and despite the snafus within her school years, Lisa Orban, the author, grew up and bettered herself. From the opening chapter regarding her grandparents, with the overarching message from her narrative of her grandfather that it instilled in her a certain innocence and love that, deep down, permitted her to survive the grief that was to come. The author shows us her perspective on what it is like to live on the 'wrong side of the tracks,' if I can put it in a common vernacular.

Her authentic voice rings true to her inner fears and a life as a foster child being raised, occasionally, by both folks with little concern for her welfare and rights as a human being, and, at least once, by a woman of sincere empathy who exercised real, true, love and understanding. I believe, with all my heart, based on observations I have regarding the foster care system we have, and based on the transition of our society from one set of biases and prejudices and moral shortcomings, to that besetting current society, that this is a must-read book for all stakeholders in the foster care and education fields. There is a bit in this memoir that, while it is hilarious in the reading, it speaks volumes in terms of the prejudice and inherent profiling (racial and otherwise) that pervades our education system.

I appreciated this memoir perhaps more than I can satisfactorily express. Suffice it to say, I am convinced it will go a long way towards improving understanding and love for one another, free of excess prejudice or morality encumbrances. My opinion, as stated above, though, has pertinence to the appreciation of a rollicking good roller coaster ride through life by someone who has dared to open herself up to ridicule in order that we can enjoy the trip with her, or share the joys, heartbreaks and fears with her. This is a must-read story that should be compulsory to all foster-care homes and the entire educational system. There is a wealth of education between the covers of It'll Feel Better When It Quits Hurting.

*-Freelance writer, Journalist, member of the Outdoor Writers Association of America and Top 500 Amazon Reviewer*

Dear Reader,

This book you are holding in your hands has been a labor of love, and sometimes insanity, started alone, but finished with the help of many others.

When I started this project in 2013 I had no idea what I was getting myself into. And so, completely naive to the task I was undertaking, computer open, I gathered my thoughts and began to write. Taking the book apart, again and again, dividing it up, and then massive rewrites after I completed my first round of word spillage. Printing up copy after copy as I X-ed out sometimes entire pages, trying to get the right feel for the story I was telling.

It was my intention to bring you the story of my life, not as someone looking back, but from my singular point of view, as it was happening. I tried very hard not to foreshadow upcoming events, nor did I want to interject the present into the past. I wanted you, dear reader, to experience my life as I did, unknowing of the future, learning as I went, growing and maturing in each story. I am not always the hero of my narrative, I did not always make sound judgment calls, and I have made some truly astounding mistakes. But life is like that for everyone, and it would not be an honest telling if I did not share the dark moments along with the light.

After two long years and many rewrites, and what was beginning to seem like forever lost in my own past, I had what I thought was a copy worth sharing. Gathering my courage (and postage stamps), I sent it off to friends and family, asking (begging) them to read, edit and make suggestions. At around the same time the book was sent off, I enlisted the help of a friend who designed the illustrations for the book, asking him please, please, pretty please, help me out. And he graciously agreed. Then, I sat back and waited (squirmed with impatience).

After months of input, I put together the first copy of the book and submitted it to Amazon. I was (and am) proud of what I had created. But, like many Indie books, no matter how hard my small group of dedicated helpers and I had tried, there were still many errors to be found in the pages of my book.

And that's when strangers who had read my book, stepped up and said, "I'll help." Each believing in what I'd written, they offered advice, editing and spelling corrections, and promotion/marketing pointers, each in their area of expertise. I cannot tell you how grateful I am to each and every one of them for all their help and encouragement to an unknown author, simply because they believed in my book as much as I did.

This is (I hope), the final re-edit of my work.

If there are any further editing errors, I am truly sorry. English is an unwieldy language, even for native speakers, only made worse by my dyslexia, and my fast & loose use of the language at the best of times. To paraphrase James Davis Nicoll, "*English doesn't borrow from other languages. English follows other languages down dark alleys, knocks them over, and rummages through their pockets for loose grammar.*" I hope in this incarnation, English is done having its way with me, and there won't be any more pilfering needed. But, if there are, please know I have put my heart, soul and every minute of spare time I had over the last several years into the creation of this book. It was not for lack of care that any mistakes remain in the book, and you will forgive me for them if there are any still lurking within these pages.

Before you begin this book, I'd like to share this with you as well. I almost stopped at my graduation. Those final chapters were taken out and put back in a dozen times before I finally decided I was ready to share those stories with the world. Many of them I had never confided to anyone, and now I was considering exposing them to the world. It left me with a painfully naked feeling even while writing them. But in the end, I knew they were stories worth telling. And so, after many agonizing weeks, I placed them back in the final copy, and there they stayed.

In the beginning, I wrote that I did not know if there was any wisdom nor inspiration in this telling, but with my choice to leave those final chapters in perhaps that is not entirely true, there may be a bit of both hidden within these pages. You'll have to judge for yourself if is true, and I leave it to you to decide.

But mostly, what this book is about is laughing at the absurdity that is life, feeling joy in the simple act of being, accepting even when life isn't perfect, it can be wonderful. It is simply, my life as I have lived it, and I hope along the way you will laugh with me, maybe roll your eyes, groan and shake your head, eager to turn the next page to see where the train wreck ends. And as you reach the end and close the book, you pause for just a moment and think, "Damn, that was a helluva ride!" And in that brief moment, you can imagine me standing before you, with a grin on my face, nodding in agreement.

Before I end this, I would like to thank every person who willingly read my first drafts. Alex for his wonderful illustrations. Cory for helping me laugh when I wanted to cry. To Best Kept Secret for allowing me to use their music in my promo videos. To Bill for his editing help, and also to Steve for his as well, and all their support along the way. To Amanda, my soul-sister I've never met, and all her help in getting the word out about my book. To my family, who at first reading, hated it, but later realized an honest account can't always be kind or flattering, and then decided to love it anyway. But most of all, I would like to thank you, dear Reader, for taking a chance on an Indie author. I know you have chosen to spend your hard-earned money, and precious time with me, and it is sincerely appreciated.

And now, without further ado....

It'll Feel Better when it Quits Hurting
I promise

## ARE YOU READY? HERE WE GO...

## I'm all that remains of my bizarre childhood

When I was in high school, I attended an Alanon meeting that had a guest speaker from outside the local group. Nothing unusual in and of itself, but he made an impression that has stayed with me to this day. He was a recovering alcoholic, and as he shared his story from its beginning, at the end of each little story he would add, "And then it got bad." He had a gift for making people laugh with him as he recounted all of his bad choices and the ever-increasing disasters in his life. As things escalated, seemingly unable to become any worse, he would add, "and then it got bad".

Looking back at my life, it could be summed up much the same way.

Often, at the end of each of my stories, I am sometimes almost compelled to add, "and then it got bad". I am not an alcoholic nor am I a drug addict. This isn't a story of redemption through religion or even a morality tale of bad choices. Many of the circumstances I have found myself in were beyond my control.

I was simply trying to cope the best I could while maintaining a smile.

This book is a bit darker than I initially intended, but I hope that while reading this I can make you smile, on occasion laugh out loud, and maybe even roll your eyes at the ridiculousness of the situations I have found myself in over the years, and near the end, as you finish each section you might, in the back of your head, hear the echo of, and then it got bad. And that's okay because it did get bad, but in the end, I survived to tell the tale and I do not regret any of it. This is my life, and I wouldn't change a single line.

For better or worse, this is the mostly true, fairly accurate, and almost completely factual account of my life. Some liberties have been taken to protect the somewhat innocent and a few small embellishments were made for the sake of a good story.

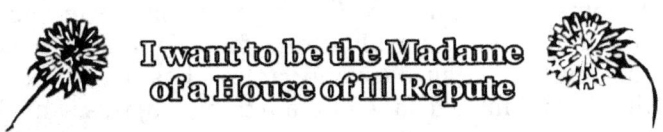

## I want to be the Madame of a House of Ill Repute

When I was twelve my English teacher gave us an assignment to write about what we wanted to be when we grew up, as I'm sure many of you were given at some point in your schooling. But of all the papers I wrote as a child, this is the one that stands out in my memory. I'm an adult now, and a mother of five, I no longer have the paper I wrote from that far away time but I do remember the title and for one perfect moment in my life, I knew exactly what I wanted to be.

I didn't actually know per se, what a Madame was, or what it meant to live that kind of life, but I did know it involved pretty dresses, expensive houses, and gentleman callers. Not that I knew what a gentleman caller was either, other than someone who brought flowers and money. Since most of my knowledge of what a Madame was coming from the endless Spaghetti Westerns my father watched on TV, it's easy to see how I may have gotten a somewhat skewed view of what it really meant.

It was the most glamorous career I could think of at the age of twelve when the world felt awkward and so did I. Boys were mean, we were no longer young enough for the playground, but not old enough to date, and we all lived in that horrible never-never land of not quite. To be a Madame was to be the pinnacle of adulthood with all the glamour, power, beauty, and grace that can only be sustained in the mind of a child. Why would anyone want to do anything else, if a career such as this existed? Now that I am older I can look back at that childish image and smile, but at one time this was what I wanted to be more than anything else.

I am an adult now, and I didn't grow up to be a Madame of a House of Ill Repute. In my life, I most often resemble the ringleader in a madhouse of anarchy. But sometimes, I wistfully remember the longing for flowers, gentleman callers, and enchantment I think all of us have had at one time or another. Whatever your childhood ideal of adult life may have been. My life is not glamorous, no high society people come to call, and any dinner party I have ever had has ended in the verbal equivalent of a food fight. But, looking back on my life I realize by and large it has been a helluva ride that I wouldn't exchange for anything. So, this is my life, for better or for worse. I hope you enjoy the ride as much as I have enjoyed the roller coaster.

 ## Twiddling thumbs & peanut butter cookies

When I was young, and an only child, I spent many summers and school vacations with my great-grandparents. They lived in, what was to me, a magical house full of things to distract, entertain, and amuse. There was an attic full of boxes, each filled with a treasure waiting for me to discover. Exotic hats, dresses by the dozens, old dolls and even a wood burning kit not fit for anyone who didn't have heavy leather gloves and a full face mask that I loved to play with. It had a screened in porch, covered in ivy and a backyard full of climbable trees and wild rhubarb to dig up. At night, I went to sleep to the sounds of trains in the distance and awoke each morning to chirping birds when I slept upstairs in what my grandparents called a sleeping porch. My Grandmother taught me to knit, play cards and the wonders of Lawrence Welk, and my Grandfather taught me how to drive my Grandma crazy.

By the time I arrived on the scene of my grandparent's life, my Grandfather was retired and mostly puttered around the house that was my Grandmother's domain and sometimes I would putter with him. We would poke around the basement for things to fix or rake the leaves in the backyard for me to jump into, but mostly we would sit side by side in my Grandfather's favorite chair and twiddle our thumbs.

For anyone who doesn't know what this is, I'll explain. Fold your hands together as if you were praying, fingers down and then rotate one thumb over the other in a circle, and nothing in this world could drive my Grandmother as crazy as twiddling our thumbs. Each time my Grandmother walked into the room and saw us doing it, she would immediately stop in her tracks, hands on hips, and with a tapping foot demand, "Arnold! Quit twiddling your thumbs!" and we would obligingly stop. But the minute she walked out of the room to continue her interrupted travels, he would calmly watch her retreating back, then smiling down at me, we would begin again. Sometimes, I think he did it just to drive her crazy, and he taught it to me so I could join the fun. If there had been an Olympic sport for synchronized thumb twiddling I do believe my Grandfather and I would have won gold medals for our performances.

My Grandfather indulged me in almost any activity a young child could dream of, we had tea parties where he would sit folded up in a chair, at a table made for midgets, and drink water from a cup while toasting me for being such a gracious hostess. He applauded whatever I played on the piano, and hung any number of drawings I gave him in his upstairs office, and occasionally, allowed me to lead him into trouble with my Grandmother.

On one such occasion, while Grandmother was out shopping, I announced I wanted to make peanut butter cookies. Now, you have to understand, I don't believe my Grandfather had ever made so much as toast without my Grandmother's blessing, but, all he asked was, "Do you know how?"

Well, of course, I did!

So my Grandfather, who hated all things sticky (he would get up at least once in every meal to wash his hands), agreed to help me. I decided the formal dining room was the perfect place for our experiment and brought in all the ingredients I believed you needed for cookies. I spread flour on the dining table, followed by peanut butter, a huge scoop of butter, and a generous coating of sugar over the whole thing and, plunging my hands into this sticky mess, said, "Help me mix it up, Grandpa!"

With an indescribable look of horror, my Grandfather put his hands into my concoction and tried to help. We smooched and smashed, kneaded and patted in an attempt to get what I considered the right consistency for cookie dough as it slowly worked its way up from fingertips to elbows, while he asked me over and over again, "Are you sure this is how you make cookies?" As our attempts to make the cookies spread up our arms and across the table my Grandmother walked in, stopping dead in her tracks in front of us, exclaimed, "Arnold! What are you doing???" Instantly turning, my Grandfather pointed at me and yelped, "She said we could make cookies!" As if somehow that would save him from my Grandmother's displeasure.

As my Grandmother continued to stare, with crossed

arms and tapping toes, my poor Grandfather slunk away to the bathroom to clean up, partly to wash the gooey, sticky mess from his arms, but mostly I believe, to avoid any further dispute with the reigning ruler of the house.

 ## Earning Sainthood

When I was about seven I learned from my great-aunt how to make scrambled eggs. With this new found knowledge, I decided one morning I wanted to treat my grandparents to breakfast in bed. I made eggs and toast, I sliced a grapefruit and gave each half and even made fresh squeezed orange juice. Since I had been helping my Grandmother make breakfast all summer, I knew how to do each of these things, except for one. How to make coffee.

They owned a silver percolating coffee pot that I had never been taught how to use. But my Grandfather always had coffee with his breakfast, no exceptions, every morning. As I tried to figure it out, a commercial I had recently seen came to mind for Folgers Instant Coffee, where all you have to do is add water to a scoop of coffee. Smiling with my own resourcefulness, I began making a cup of coffee. But with only one scoop it didn't look dark enough no matter how I stirred it, so I kept adding coffee to the cup until it had achieved what I considered to be the right color. I then took breakfast up to them on a tray filled with the eggs, toast, grapefruit, orange juice, and my Grandfather's coffee. I even added a small vase with flowers I picked earlier in the morning to make it all look nice.

As I presented all of this to my Grandparents, they both expressed how happy and pleased they were with all I had done for them. Serving them breakfast, my Grandmother commented she was surprised about the coffee, when had I learned to use the coffee pot? I, of course, told them of the problem and of my solution to it, and bless that man; he choked down every bit of his coffee with a smile on his face and with nothing but praise for what I had done. Although, he did refuse a second cup when it was offered.

If ever there was someone who met the criteria for sainthood, I do believe my Grandfather's ability to drink that cup of coffee and make me believe it was perfect, without a single grimace or sign of distress, should have qualified him instantly.

But, what I love my Grandfather for most of all is not what I knew then about his love for me, but what I only began to realize as I grew older. His endless patience, his grace under difficult circumstances, and his boundless love for me that he never failed to show, no matter how tired, sick or hurt.

And this is where we will leave my Grandparents. A few years later, my Grandfather became ill and eventually had to be put in a nursing home, and my Grandmother followed shortly thereafter. But I prefer for you to remember them like this, as I do, when Grandma ruled and Grandpa puttered, and they lived in a magical house full of treasures just waiting to be found. As with all roller coaster rides, there's always a staging area, it's a quiet place as you move slowly forward, but it's also full of excitement and hope for the ride ahead, and maybe with just a little fear of the unknown as well. Now that we've reached the head of the line, we'll wave goodbye to them as they smile and urge us onward, knowing while it may be scary at times, it's going to be a great ride.

**HANG ON TIGHT AND ENJOY THE RIDE.**

## I'm all that remains of my bizarre childhood

When I was very young, maybe three or four, I saw a movie about a small voodoo doll that came to life. With an equally small spear, the doll ran around a house, spending most of the movie hiding under furniture, where it would launch sneak attacks at the main character's feet. The heroine of this god-awful movie eventually tossed the small terror into the oven, baking it to death. As silly as it sounds, this horrible horror movie affected me until my late teens. For years I couldn't put my feet down on the floor after dark without fear or reach for anything under the bed without a flashlight.

Even now as an adult, I sometimes feel a remote twinge putting my feet down on the ground in the dark. I know rationally my fear comes from the leftovers of childhood imagination, there is no basis for it in reality, but it doesn't stop the small hesitation I still have. Somewhere deep inside my mind, a little voice is still convinced one of these days something scary is going to come out from wherever it's been hiding all these years and get me.

We're all afraid like that sometimes, of things big and small, real or imagined. Sitting paralyzed in the dark, with the fear of the unknown, of change, of the thousands of what-if's that inhibit us from taking our first step up off the safety and familiarity of the known, and putting our feet firmly on the ground. It's a leap of faith against the small voice that says, "I know you're probably right, but... what if you're wrong? What if the monster *is* real?"

 ## Sister for Sale

Shortly before my 6th birthday, I began to notice Mother was getting fat and the closer we got to my birthday the fatter she got. She began having troubles seeing her feet, waddled like a duck when she walked, and was often sick or tired during the day. I was told sometime around my birthday I was going to receive the greatest birthday present I could ever hope for, and as my mother got bigger, my excitement grew. Along with the changes to my mother, there came changes to the house as well. New furniture arrived and was set up in my old room because my parent had moved my bedroom to make room for the soon to be arriving present. The house smelled of new paint and cleaning supplies, and as all these things were going on around me I became more and more excited. They must be right, with all that was going on there had to be something wonderful waiting for me at the end of it.

A week before my birthday Mother disappeared, other family came to stay with me and excitement was everywhere around me. There were presents stacked in the corner, full of ribbons and pretty pastel colors, and in the room that had once been mine, began to overflow with all sorts of things both bright and mundane. I was informed by everyone my present was about to arrive! A few days later, my parents came home to the fanfare of family and I was presented to my present, a new baby sister. She was small, she was sleeping, and she was to be the greatest gift I would ever receive, and she was all of those things. For 24 hours.

The first day she was home, Mother sat rocking my sister in her arms as I stood by and watched the small, sleeping wonder. People came and went, and my parents beamed and talked about how quiet she was, what a good baby she was. I followed them upstairs that night as they put her to bed and stared down at her as she slept in her crib, and thought to myself, yes, this *was* a good gift. Not only did I have a new sister, but Mother no longer waddled as she walked and could see her toes again. I began to believe my life would go back to how it had been before, but with the added happiness of someone else to share it with.

The following day, the gift began to cry, and cry, and cry, and it wouldn't stop. She cried from dawn to dawn with only short breaks as she napped, but never long enough for anyone else to get any real sleep. We rocked her, sang to her, put her in cars and in the swing, we patted her back and rubbed her belly and tried everything but put a cork in her mouth. Which I thought would be a great idea, but it was not a well-received suggestion by my parents. My parents wore ruts in the carpet from walking her back and forth in a vain attempt to make her stop; trading her back and forth like some bizarre game of Hot Potato, so one of them could take a break from her never-ending wailing. I thought to myself, no, this would not do.

This was not right. This was my present and I no longer liked it. I wanted to take it back, right now, and get something else. But I was told this was not the kind of gift you could return or exchange, she was staying and there was nothing that could be done about it. As the days turned into weeks, and the crying continued, my parents' attention was focused solely on the new baby with no time for play. I began to think about how this could be fixed; there had to be a way.

One late summer day, when my sister was about a month old, she fell asleep in her pumpkin seat and my mother fell asleep immediately afterward. I stared at her for the longest time, and then slowly, quietly, not to disturb either her or Mother; I carried her out to my wagon in the front yard. If I could not exchange her and I could not return her, then I would sell her! I loaded her into my wagon and set off down the street to the corner, where I had to stop because I wasn't allowed to leave the block, and began hawking to oncoming cars, "Sister for Sale! Sister for Sale!" until a neighbor noticed me.

Out of the house and down to the corner she ran towards me and the sister. Stopping before me, she looked down at my sleeping sister and inquired what on earth I thought I was doing? "Selling her," I responded, looking longingly back at the passing traffic, hoping one of them would stop to take this problem away. Shaking her head, I was informed once again, I could not exchange her, nor return her and I definitely could **not** sell her.

I slowly followed the neighbor lady home, the sister in her arms, a small parade of three with my wagon trailing behind me. I came to the sad realization the sister was here, to stay, forever, and nothing could be done about it.

# IT'LL FEEL BETTER WHEN IT QUITS HURTING 31

 ## Song to Soothe the Savage Beast

Life with the sister was definitely different. No longer were there quiet moments to share, relaxing outings with my parents or unbroken sleep during the night. Music played and vacuums ran continually, loads of laundry were washed, partly because the sister leaked at both ends, but also so she could be sat on the dryer in another vain attempt to quiet her. The center of my parent's universe had shifted to circle around the baby. All activities were done to placate her, and nothing was ever done without first considering how it would affect her because there was no other consideration in the world but whether or not it would make her cry.

When Christmas came, we all loaded into my parent's car to spend the holidays with my mother's family out of town. When we arrived, the house was decorated for the season and everyone was waiting for us with happy smiles and welcoming embraces. There were cookies and cocoa, big meals taken in the formal dining room, cousins and aunts everywhere. There was laughter and large, pretty bows, and even the sister was, mostly, quiet. We sat by the Christmas tree with the snow blowing outside and a fire going in the evenings while I dozed on the floor by its warmth and listened to the calm normalcy of adult conversations around me as the sister slept in another room. This was peace, this was Christmas, and this was wonderful.

And all was good and right in the world until we climbed into the car to return home. It was cold, the radio was broken, and the sister began to cry. As the miles passed, the crying turned into screaming and the screaming became howling. As we rolled down the road, my mother's grip on the steering wheel became tighter, her face more drawn and her foot became heavier by the mile, while the sister cried on, oblivious to the rising tide of frustration growing around her.

Mother begged me to do something, do anything, to make her stop, by the love of God, make it stop. I turned around in my seat and tried playing peek-a-boo; she just stared at me and continued to howl. I tried rubbing her belly and I tried to give her a pacifier, I tried "get the nose" with a toy and I tried "this little piggy", and still she continued with the never-ending wail that seemed to resonate up from the base of the spine until it ended in a spike in the center of your head. Out of desperation, I began to sing to her the only song I knew all the way through, *Jesus Loves Me*. The cry turned into a whimper, and so I sang it again and the whimper wound down to a sniffle and then to golden, blessed silence. Happy she stopped crying, I turned back around and sat down in my seat, when the silence was once again shattered by her crying.

Back up and back around I turned and sang to her again, and again she quieted, but only for as long as I would continue to sing. Throughout the two hour ride back to our home I sang. I sang until my throat was raw, but sing on I did, continuing an endless cycle of *Jesus Loves Me* until we pulled up to the house.

By the end of the ride, I honestly don't know if my mother had been driven crazier by my sister's crying or the non-stop song loop, monotonously sung by a 6-year-old. But I do believe that may have been the longest car ride in the history of car rides, ever.

 ## I could read the Mayo on the wall

One fine day Mother took me shopping with her, just the two of us. We picked out groceries, and I helped her find items on the shopping list, and on the way home, we discussed what we were going to make for dinner. Walking in the door, we heard Father in the kitchen. While we were gone, he decided to be nice to my mother and make dinner for us, and the stove was busily bubbling with his efforts. I'm not sure if any of you are familiar with this type of food, but in the days before TV dinners or microwaves, there were "boil-a-bag" foods. Mostly things like mashed potatoes and some kind of meat, often with gravy, sealed in bags and then boiled to cook them.

As Father turned and grinned at us, I thought Mother was going to have a stroke as she stood there turning red, staring at the dinner Father had made. To this day, I'm not sure why Mother was so mad or why this upset her so, but take my word for it, she was livid.

My father's grin faltered as he stood there before the steaming, pot covered stove and announced, "I've made dinner for us." As if somehow Mother had not gotten the memo, and he was trying hard to deliver the good news.

For an awkward moment, we both stood in the doorway in silence, and then I was told to take my place at the table for dinner. We had a short, oblong table where Father sat at one end, Mother on the other, and I sat in the between the two of them. It was a very quiet, tense meal, where I ate in silence watching my parents glare at each other across the table. Until the moment, Father asked Mother to pass the mayo.

She stared at him for a few seconds, and then with calm deliberation picked up the glass mayo jar and launched it at him. That jar sailed across the table with a gentle tumble at the midway mark, straight to where my father's head had been the moment before he ducked. As the jar exploded behind my father, he popped back up and grabbed the first available item on the table and returned fire. And so began the Great Food Fight of 1976. Mashed potatoes, peas, and chipped beef flew with equal ease back and forth across the playing field of our kitchen table.

As the ammunition began to dwindle and the volleys became more sporadic, an uneasy truce settled over the kitchen as each of my parents stared at one another and the mess they had made. Even as young as I was, I needed no help reading the mayo on the wall to know that this was the beginning of the end of my parents' marriage. And nothing in this life would be the same again.

# HOW'S IT GOING? ENJOYING THE STORY SO FAR?

## The Descent

My parents' marriage limped along for a few years after that. Until one day, I was sat down by both of them and informed they were getting a divorce. Did I know what that meant? Taking turns, my parents told me they could no longer live together, for various adult reasons I wasn't old enough to understand yet, and they would be moving into separate places. Apparently, their imminent separation was much more of a surprise for them than it was for me, and they were very concerned I understood what was happening.

Oh, I got it all right. No more tense dinners or hissed comments, no more glaring stares or uneasy silence pervading the house, no more biting conversations or barely submerged hostility. Yeah, I got it, and "Thank God" was all I could think. It may have been, quite literally, the happiest day of my young life, where we could all quit pretending everything was great and we could all just get on with our lives.

The end of my mother's second marriage began the first long climb of my roller coaster. Where we were all strapped in, and like it or not, committed to the ride. Now begins the descent...

 ## A new Daddy for Lisa

Whenever my mother was between marriages, she developed a passion for packing boxes. No move was too far, and no apartment left unexplored during these times. As my mother relentlessly searched for the perfect place to live, she was also searching for the next perfect husband to make her life complete. New daddy #3 came along less than two years after old daddy #2 was left by the wayside.

The new daddy, who at this point was just the new boyfriend, came upon the scene with no fanfare. He was simply there, sitting on the couch one day when I came home from school. Introductions were made, and I was encouraged to like and be nice to, this new person and make him feel welcome.

Life went on close to normal for a while, with the only change of the new boyfriend being a part of the daily activities. He would sit on the couch and watch TV, tell my mother how things should be done, and on occasion disappear to unknown locations. Sometimes while out driving, we would park on a particular street and he would leave us to go somewhere that I couldn't see, then come back with a change of clothes or some other item and off we'd go again.

He loved sports. He'd been a professional baseball player a few years earlier and tried very hard to teach me the finer details of hitting a ball with a stick. I had no interest in sports of any kind, but I indulged him in his fervor for this game and played along whenever asked. I had, after all, been told to be nice to him, and while I thought it was a silly activity, my efforts seemed to make him happy.

Then one day came the announcement; the new boyfriend was going to become the new daddy. Oh, how wonderful it was going to be. I was going to get a whole new family, and we were all going to be one big happy family together.

Now that the new boyfriend was going to officially

become part of the family and be the new daddy, we were to meet his family for the first time. That mysterious place, his parent's house, that we had never been allowed to go before, was now open to us. In timid anticipation, I entered this new place, full of new people I didn't know. These new people were to become "family" and I was expected to be nice and pretend that I loved them. I was suddenly going to have new grandparents, aunts, and cousins, and I was expected to gracefully insert myself into their way of living without causing a fuss. Because, as my mother pointed out continuously, this was something wonderful and we should all be as happy as she was about it.

This new family was very different than my old family. There were rules for everything, from how you ate at the table to the correct way to brush your teeth in the bathroom. The rule was to never look up, always down into the sink so you didn't get the mirrors dirty. Their house was always spotless, and you didn't sit in the sitting room, you only passed through on your way to somewhere else and never stopped to look at anything. There were no comfortable couches or approved places to play. This was a quiet place where children were only barely tolerated.

Sports were prevalent in every conversation or activity. Everyone was expected to know about every team and all the details of every player's stats. Grandparents did not play or indulge, and all things were regulated for order.

And so began the quiet before the storm. Packing boxes were put away in exchange for a new house. Meals were served at a table and usually on time. Family gatherings were common, with the constant bray of a sportscaster droning in the background wherever we went. In the way I image happens in the lives of most people, the days started to blend together with little to distinguish one day from the next. Looking through a window at our lives, we would have appeared to be the live action version of a Norman Rockwell painting.

Not long after their wedding, another big announcement was made to the family. There would be yet another bundle a joy soon to arrive. Once again, I was told what a happy occasion this would be, how wonderful for all of us, we would now be a "real" family. As I was still coming to terms with the last bundle of joy, it was understandable that I had some reservations about yet another coming to live with us.

Space was made for the impending bundle. A new room created out of an old attic. Walls were put up, and the air filled with the scent of fresh pine and new paint. Furniture was added, final touches were made, and then we waited for the new arrival. The wait was not long, and on a cold spring morning, a new brother came to be. This one was different than the last. He was quiet and slept, mostly, through the night. I was delighted. This one could stay with my blessing.

I took much more interest in the new brother than I had in new sister. It was more like having a lively doll than a screaming shrew. On occasion, I brought down the wrath of my parents in my interest in playing with him. Apparently, dressing him in frilly dresses and putting his curly locks in pigtails was not an acceptable form of play.

For several years, we played our respective roles as a family. But, as time went on, the edges of our Rockwell painting began to fray. Small things at first, a tense meal, low sharp words, less time spent with the extended family and more time left alone in the house. The dissolution of this marriage was much quieter than the last. No food fights at dinner. No shouting matches in the bedroom wayfaring up through the vents. But a slow, inevitable, march towards destruction nonetheless.

Then one day, the boxes were brought out once again, and the search for the new perfect place commenced amidst the chaos of packing. In a deal made behind closed doors, my sister and I would go with my mother, but brother was to be left behind. I would gladly have traded sister for brother, but my opinion wasn't asked for and would have been ignored if volunteered. So once again, new daddy became old daddy, and he left our lives with as little fanfare as he entered it.

Which is to say, none at all.

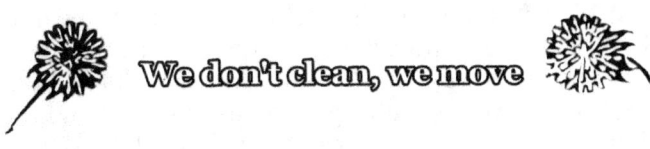

## We don't clean, we move

"A new life", my mother announced as we walked through the apartment she'd picked for us. It was old, with worn carpeting, and smelled moldy. It had a decided 70's porn film feel to it, complete with a plastic stained glass wall for my sister's room, separating it from the living room. In my room, a patchwork of shag carpeting covered the walls and cracked glass adorned the window frames. One dim light hung in from the ceiling that wasn't bright enough to reach the corners of the room told me all I needed to know about our new home.

A new life was all well and good, but it certainly wasn't an upgrade from the old one. I didn't let myself get too distressed by this turn of events, after all, how long could it last? My mother was the reigning champion of the pack & move maneuver, and we had the boxes to prove it.

We moved into our new life with barely a break from the old. There was more time alone and very little family to socialize with since most of my mother's family lived out of town. I was often left in charge of my sister while my mother went to work, and it fell to me to put meals on the table when my mother worked late.

Life settled into a new routine very different from the old. It was not as comfortable as it had been. There were fewer activities and little money for going out to dinner or movies as a family which had once been more common in our old one. It was a little sadder, a little shabbier and a little more frantic than before. But every new life needs a beginning, and not all beginnings are easy. This one, certainly, was not.

Of the many things wrong with our new home, my mother blithely ignored them, often stating this was just temporary. Even though it was as hot as an oven in the summer and you could have stored fresh meat without spoiling in the winter, if I complained that I slept in my winter coat and I could see my breath while in my room, my mother reminded me we should all be grateful to have a roof over our heads. If the water sometimes tasted funny and had a red tinge to it she waved aside with little comment. That the stove didn't always work right and the pilot light often went out was solved by putting matches next to it and told to simply keep an eye on it. Since my cooking skills were such that the stove wasn't required for much I thought very little of it, other than making sure the pilot light remained lit. An exploding house, after all, was never a fun way to end your day.

There were bugs who shared our home with us as well. They were most often seen when dark turned to sudden light in a room, to quickly scatter and disappear to unknown locations. But they were annoying nonetheless. You knew they were there, even if you could no longer see them.

I don't believe the state of the house affected my mother as much as it did my sister and me. She began to spend less and less time at home with us. She did work more hours, but my mother's bed began to remain empty throughout the night more frequently as more of her time was spent away from us. She was once again in earnest pursuit of the new perfect life, and it didn't always include my sister and me.

After three seasons of bitter cold and sweltering heat, my mother decided one weekend it was time to clean house. She embarked on this crusade with gusto and soon the house was filled with the smell of disinfectant. Working her way through the apartment with dogged determination from one room to the next, until finally, she made her way into the kitchen.

The counters were scrubbed and floors were swept. Stopping at the oven, she decided it too needed a good cleaning. She cleaned the top, eventually moving onto the burner plates, discolored and crusted with the blackened remains of many mealtime disasters. As my mother popped the top of the stove to remove the plates, a black wave of roaches erupted from their hiding place. In a black fountain of moving insects, they hit the floor to scurry off to whatever secondary hiding places they may have had, occasionally hitting my mother in the process. With a screech, Mother slammed the stove closed and announced, "We're moving!"

Two days later, after a flurry of boxes and chaos, we moved into our new home, a trailer on the edge of town.

 ## Marcus O'Realious

To the screech of tires and the clatter of rolling trash cans, followed by the final thump of car doors slamming outside the trailer, LeeAnn and I were pulled from sleep. With the engine noise now quiet, we could more clearly hear the sounds of laughter and slurred shouts outside my bedroom door, announcing to all within earshot, my mother was home. With company.

Soon, the trailer was filled with loud conversation and my mother's piano playing. From the noise level, the remains of the bar crowd must have followed her home. And with the party in full swing, they seemed more than willing to go until dawn. Since this was not an unusual occurrence in my life, and both of us were used to it, we fell back asleep not long after the festivities began.

Loud shouting echoing through the trailer pulled us once again from sleep. Over the din of revelry, I heard my mother's voice raised in protest, "No! No! Not in there! The toilet's broken!" Earlier in the week, my brother had flushed a toothbrush down the toilet, after filling it with food to "feed the fishes."

Random crashing noises, more clearly heard as movement brought whoever closer to the front of the house. Once again, my mother's voice raised above the crowd, decrying, "No! No! Not there! There's dishes in the sink!" Pitiful moaning could be heard as my mother shouted, "In there! In my daughter's room," a pause, then, "There's a second bathroom in there."

My door slammed open, only to bounce against the wall and shut on its own behind a shadowy figure barely visible in the low light of my room. In a mad dash, the blur ran through my bathroom, little could be seen of this poor soul, but from the sounds, he'd obviously had too much to drink this evening. Then the bathroom door shut, closing him off from further view. LeeAnn and I talked for a bit about the stranger in the bathroom, but when we heard nothing but silence, we soon lost interest and after a while, drifted back to sleep.

Some dark time later a vague sensation pulled me awake once more. Not loud noises this time. The sounds of the party had long since died down when movement at the end of my bed caught my eye. There stood a naked, youngish looking man doing calisthenics, completely oblivious to everything else around him. Quietly, I nudged my friend awake, and together we watched his antics with barely contained amusement wondering what he would do next. When he began doing jumping jacks, the silence that had prevailed while watching him, quickly fell to our howls of unconstrained laughter. His naked bouncing was too much for us to remain silent anymore.

With a grunt and trip, he fell to the floor. Our presence had, seemingly, gone unnoticed by him until that moment. And, by his reaction, I do believe we scared him much more than his presence had us.

Our drunk, naked friend rallied and, once he recovered from his shock, stood back up and resumed his exercise routine. Toe-touches this time. Our presence, once again, forgotten.

After watching him for a few minutes I decided some questions were in need of asking. Because, as fascinating as this was, it was the middle of the night, and I was, to be truthful, tired. During a pause between repetitions, I asked, "Who are you?"

With a start he stopped, falling forward this time in his surprise, landing between me and LeeAnn. After several minutes of wiggling and a bit of prompting from us, he eventually replied without much conviction, "Marcus?"

"Marcus what," I inquired.

Gaining some confidence in his answers, "Marcus O'Realious Tired," with a big smile and a nod of confirmation for his efforts.

Hmm, now this was an interesting response that definitely required additional questioning. "How did you get here Marcus O'Realious?"

After a few pokes to wake him back up again, his response once again amused, "I took the frog express, but I'm planning on hopping back in the morning," closing his eyes to the world once more.

LeeAnn and I discussed our options at this point over the

soft sounds of Marcus's snoring. We could ignore him and go back to sleep or we could wake him up and question him further to see what else he could have to say. I could, in theory, go find my mother and ask her to take the strange, naked man out of my bed, or we could relocate to the couch and sleep there for the rest of the night.

The two of us sleeping on the couch had no appeal. It was small and uncomfortable. Marcus was laying on my only blanket, and there weren't any others in the house within range of reasonable acquisition. Not to mention, there had been a party, not that long ago out there, and the realm of possibilities we could walk into was infinite. Who knew how many other strangers slept outside the walls of my room?

Finding my mother had no appeal. I had no idea what state I would find her in, or even if she could be woken up if she was passed out. It would also require us to traverse the unknown territory of the now darkened trailer, something neither of us found the least bit appealing.

Ignoring him and going back to sleep seemed like a wasted opportunity for someone who answered questions so wonderfully randomly. Besides, how often does a man just drop naked into your bed? To stay awake and annoy, we decided, would be our course of action for what remained of our night.

Before awakening him again, we felt we probably should cover poor, shivering Marcus up with something first. There was something mildly disconcerting about watching the moonlight reflect off his bare ass as he moved about. Taking the top cover in hand, we folded him into it like a burrito and then added a few stuffed animals for company and our own personal amusement.

Waking him was not as easy as we'd hoped. The snoring by this time was quite loud and pronounced, but dedicated to our course of action, we continued valiantly on.

Poke.....

Poke.....Poke.....

Poke.....

until the snoring ceased and the complaining, in almost English, began.

As consciousness returned, he gave a mild struggle against the burrito covering. But, after a few feeble attempts at freedom, he subsided in defeat, settling into resigned compliance. Both of us were quite pleased with that. It alleviated the possibility of any more midnight calisthenics. Or sudden, random actions while he was in our presence.

Now we could begin our favorite guessing game, 20 questions...

"Where'd you come from Marcus?" we asked.

"Albuquerque."

"How did you end up here?"

"In a car," squirming, once more.

"Whose car?"

"Somebody's." Lifting his head up to look around, he let it drop with a sigh, "Can I please go back to sleep now?"

We briefly mulled over his request. We weren't actually getting anywhere with our questioning, and most of what he had said to us had to be lies. He seemed to earnestly believe he was a frog named Marcus, was from out of state and was completely oblivious as to how he'd arrived naked in my bed. But his answers were funny, and it was my bed after all that he'd so rudely crashed onto. So, rejecting his heartfelt request, we continued on.

Throughout the night, we talked to him, questioned him and, on occasion, poked at him if he began to drift off back to sleep. We never really did find out a whole lot more. He was vague on details such as age (young), occupation (frog) or even as to why he had been standing naked at the end of my bed exercising (excessive alcohol intake). But, the answers were, for the most part, amusing, even if they were lies and fabrications derived from an alcohol soaked brain.

Towards dawn, our attention began to wane in our torment of poor Marcus, and we finally left the poor bastard alone to get some sleep. Crawling over Marcus to get out of bed, an activity he barely noticed, we headed out to inspect the state of the rest of the trailer and see if we could find anyone else interesting.

Cautiously, we opened my door and peered out where the remains of the party could be seen scattered here and there. The early morning light sparkled on full ashtrays and empty bottles, but no other movement could be detected. With cautious steps, we slipped through the door into the living room to the sounds of silence, as loud, in its own way, as the party in full swing had been the night before.

Coffee, we agreed, was needed now. At some point, we assumed others would emerge from whatever location they had crawled to in the night and coffee would be good. We set up the coffee pot and while it brewed we began to gather up the party leftovers, depositing most of it in the trash. We cleaned up spills of alcohol; wayward cigarette butts that had escaped the ashtrays, and began a small pile of lost & found items next to the front door. Hopefully, to be reclaimed by their rightful owners at some later time.

By the time the coffee finished brewing, order had been restored and little evidence remained of the invasion. Looking around in satisfaction, we each poured ourselves a cup and settled in on the couch to wait and see who might appear.

We didn't have a long wait before footsteps from the back of the trailer could be heard, with the occasional soft bump of unsteady movement against the wall, allowing us to follow their progress through the trailer. There was a pause before my sister's room, and we heard the door swing open. She was gone for the weekend and, in theory, that room should have been empty. But, any number of fallen drunks could have been left in there to sleep off the night's excesses. After a brief pause, the unsteady sounds continued onward toward the kitchen. As my mother emerged from the hallway, blinking like a mole at first light, she was followed by the new friend she'd made the night before, looking this way and that in confusion.

"Good morning, Mom, there's coffee," I said brightly to her, pointing towards the coffee pot.

"Where's Marvin?" She continued to look around in confusion, as if unsure of where she was or even why she was there.

"Marvin?" Beginning to suspect that the Marcus in my bed was the Marvin she was looking for.

"Yes, Marvin. He was here last night, have you seen him this morning?" A look of concern settle onto her face and spread to her new friend.

"Oh, you mean the one who was throwing up last night?" Waving in the general direction of my bedroom, "He's passed out in there."

At this point, my mother went from pliant confusion to livid anger, "In your room???"

At the beginning of my nod, she stormed off into my room. With a slam, my door was shut behind her and righteous anger could be heard through the thin walls. Poor Marcus was once again forced from his slumber.

"What are you doing here?!?!" My mother screeched to wake the dead, and I doubt anything less could have awakened him at this point.

"Trying to get some sleep." came his pitiful reply.

"In my 13-year-old daughter's room?" she shrieked, "What were you thinking?"

"Oh please," he moaned, "I just wanted to get some sleep, they kept me up all night and I just want to get some sleep."

Storming back into the living room, my mother glared at me with bloodshot eyes narrowed in suspicion, "What exactly happened here last night?"

Now, as to what happened last night was that Mother had drunkenly brought home the bar to throw an after party at her house, then sent a drunk into my room to throw up. Whereupon she forgot he was there and continued on with her own activities while LeeAnn and I tormented our naked guest for the remainder of the night. But, I did not believe that was the answer she was looking for.

"Marvin passed out naked in my bed after throwing up in my bathroom," I responded with a shrug, "so we decided to question him to see who he was and why he was there. We covered him up and let him go to sleep when he started to pass out. After that, we came out here to clean up your mess and make coffee. Would you like some?" Tipping my cup in the direction of the coffee pot.

My mother walked slowly back into the kitchen and looked around, nodding to herself as she poured a cup of coffee. Looking up at the silent man still standing in the hallway, she sighed, "Well, it seems they found your brother."

Looking distinctly uncomfortable with the situation he found himself in and his role in the entire affair, he took his leave and headed for my room. Poor, sad, tired Marvin/Marcus was, once again rudely awakened, and forced into sweats and a t-shirt. Not even stopping to say goodbye, he was pushed out the door by his brother and without a backward glance from either of them, they left the trailer.

Neither was seen again in my home. But I would like to believe they hopped on the Frog Express and went back to Albuquerque with a story as good as mine to share with friends.

The clothes he was forced into, by the way, were not his but mine, that I had left at the foot of the bed the day before. I later found his in a pile on my bathroom floor and wore his jeans for years until the seams ripped beyond repair. Though the years I've wondered, on occasion, if he kept that pair of sweats and t-shirt, as I kept his clothes. A small memento to his drunken trailer adventure.

##  How to get an Atari

I have always been an early riser. I have tried to sleep in, and I understand that doing so can be wonderful. But, sleeping much past sunrise has always eluded me. This can be a very helpful thing, especially when you have a mother who is anything but an early morning person. So over the years, I'd fallen into the habit of waking my mother on my way out the door for school, when she was at home.

Generally, this consisted of me knocking on her door, and a quick peek to make sure her eyes were open before leaving. Most mornings this worked out well for both us. It only took me a few extra minutes to knock and check, and it ensured she didn't sleep through her alarm clock yet again and be late for work.

It was a well-established routine I did without thinking, knock, peek in, check, leave, done hundreds of times over the years. On a morning, like any other weekday morning after getting ready for school, I looked out the window, saw my mother's car and headed towards her room to complete our morning ritual. Knock, open the door... and stop. Instead of my mother sound asleep and ignoring the alarm clock, I see, perfectly centered in my line of sight, a white, naked ass. One that, most assuredly, did not belong to my mother.

After a moment's pause, I hastily remarked, "Oh, I see you're up already." and promptly turned, closed the door, and immediately headed out to the bus stop. There were a few distant sounding squawks from the direction of my mother's bedroom, but I ignored them. I felt any stopping for conversation or explanation would do nothing but cause me to miss my bus, a much higher priority than listening to flustered adults explain their behavior.

Returning home after school, I'd honestly forgotten about the early morning naked ass. Until I walked back through the door and there sat a very embarrassed looking, but dressed, man. Standing up as soon as I walked through the door he launched into a very incoherent, but sincere-

# IT'LL FEEL BETTER WHEN IT QUITS HURTING 51

sounding apology for his part in this morning's activities. I listened politely to his nervous rambling, wondering at what point I could jump in with an "it's all good" spiel of my own. As his torturous explanation began to run down, he reached behind him to the side of the couch and pulled out a box; handing it to me with a very earnest "I hope this can help make up for this morning!"

Well, this was certainly different. Sitting down, I opened my gift. A brand new Atari emerged from the wrappings, something that none of my friends even owned. They hadn't been on the market for very long and, truthfully, none of our parents could afford to buy one.

The strange gift-giver had nervously hopped from foot to foot watching me open the box, and as soon as I pulled the Atari free of its wrappings, he immediately launched into explanations about each of the games he'd gotten to go with it, several of them prototypes. As he continued his excited explanations, I began thinking I should catch my mother like this more often if this was going to be the result.

Waiting for my mother to return home from work, he set up the gaming system, needing some further distraction from his continued discomfort in my presence judging by the flush of red that danced across his face every time he looked at me. Set up complete, he slapped in a cartridge, handed me one of the two controllers, and hit start. Playing a few games, he showed me how the controllers worked and the different combination of buttons to use for the various games. In short order, we became completely engrossed in our play. A friendly competition began to emerge between the two of us as we moved through the levels, happily replacing the awkward memories of our early morning introduction with our gaming.

In our play, the afternoon turned to evening without much notice by either of us. Even the sound of my mother's car pulling into the carport did not dissuade our attention from the bright, flickering joy of electronic entertainment splashed across the TV. My mother, walking in on our antics, stopped short in the doorway, confusion on her face as she saw the two of us cross-legged on the floor yelling insults and encouragement to each other as we made our way through the increasingly harder levels, and her presence ignored in our efforts to lay waste to one another.

Unwilling to be ignored any longer, my mother

demanded, "What on earth is going on?" Quickly shifting our attention away from the TV to her.

Pausing the game the gift-giver looked up to her, once again uncomfortable, "I, uh, bought an Atari for your daughter," beginning to show his nervous embarrassment once more, "to uh, you know, make up for this morning?"

"Oh, I see," looking over the pile of games scattered between the TV and the Atari.

"I was also planning on taking everyone out to dinner tonight as well." Yet another peace offering in the making, "Where would you like to go?" Standing up to go to her, he slipped his arm around her waist and offered her a smile. Gaming was no longer foremost in his mind now that my mother was home.

As the adults moved away to discuss the evening's activities, several thoughts danced through my head as I turned the controller over in my hand. Things were definitely looking up. An Atari, a ton of games and now dinner, best of all, I'd learned something new from this experience, guilt was good.

# IT'LL FEEL BETTER WHEN IT QUITS HURTING

 ## Your Mother sent me to you

One Sunday evening, while doing my homework for school, my mother arrived home in the company of a woman she'd met at the bar. Mother had been out most of the day, and I'd been expecting her arrival for some time already. My sister was in town, having spent the weekend with a friend, but it was Sunday now and she needed to be brought back home for school tomorrow.

Not seeing my sister as they entered, I inquired if she remembered she needed to pick Sister up while out and about today. Shaking her head no, it seemed they'd only come home from the bar to pick something up, but not to stay. My sister had been forgotten in their quest for whatever it was they were there for. Now that she was reminded of it, we still had one problem. Mother couldn't remember where the house was.

Living at the edge of town did have some distinct disadvantages, and this was one of the big ones, I was no longer within reasonable walking distance of anything. While living in town I walked almost everywhere, but we lived on the side of the highway now without so much as a sidewalk for miles. I remembered where my sister was, and if we were in town I could have walked to get her, but that wasn't an option anymore. I didn't know the address, only how to get there, and my mother couldn't remember even that much. She vaguely recalled the area my sister was in, but not the house or address. I would have to go with them if she was to be retrieved; it was our only reasonable option.

Back into town we went. Giving Mother directions to the house, we arrived with no trouble but ran into another snag as soon as we arrived. Sister was not there. She'd gone out to dinner with most of the family, and they weren't expected back for some time. We sat outside the house, hoping the family would return soon while my mother and her friend waited with increasing anxiety for their return to the bar.

Eventually becoming impatient, my mother went back up

to the house to talk with the family member who had stayed behind, and arrangements were made for my sister to stay there another night. Once my sister had been taken care of, the question of what to do with me came up. Returning to the trailer at the edge of town just seemed like a waste of time for two people who were so eager to return to their drinking.

"I don't live far from here," the friend said, "we could drop her off there." My mother nodded in happy agreement as her friend took off for her house. A solution, made without any consideration to my opinion on the matter, and over my loud protests.

A few blocks away we stopped in front of a house, and the friend pointed towards a set of outside stairs, "I live on the second story, my son is home. Knock on the door and tell him I sent you." Great. Having no other choice, I exited the car, walked up the stairs, and knocked at the door.

As the door opened, a boy vaguely familiar from school appeared "Yes?"Looking confused at my late night arrival on his doorstep, "Can I help you?"

"Uh..., your mother sent me to you and said I should stay here for the night." Sighing, I shrugged my shoulders, "She's out with my mother."

"Ah. Well..." he seemed as flustered, yet resigned, as I was. Stepping back, he waved me in, "I guess come on in then."

The awkwardness of the situation was apparent on both of our faces as we looked at each other wondering what to do next. We'd seen each other around school, but couldn't exactly be called friends. Vaguely recognized strangers was the best we could be called. Standing in the kitchen, I look around and wondering what I should do. There was school tomorrow; I didn't have my books or my homework. I didn't even have a change of clothes and I was stuck here for the night.

He looked equally as uncomfortable, shifting from foot to foot, and looking randomly all around, at a loss for what to do. What do you do with a stranger that comes to the door? This was definitely not a situation either of us had encountered before.

"Hi, my name's Lisa." I finally offered, as the silence began to stretch beyond comfort.

"Uh, my name's Brian, we go to school together, right?" He halfheartedly raised his hand, probably wondering if this was a handshake occasion, but dropped it before it reached the halfway mark. Guess not.

"Yeah, I think we may have had a class or two together." Another awkward pause on my part, "I... I... think I've seen you around."

"So, uh... do you want to watch TV or something?" I had to give it to him, he was rallying. I looked around the kitchen where a small black & white TV sat on a counter next to the table, but only one chair.

With a somewhat guilty expression he added, "Uh, yeah, this is the only one in the house... but uh, we can share the chair or whatever."

"Oh, no, I can't take the only chair," I protested. "I can sit on the floor. I do it all the time at home."

For the rest of the evening, we sat in the kitchen eating popcorn, him in the chair, me at his feet using his legs as a backrest watching old movies. We both agreed we liked *The Blob*, but *Attack of the Killer Bees* was a bit over the top, even for a B-movie. With the TV as a buffer to our awkwardness, we began to relax in each others company. Still not friends, but at least comfortable acquaintances.

As time stretched out, the lateness of the evening began to affect both of us with suppressed yawns and eye rubbing. "Umm, I suppose we should probably get some sleep, uh, right?" Turning a pale pink as he said it.

"Uh, yeah, since we have school and all tomorrow, that's probably a good idea." Looking around wondering what to do next.

Standing up with a bit of self-conscious shuffling about, he eventually led me through the rest of the apartment, stopping at his room, "I uh, have a t-shirt and some sweats if you'd like to wear those and I can give you some of my blankets for the couch too."

Without waiting for a reply he quickly darted into his bedroom and returned with a wad of blankets and clothes for me. Walking over to the couch with my bundle, I found the clothes tucked in among the bedding. They were much too big, but preferable to wearing jeans to sleep in. After sorting out the clothes from the blankets, I headed to the bathroom to change.

When I returned, I saw he'd made up the couch, and even found an extra pillow for me. I was touched by his gesture, and his awkward shyness, while we tried to make the best out of the situation. I thanked him and assured him that I would be very comfortable on the couch. When, at the last minute, he offered me his bed instead. I waved off his kind gesture with a shake of my head. Things were weird enough without me also taking over his room, even if it was just for the night.

The following morning, I realized Brian had gotten up early to make sure I had time to shower, and found me some of his older, and smaller, clothes to wear to school. I weighed barely 80 pounds at an even 5 foot, and, while he was not fat by any stretch, I was tiny compared to most of my classmates.

While I showered and got myself ready for school, he kept himself busy by making us both breakfast, cereal, and toast with orange juice. I appreciated his efforts to offset what was probably going to be a very strained day, trying to find a reasonable explanation for my teachers as to why I had neither homework nor books to bring to class.

Ready for school, he gathering up all of his school things and we headed out the door. He lived only a few blocks from the junior high and walked to school each day. Descending the stairs there was one last uncomfortable moment. One avoidable, yet unconsidered by both of us up to the time we walked out of the door. Walking out onto the landing, we saw his friends waiting for him at the foot of the stairs.

Seeing the two of us come out of his apartment caused a ripple of conversation to spread throughout his friends. They noticed our wet hair and the clothes I was wearing. Each small thing noted, brought another round of nudging, raised eyebrows and inquiring looks as possibilities were discussed among themselves. The most likely possibility was so improbable it was rejected almost as soon as it was broached, while Brian and I stood in silence during their scrutiny, unsure what to say about our unlikely evening together.

As the moment stretched uncomfortably, I turned to Brian, winked, and announced to the group, "His mother sent me to him."

A look of awed wonder spread among his friends as they looked back and forth between the two of us wondering if they'd heard me correctly. Such an unlikely scenario was so outside the normal realm of reality to cause disbelief even while it was being confirmed.

Slowly, Brian and I descended the remaining stairs that separated us from his friends waiting below. Stepping off the stairs, they enveloped us in the group to continue their questioning as we drifted towards the school. While confirming I had indeed stayed the night, we both remained stubbornly silent as to why it had occurred. Self-preservation kept us vague in our explanations of our parent's behavior, both of us long used to finding acceptable excuses for unacceptable situations.

I would like to say we became good friends after that. But the truth is, other than exchanging our clothes the following day; we once again became vague strangers who went to the same school. An occasional wave was given when we randomly ran into each other, but no phone numbers were exchanged or promises made to keep in touch. Eventually, I no longer noticed him around the hallways. I don't know if he moved to another school or if our paths simply didn't cross anymore. Nor do I know what stories he told about our night together or if he ever did say, preferring to leave it a mystery to his friends. We ran in completely different circles, but I don't believe he did.

Sometimes people come into our lives unexpectedly. On occasion, a bit weirdly. But even after all these years, I can vividly recall the cracked black & white linoleum, and the small TV with the giant bees playing on it while I leaned against his legs, laughing and eating popcorn, pretending this was just another normal night in our lives, nothing unusual or out of the ordinary. And for us, maybe this was and we both understood that.

 ## What a Riot

Hanging out at my house one evening with Cindy and Ginny, we became bored. Nothing was really going on and we were feeling restless. My sister was staying the night at a friend's, so I was technically free to do whatever I wanted until it was time to pick her up in the morning. Not wanting to spend any more time at my house, we decided to head out for Ginny's house across town. From my house to hers was about an hour's walk, but the evening was pleasant, and the walk not horrible. And while we knew it would be dark before we reached her house, it didn't deter us from our decision.

Before deciding to walk, Cindy made a call to her boyfriends, twins, to see if maybe we could get a ride from their older brother, but he wasn't around to ask. She let them know we were on our way across town and to stop by later if they wanted to hang out. They lived only a few blocks away from Ginny, and if we wanted to come back across town, they could always escort us back or maybe catch a ride with their brother. Hanging up the phone, Cindy joined us as we headed out the door.

We strolled across town, not in any big hurry to get there, laughing and talking as we went. By sunset, we were approaching the midway point between the north and south side of town. The streetlights were beginning to turn on as dusk descended, but with less than eight blocks left to go, we weren't concerned with our progress.

In the gathering gloom, we started to hear something unusual, a kind of steady roar we couldn't place but was definitely outside of the normal range of noise. Crossing Broadway in the dark, we began to make out occasional shouts, car horns and maybe something that could have been firecrackers being set off. The three of us glanced at each other more than once with worried looks. No one really knew where we were, and something was not right in this area, the whole feel of the neighborhood was off. But we were much closer to Ginny's house than to mine or Cindy's, so we decided to cautiously continue on.

As the noise continued to get louder, the feel of it began to tug on my memory of the time I was in a huge stadium watching a football game, with the same dull roar that filled every space around it. At this time of night, the city was normally quiet. You would hear the occasional traffic noises, maybe some music coming from a house or a bar with its doors open, children playing in yards before being called in for the night. But, this was not what we were hearing at all. This was like a caged animal wanting to get free. This was a stadium filled with unhappy fans. This, whatever *this* was, was very, very bad.

Moving out of the streetlights and into the shadows, we continued north towards the safety of Ginny's house. Our casual stroll now a determined fast walk, stopping occasionally to glance around, trying to pinpoint the source of the sound to, hopefully, avoid it. In the distance, we could see shapes take form down the center of the street ahead of us, moving quickly in our direction.

Stopping where we were, we knew there was no place to really hide, but we didn't want to draw any more attention to ourselves if we could avoid it. Coming closer the shapes began to resolve themselves into several people, male, all looking around as they walked. We were too far away to hear what they were saying, but the closer they came the more worried we got. Silence and shadows wouldn't hide us for much longer if they got much closer. Something was going on, and we wanted no part of it or them.

Less than half a block away we started to hear bit and snatches of their conversation.

"...they should be around..."

"...can't be far now...."

"...are you sure....?"

The three of us, getting ready to bolt if needed, watched them steadily walk closer to where we were standing. Less than six blocks now separated us from the safety of Ginny's house. It might as well been on the moon for all the good it did us.

Then, stepping into the streetlight, we got our first clear image of them, and relief spread instantly throughout our little group. Stepping forward I called out "Will! Wes! What are you guys doing here?"

The entire group stopped and swung around to look at

us, "Thank god! We've been looking for you guys and hoped this was the way you would take." Will said, "We were worried we'd miss you!"

Walking out of the shadows Cindy walked up to Wes and Will, giving each of them a kiss, "What's going on?" Looking around the biggish group of guys, their older brother was with them, along with about 4 or 5 others, a couple we knew, a few we didn't, but all of them had been apparently looking for us.

Forming a circle around us, one of the guys responded, "Riot." Continuing to scan the area around us, their nervousness evident despite their attempts to play it cool for our benefit.

"Huh?" Came my clever response to his announcement.

"There's a riot going on right now, not far from here." Their eyes darted this way and that, trying to spot anything out of the ordinary, "We need to get you guys back to Ginny's before they get any closer."

"It started shortly after you guys called us saying you were walking this way," Will said as they started to get us moving, "when things got bad outside, we decided to come looking for you."

"We hoped this was the way you would come," Wes said. "So we gathered up a few of the guys and started this way hoping to find you before anyone else did."

Walking briskly, we picked up speed, staying more or less in the middle of the road. There was no traffic moving anywhere near us and the guys felt better with us in the center and able to completely surround us while on the move. We stepped quickly and with a purpose as the sounds of the nearby riot continued to grow, off to the left now, but coming closer.

Gathering closer and herding us faster towards the house, we were almost running by the time we reached Ginny's house. We could see flashing lights, noises that could have been fireworks, but probably weren't, mixed in with the sounds of sirens and shouts, and the occasional whiff of smoke.

Almost throwing us into the house, the guys went around locking all the windows and doors. Herding us into a center room with no outside windows, they turned off all the lights except for one table lamp in the center room trying to make the house appear unoccupied and diminish any interest in it.

And there they set up watch, some staying inside with us, others slipping out randomly to check on the progress of the riot going on outside and see how close it was getting.

They stayed with us the rest of the night, never leaving us all alone. The riot passed us by without harm, and in the glow of morning, it had completely run its course.

I have no idea what caused the riot, who started it, how many were actually involved or any other details. We heard it all from a distance, kept safe by our self-appointed bodyguards. They did not join in the fray, choosing instead to stay with us and keep us out of harm's way.

They were all considered "bad boy's", each and every one of them. They had reputations for violence and thuggery, and had the police records to prove it. If you asked around, very few would have had a good word to say about any of them, dismissing them out of hand as worthless juvenile delinquents. But on that night, they were our knights in shining armor, swooping in to protect us and putting themselves in danger to keep us safe.

In the years to come, some put aside their past and went on to make a good life for themselves with jobs, wives, kids, and homes. Others, as had been predicted in their youth, ended up in jail or other bad circumstances. But I'll always remember each of them fondly as they had been on that night, fearless and bold, our gentle protectors who came looking for us and kept us safe throughout the night.

 ## Ante Up

For a brief period of time, my friends and I started playing poker. It was a fun way to pass the time, and mostly, we would play for pennies. But, we also allowed other non-cash items to be used as well, marbles, paperclips, pretty rocks, hair ties, basically anything in our pockets when the game started was allowed if we were low on cash. They had no real assigned value; we'd just flip whatever into the pot, and collect our trinkets with each round we won.

On a rainy summer afternoon, we were all hanging out at Cindy's house. We had the place to ourselves, and in no particular hurry to be anywhere else, we decided to kill some time until the storm passed. Sitting down at the kitchen table Ginny pulled out a deck of cards, (at least one of us at any given time had a deck shoved into a back pocket) and began yet another round of poker. Laughing and joking, we played blackjack, stud poker, 5 card draw, and other varieties of this game. Basically, whatever the dealer wanted, so it often changed with each new round.

I was having unusually good luck, while Cindy, unusually bad. Everyone else was doing moderately well, but I had won a good sized collection of things in front of me, while Cindy, on the other hand, was slowly drifting down to nothing. During a badly played bluff, she lost the last of her trinkets, with nothing more in her pockets to ante up with. Usually, this was the point we called the game. It just wasn't as much fun unless we could all play, and Cindy was flat busted.

But on occasion, along with things found in our pockets, we would offer a paper promise for the pot. It was usually things like, "wash your dishes next time at your house" or "help clean your room", things like that. Something any of us would honestly do anyway if we happened to be at each others' house for the day, but there were also offbeat antes as well. The ones with things like, "I will sing *I'm a Little Teapot* in the lunchroom" or other such bizarre but harmless funnies. Things that were fun to call in at a later date whenever we wanted to, and each of us had a stack of paper promises from each other. Usually, they were kept in a back pocket along with all the other random things we started to keep with us with our new found love of poker. It wouldn't do if a spontaneous game started and you had nothing to offer up to play with.

Not wanting to throw in the towel so far behind in the game, Cindy decided to continue playing with a short stack of paper promises and try and recoup some of her loses. Writing down a few things that she had to offer, we all agreed they were poker worthy and the game could continue. As another hand was dealt, I looked over my cards, and anted up a couple of marbles, a paperclip, and a rubber band, pushing the pot up as others choose to match or decline. Cindy, looking at me a few times, decided to go for broke, and put in a paper promise of high value. She seemed secure in her hand and decided I had to be bluffing. The pot was enticingly high, and if she won, she would be set the next time we played for trinkets.

After setting the bets, she called, laying down 3 Jacks, Aces high. Grinning as she looked around the table, reaching for the pot, sure that she had won. Slowly, I laid down my cards one at a time, a royal flush, and grinned back.

Pausing, Cindy looked the cards over unable to believe her bad luck. Shaking her head at how quickly her good fortune had flipped, she sighed, "Well damn. Looks like I have a phone call to make after all."

Getting up from the table I followed her to the phone hanging on the wall and watched her dial the number. Waiting for the other end to pick up, she stuck her tongue out at me while I laughed. "Hello?" a muffled voice asked when the ringing stopped.

"Hey Wes," pausing to regroup before plunging in, "I have some bad news."

"Okay?"

"I uh..." after pausing to swallow, she rushed to the finish, "lost you in a poker game."

"You *WHAT*?" A reaction that could be heard from across the room, making everyone left at the table laugh.

"Well, yeah," Cindy rallied, "I was losing, but it *was* a good hand, and I was out of things to bet, so... I uh, well... lost you."

"Uh huh," Wes sighed, "and who did you lose to?"

# IT'LL FEEL BETTER WHEN IT QUITS HURTING

"Lisa,"

"For how long does Lisa now own me?"

"Um... a year?"

"A year." Nothing but silence came from the other end of the line for several seconds. Putting his hand over the receiver, a muffled conversation with someone else could vaguely be heard, as he shared his new status. A peal of rolling laughter in the background came through loud and clear when he dropped his hand, "And what do I have to do now that she owns me?"

Cindy turned to look at me and shrugged, waiting for my reply. This wasn't something we had discussed and none of us had been silly enough to throw a boy into the pot up til now. I shrugged back and shook my head. I'd never won a human being before, how was I to know?

"Umm..." pausing, she said, "we'll work out the details later."

"Oh, this should be fun." His voice heavily laced with sarcasm, causing even more laughter from his side of the phone. "I should be around in a few days. Talk then?"

"Yep, sounds good." Hanging up the phone she turned to me and stuck out her tongue, "Have fun." Then, unable to hold a steady face, laughed with the rest of us and shook my hand at a hand well played.

*I still have that piece of paper around here somewhere, even after all these years. Kept safe in a small treasure box along with other small mementos from that time.*

## HAVE YOU NOTICED MY NOTES YET? LOL

## The Rebellion

Living with my father was much different than living with my mother. Not better, just different. Gone were the late night parties, long parental absences and the ability to order my life as I wanted, so long as I went to school, did my homework and watched over my sister. My father, a police officer, believed in order, believed in discipline and, most of all, believed I needed structure. And he was going to provide it to me, in spades.

He lured me into his home with promises of food and taking the burden of caring for my sister off my shoulders. And while the first part was true, the second was not. As soon as I moved in, not only was I was still responsible for my younger sister, I was also given my baby sister, recently arrived from my father and his new wife, to care for as well.

My rehabilitation became my father's personal crusade. With brutal efficiency, he went through all my friends, deciding none of them were good enough for me and began his campaign to cut me off from them. Unmonitored time away from home was rarely, and only grudgingly given, in intervals of 10 minutes or less at a time. I could basically walk around the block once a day before being subjected to lock down once more. Phone calls were monitored and often listened in on, to ensure I was not saying anything I shouldn't.

The room I was given, prior to my occupation, had been an office/walkway to go from the living room to the kitchen. And, while there were doors at either end, I was not allowed to close them. Privacy that had once been a normal part of my life was now a thing of the past. I quickly came to realize I had exchanged a full larder for an empty life.

Time at school became my only social interaction. Never

before in the past had I shirked my duty in going to school or in doing my homework. But now, I clung to it like a shipwreck victim on a life preserver. It was only during those hours that I could speak to my friends, have an opinion or move without intense scrutiny. It was my only haven from the miserable existence my life had become.

There were no more school dances or after school activities. No more movies, even if I could scrounge up the cash. No more hanging out with friends or going to the mall. No form of teen socializing was acceptable since there might be someone my father didn't approve of there as well. He even went so far as to try and pick friends for me. I often went along with it since it was better than nothing, but none of the people he chose were people I would have picked on my own.

Each day blended into the next with little variation. The weekends became an endless vacuum of time split between chores, homework, and caring for my sisters. My world became immersed in charts, chore lists and an endless stream of rules that had to be followed. All time was accounted for and every movement was followed to see if there was any deviation from what was expected of me. My confinement was so complete, I spent most of my free time sitting in a chair staring out the window.

During this time, I learned two things that would affect the rest of my life, and the choices I would make forever after. The first was, if you back someone into a corner and take away all their options, there are no consequences, since all actions, good or bad, lead to the same results. The other was, chaos was good and I wanted it back.

 ## Freedom

Time at my father's house had slunk on from moment to moment, in its endless repetition of mindless nothingness, for months by the time Halloween came around. I had already resigned myself to sitting at home, alone, handing out candy, and not feeling very happy about it, when a knock sounded at the door.

Answering it, there stood one of the "friends" my father had picked out for me with a giant grin and a plan to escape for the evening. Her church, right behind my father's house, was having a teen activity for Halloween, probably with the thought of keeping us away from any "godless" secular (i.e. fun) activities. Church buses would take everyone to a farm for an evening of chaperoned bonfires, singing, s'mores and hayrack rides. Perhaps, if the stars aligned in my favor, we could convince my father this was something I could do.

Together, we presented the idea to my father. After several phone calls to both the church and other parents, he decided yes, I could go. Following us to the buses, he watched us board and take seats, then stood around for a bit talking to the other parents until the youth leader announced we'd be leaving in the next few minutes. Hearing that, he departed back to the house after tossing me a wave when he passed our window. As soon as he was out of sight the friend grabbed my hand, rushed us from the bus, out of the lot, and down the block. We were free!!!

I hadn't been aware this was actually part of the plan. I'd have been happy just to get out of the house for the evening. But, the idea of absolute freedom for a few hours had an appeal I cannot even begin to describe, and gleefully, I followed wherever she led.

Our first stop was to the store down the way for rolling papers and a bar of soap. Once that task was accomplished, we started wandering around town with no particular destination in mind, just enjoying this unfamiliar freedom of movement. In our wanderings, we began to run into people we knew, hopping from group to group as they came into contact with each other. Rambling aimlessly, we smoked and gleefully ate candy, so thoughtfully provided by random strangers on this night of begging. For a few blocks, we drew holiday appropriate pictures and well-wishing messages on the windshields of cars until our soap ran out, and we became bored with the activity.

As night descended, the number of young children started to disappear from the streets, but larger numbers of teens came to fill their place. Drifting, we encountered more people we knew, trading candy and pot with equal ease as our laughter filled the air. The friend my father had chosen for me, was a well-connected drug dealer, and I was having more fun than I'd had since moving into his house. Standing with a group of people I vaguely knew, but well known to my friend, a car squealed to a stop in front of us. Before the engine died, an angry group of four piled out, heading straight toward us.

A confusion of shouting erupted from this group, directed toward who, we did not know. To be truthful, I'm not sure they did either. The closer they came to our group, the less aggressive the shouting became until it dwindled and died by the time they reached us. A case of mistaken identity it seemed; well, no harm, no foul. We offered them some of our candy and they offered us a smoke, and a peaceful truce was achieved.

Quickly becoming restless, they were ready to be on the move again. Following them to their car, they offered us a lift. At first, we declined. We had no particular destination in mind, but they didn't care, neither did they. So, in the same spirit of rash decision making that had chosen our path the entire night, we happily accepted their offer.

Now, I should mention, as we climbed into the car, I was under the impression my friend knew who these people were, and she thought I had some clue who they were. Neither of our assumptions were correct. And honestly, I'm not sure it would have mattered anyway. In we climbed, and away we went, free as birds and with even less care about where we were going. Much of that ride was a blur of bright lights, thick smoke and the taste of candy, as we sang loudly to the music and screamed out the windows.

After such a long confinement, any idea of restraint or caution had been thrown to the wind. I no longer cared if this was a good or bad choice, or even what the possible consequences were for my behavior. I was free, Free, FREE!

At one stop, I put my jacket on upside down and ran with my arms straight in front of me, crying out, "I am the Blue Avenger! Feed Me Candy!" Knocking on doors to beg for candy every time we piled out of the car, we made quite a haul between the six of us. At another stop, we jumped out of the car and attempted to reenact "*We're off to the see the Wizard*" arm-in-arm. But we couldn't coordinate our movements well enough, falling down repeatedly in a heap of laughter and elbows.

The following morning I woke up with a horde of bruises I couldn't account for, but the two large ones on my knees I had no trouble figuring out. Late into the night, our joyride took us into a supermarket parking lot, simply to run and chase each other without the worry of traffic or disgruntled homeowners. One of the guys started pushing a shopping cart around, and in a feat I would never try to replicate, nor even figure out afterward how I accomplished it in the state I was in, took a running leap and landed in the cart. After a great deal of cheering from my companions, they started pushing me all around the parking lot, with my jacket still on backwards and arms spread wide, we flew. With dizzying speed, we whooped and hollered and screamed, racing through the spaces in between cars, up and down the small hills of our new playground.

And all was well in the world until someone inside the store noticed our behavior and came out to stop it. Several people exited the building, all looking less than impressed with our antics, demanding that we stop, stop right now! My cart driver ran one last loop of the parking lot and then headed back towards the cart rack. Sitting back in my cart I noticed the rack ahead of me had a bar just barely above the cart handle. With a gasp, I slid down into the cart, but in saving my neck, I exposed my knees to the impact. Once again at rest, I jumped up, screaming my defiance at the world, and leaped from the cart to land beside the car.

Pealing out of the parking lot, my friend stuck her head out the window and shouted, "May the fleas of a thousand camels infest your armpits!", which struck everyone in the car as hysterically funny, leaving a trail of laughter behind us as we drove off.

As with everything else, all good things must eventually

come to an end, and shortly after the parking lot adventure, I was dropped off at the church behind my house. Walking through the back gate, I noticed the house was completely dark except for one light moving restlessly through the downstairs. It was my father with a flashlight pacing back and forth in the dark.

The closer I came to the house the more dread I felt. The church was dark, the buses all parked and the lot completely empty. There was no way to know when they had returned, it could have been hours or minutes, but either way, I was caught, no doubt about it. Before entering the house I decided to tell the truth, more or less, and throw myself on the mercy of the court. Not much chance of that, but I didn't see any other option.

Opening the back door I was greeted by my father, flashlight in hand pointed at me, "Where have you been?" Oh, he was angry all right.

"I've been out getting high and begging for candy," talking fast and hoping for the best. "Then we got into a car with strangers and drove around town. I went for a ride in a shopping cart, and bruised my knees," pointing at them as I spoke, "then they dropped me off after that, and here I am." Short, concise and to the point.

"I don't believe you," he shouted, "I can smell the alcohol from here!"

Well, I wasn't sure what to say about that. The closest I had come to alcohol all night had been walking by the liquor section at the grocery store earlier in the evening. "Dad, I'm not drunk, I'm stoned. I haven't touched any alcohol at all."

"Don't lie to me!" Pointing the flashlight in my eyes, "Tell me what really happened; and don't make up ridiculous stories about being in town when I put you on that bus myself! And why weren't you with them when they returned?"

Hmm, well, so much for the truth setting you free. Taking a moment to consider all my options, I decided to go for the big lie. "Okay, fine Dad, you caught me. We went with the church group, but once we got there we found an older crowd who managed to sneak alcohol onto the bus with them. We sat around the fire and got really, really drunk, but I got sick and we went off into the woods to keep anyone from seeing. We were gone so long we missed everyone getting back on the bus so we had to walk back into town and then one of the guys called for a ride. When their ride showed up they gave us a ride as well, dropping me off at home and here I am."

"Finally, the truth. When will you learn that you can't hide anything from me?!" Nodding to himself, he seemed deeply satisfied with his conclusion.

"Yes, Dad, you're right," Hiding my eye roll, but unable to suppress the corresponding sigh, "I can't hide anything from you." I was in trouble anyway; I might as well try to humor him in the hopes of a lesser punishment. It was a vague hope since all infractions were treated as capital crimes. But, it couldn't hurt.

"It's good to see you're finally beginning to realize that." Mollified somewhat by my words, he waved me on, "Go to bed and we'll discuss your punishment in the morning." And with that, he clicked off the flashlight and went upstairs to bed.

The next day, punishment was handed out. I was grounded for a month with no contact with anyone except when at school. I was given extra chores, and told unless it was for meals or chores; I was confined to my room. Which was my standard punishment for just about everything from being a few minutes late coming in from my 10-minute walk to, well, my outrageous behavior the night before. There were no real attempts to make the punishment fit the crime. It seemed my father was a one size fits all kind of guy.

Having lived my life in a perpetual state of "in trouble" since I'd entered my father's house, I decided my night of freedom had been worth the consequences. Content, I walked to my room with a smile on my face, happy to begin my grounding.

 ## You can lead a horse to water...

My father, during the time I lived with him, was a devout Catholic. I had been baptized shortly after my parents' wedding, was enrolled in a Catholic school for part of the first and second grade, and went through First Communion when I was around 6 years old. But the older I got, the less I believed.

Part of this doubt may have come from my mother. She switched religions regularly, depending on who she was married to at the time, giving me a broad, if unintentional, exposure to multiple faiths. She was raised a Methodist, switched to Catholic with my father, and Evangelical with her third husband. And with each switch, I'd been taken along for the ride. Each of these faiths claimed to be the "one true path" to God, while denouncing their counterparts, even when I could see very little difference between them. When I was young, I secretly hoped at some point she would fall in love with someone Jewish because I really wanted to see how a Synagogue worked. She never did, and I was left sadly disappointed over it for years.

But now that I was living with my father full-time, he decided it was time for me to fully embrace the religion of his choice and go through something called Catechism where, as an adolescent, you are sent to a class that explains your religion to you, while reaffirming your devotion and faith in it.

To say I was opposed to it would be a gross understatement. I no longer wanted to be Catholic. I'd already stopped taking communion years ago, nor did I participate in the weekly rituals during sermons. I elected instead to remain seated quietly as the rest of the congregation went through their "Catholic calisthenics" as I liked to call it.

I had many objections to this religion, and to be honest, to pretty much all of them for various reasons. They seemed to be a mass of people who insisted we all do as they say, not as they do. And try as I might, I could find very few people who actually lived as they preached, and it left me feeling vaguely dirty. I wanted nothing to do with any of them any longer, not that my father gave me the option as he dragged me to and from church every week.

With his announcement that I was enrolled me in class, over all my objections, left me feeling angry and bitter. And for once, I actually let my anger show in my dealings with my father. "No, no, no... I do not want to go!" Giving voice to my objections.

But, with my father's usual attentiveness to my feelings on any given subject, he commanded, "You *will* go, and you *will* be Catholic, and that *is* the end of it."

Looking him dead in the eye after this statement and shaking with anger, I shot back, "You can force me to go, but you can't force me to be Catholic."

Shrugging his shoulders, considering it a closed subject, "You start on Wednesday." Leaving me to stew in my anger at once again being forced into something I found distasteful by my father.

And so, the following Wednesday, I was hauled off to attend class. Parking the car, he walked me into the classroom, and once he was assured I could not escape, left me. Standing around, shifting from foot to foot, I looked over my fellow classmates. I knew a few of them by sight, but most of them went to the Catholic high school in town. I'd seen them during church but hadn't interacted with most of them. After a few minutes, I went to the back of the room and slipped into a seat by myself, hoping to be left alone for the next 60 minutes, and maybe get in a short nap or something.

Instead, as soon as everyone was accounted for, the group leader asked us all to move our desks into a big circle, with him in the middle. Sighing with resignation, I moved my desk as well, joining the group, like it or not. And sat listlessly for the next hour listening to him speak on all things Catholic.

As soon as the group broke up for the evening, my father was standing in the doorway waiting for me. Approaching him, he asked, "Did you learn anything?"

"No," I responded, following him out to the car.

"Did you see anyone you knew?"

"No." Sliding into the car, waiting for him to get in on the other side.

"Do you have any questions that maybe I can answer?" Trying again to engage me.

"Yes, actually." Looking him in the eye and getting a briefly hopeful look from him, I asked, "Do I have to go again?"

His face clouded with my question and turning in his seat, he gripped the steering wheel and in a clipped voice said, "Yes. Yes, you will be going again." Leaving me to sit quietly the rest of the way home with no further conversation from either of us.

And so this weekly ritual was added to the established Sunday one. Week after week, I would go and sit in the classroom, mostly staring at the ceiling while being held hostage by religion. A few times the instructor attempted to force my participation, but after dead silence from me, and a refusal to yield, he gave up.

I did make a friend of sorts while I was there. A girl who sat next to me that I would exchange a few words with, as we sat through yet another lecture. She was as bored as I was, but wasn't the conscientious objector that I had become. She went to make her parents happy, and without the fight my parents faced every week.

After a few weeks of this, I did start talking, but not in a way that made anyone in authority happy. I began asking questions that made the instructor uncomfortable, once even referring to communion as symbolic cannibalism. And by his livid response to my statement, I did not make a new friend of him for it. It started to become a game of sorts to me, to see how many times a session I could make him sputter, turn pink or rigidly ignore me, and by my tally, I was winning.

And then everything came to a head with a movie, that I swear to you was called, *"You are a Spring Chicken"*. The essence of this movie was that we were all precious vessels of God, and our bodies were temples to him, and so should be kept pure and unsullied until the sanctity of marriage. As this movie droned on, I began my own commentary in a low but clear voice. Remarking it was much too late for that, this vessel had already done sailed. Commenting on certain types of birth control (they are a sin you know, since sexual relations are only for the purpose of conceiving a child) and which I had used up to that point. Until the instructor could no longer control himself and yelled, "Get out! Get out of this classroom now!"

Grinning to myself, I slipped out of my seat and out the door since this was what I'd wanted all along. I sat down happily in the hallway outside of the room for the remaining time until my father showed up. Seeing me sitting in the hallway and not in class as I was supposed to be, he demanded to know what happened.

Smiling again, in real joy, I pointed to the instructor, "He told me to get out."

Walking into the classroom, he confronted the teacher, and a low but heated exchange commenced. There were constant looks shot my way as I stood in the doorway and watched. The instructor shook his head often during the exchange, making other negative gestures at my father while often glancing over at me. I could tell it was not going well for my father, and in this instance, he was probably not going to get his way. It made me almost giddy with joy, I wanted to dance about, but instead, I continued to watch quietly from the doorway.

Eventually, I could see my father's shoulders slump in defeat. He was not going to be forcing me to any more classes it would seem. Turning to walk toward me, they both looked distinctly unhappy with the entire situation. Standing before me, I stood quietly and waited for the outcome of the exchange. Although I can't truthfully say I didn't have a sneaking suspicion of what it was going to be.

Looking sorrowful, the instructor said to me, "You will not be allowed back to class again."

I'm not sure what he thought my reaction to this was going to be, but remorse was not even close to what I was feeling. Nodding my head, I smiled, "Good."

"Do you understand that without this class you cannot fully participate in your faith any longer?" Trying, yet again, to get some kind of contrite response from me.

"Yes," smiling once more.

Shaking his head, and spreading his hands like Pontius Pilate, he washed his hands of me and turned away.

And so ended my father's crusade to convert me to Catholicism. You can lead a horse to water, but you can't make 'em Catholic.

##  I do believe it's time for you to go

At the beginning of my sophomore year, while hanging out in the courtyard before class, I met a boy. He was leaning against a picnic table, dressed in Army fatigues, and he looked good. I didn't know then how much this boy would influence the rest of my life and the choices I would make. All I knew was he was good to look at, and I wanted to get to know him better.

Walking up and I sat on the edge of the table next to him, "Hi," looking up to smile at him, "my name's Lisa."

"Hi," grinning back, "I'm Billy. I haven't seen you around before."

"I'm a sophomore," warming up to the conversation, "my first year here." In our school district, 7th through 9th went to the junior high and sophomore through seniors were at the senior high.

"Oh," put off just a little, "this is my last year here, I'm a senior."

The first bell rang, cutting our conversation short and dispersing the crowd. As we parted ways at the doors, he turned to me, "Nice meeting you Lisa, see you around."

I didn't have high hopes after learning he was a senior, of us seeing each other much. In the world of the teenager, there are barriers within social groups, difficult to cross without gaining social animus. As sophomores, we were considered the lowest of the low, and in general, the two never mixed.

But as the school year progressed, I did begin to run into him more often. At first, I thought it was just a coincidence. A chance meeting in the courtyard, a quick conversation during lunch, but as time went on, I started to realize all these meetings were not as accidental as they seemed. There was a definite growing interest between the two of us, and soon we started seeking out each other's company more and more often. We shared only one class together, gym. Whenever possible, we tried to join the same group as activities were rotated and different activities were offered.

During one session, we were offered a fishing class. I've never been sure how this qualified as a gym activity, but the school did have a small pond on the property and, in theory, it did have fish in it. Each day, we would head out with our fishing poles and spend an hour sitting on the bank pretending to fish. I don't believe I ever once so much as put a lure on my hook. But, it was an enjoyable way to spend an hour, and it gave us time to talk and get to know each other. We'd sit side by side, Billy actually trying to fish, and me laughing at him for his efforts.

After a few months, Billy started to push to meet me after school. Maybe take me out on a date, to a movie, or pretty much anything I wanted, all I had to do was say yes. But the situation in my father's house prohibited any socialization after school. Over and over I explained this to him, but I'm not sure he truly understood the oppressive nature of my life, or how impossible it was for me to get away.

As a compromise, I stopped taking the bus home and allowed him to drive me instead. Not home, but to my bus stop where we would sit and talk in his car until the bus showed up. Departing with the rest to make my way home, hopefully, without my father ever finding out what I had been doing. He had expressly forbidden me from accepting a ride home from anyone, insisting that I take the bus, period.

After months of persuasion and stolen rides, I eventually relented and allowed Billy to talk me into letting him into my home. Neither of my parents were ever there before 5 p.m., but I'd developed a deep paranoia that they were keeping tabs on me through the neighbors. I did not know this for a fact, but I did have my suspicions. Maybe it was my growing frustration of not having a life, not being allowed to date, or maybe I just no longer cared. But for whatever the reason, I did concede, and allowed him in the door.

We walked into an empty house. With both my younger sisters gone for at least another hour, we had the place to ourselves. Sitting on the couch in the living room, we talked for a bit, and then Billy slowly leaned over to kiss me. I was still nervous about him being in the house, frequently looking at the door, but his attention was distracting, and enjoyable enough, that I soon forgot to care.

Slowly, as we kissed, we slid from sitting to laying on the couch, our attention centered solely on each other.

So enthralled with one another, I did not hear the click of the lock or the opening of the door as my father's shadow fell across us. Only after my father's first step in the door did we realize we'd been caught. With an audible pop, Billy let go of the nipple he had been nuzzling, sitting up quickly to face my father.

My father's frame filled the doorway, in his uniform, hand resting on his gun, anger etched across his face as he surveyed the scene before him. "Son, I do believe it is time for you to go."

Billy, leaping up from the couch, looked him up and down, and said, "Sir, I do believe you're right." Grabbing his coat as he scooted around my father, he quickly exited the house without a backward glance.

Once he was gone, deadening silence echoed throughout the house as my father and I looked at each other. "Do you want to tell me who that was?"

"No," I had no intentions of giving up a name. Billy was 18, and I would not do anything to ruin his life because of my father.

"I see. We will discuss this later when I get back from work." Looking around the room once more before turning back to me, staring dead into my eyes, he said, "And don't think of leaving the house. I have the neighbor's keeping an eye on things, and they'll tell me if you attempt to leave before I get back."

Well, that answered that question, I was being watched. It had not just been paranoia. "I wasn't planning on going anywhere anyway," Flopping back down on the couch with a shrug.

It was a long wait for my father to get home that night, as I sat in the chair in my room waiting for him to return. Wondering, yet again, how much more restrictive my life would be after this. but I knew I could not accept any more rides home from Billy. To protect him, I would have to keep him away from me. My father knew most of the staff at school, his job as a juvenile officer brought him there regularly. If we were seen together too often, they'd be able to answer his questions if asked.

Throughout the rest of the school year, Billy and I drifted further apart. I explained the situation to him and the possible dire consequences for him if we continued to see each other. While neither of us was happy about it, there was also very little that could be done about it. He was considered an adult, set to leave for AIT after graduation, going on to active duty sometime after that. I didn't want to see him sitting in jail instead because of my father. By the end of the school year, I hardly saw him at all. Even during gym, we had begun choosing different activities, remaining separated to avoid temptation. On the last day of school, we talked, for what I thought was the last time. I wished him well, and he told me if things ever changed that I knew how to find him. But neither of us truly believed we would ever see each other again.

 ## A Wet Rat

During the final week of school, and in between finals, I found myself hanging out with two friends, with some spare time in between tests and nothing to do. Larry, being a senior, had a car on campus, and with a glint in his eye, reminded us of this fact. With that reminder, and after a bit of discussion, we decided that sneaking off grounds and finding something to do was a very good idea. It had to be better than sitting in study hall for the rest of the day, staring at the wall, waiting for the final bell to ring.

Making plans for our exit, Larry slipped out the front door to get his car, something that, as a senior, he could do during finals. Pulling the car around to the exit off of the cafeteria, he waited for us to make our escape, after ensuring no teachers were anywhere around to see us leave.

Springing for the door, we ran out of the building full tilt, and with a "whoop" from both of us, jumped in and off we went, to seek out some adventure. Sliding down in the seats until we exited the campus, we discussed where we might be able to go without any inquiring minds wondering why we weren't at school. South Park, we decided, was the place to go. Quincy's largest park had many places off the beaten path that weren't often frequented, and well away from any roads, paths or people.

After parking the car, we took off on a small, narrow trail down to a stream that meandered through most of the park. Leaving the trail after reaching the water, we headed further into the untamed parts of the park. Creek-walking was a fun activity we often enjoyed. Sometimes the water smelled, it was somehow linked into the city's sewage system and accommodated the overflow for that area of town. But on this day, the sun was shining, the water was clear and the day was beautiful.

Eventually settling on a shale outcropping, we lazily watched the water flow by with the trees on either side arching over our heads shading us from the full force of the sun. We laid back, using Larry as a pillow and let the world drift by, talking a bit about summer and what we would do. Larry had joined the Army earlier in the school year and would be leaving shortly after graduation. I was sorry I couldn't go to either his graduation or the farewell party his parents had planned for him. My father had already forbidden me from going when I asked, so this short escape would be one of the last times I would be able to hang out with him now that school was coming to an end.

After a while, it began to get warm laying on the rocks as the sun beat down in all of its afternoon glory we shifted over to the water to put our feet in and cool down. Sitting side by side, feet in the water, first one, and then another would bump into the person next to us, causing ripple effects up and down the line. The bumps, gentle at first, began to pick up some momentum as we giggled and started a more vigorous shove using our hands until, suddenly, I was dropped into the water. Not wanting to be there alone, I reached out, grabbed Michelle by the wrist, and pulled her in after me. Soaking wet, we both turned on Larry who tried to back up out of range with his hands held out to ward us off. Reaching out, we each managed to grab a hand and dragged him in with us.

Soaking wet, we started an all-out assault on each other, splashing and shoving, picking up mud, leaves, and bits of small debris as we rolled around in the ankle deep water. Our laughter probably could have been heard from the road a half mile away, as we continued to try and get the best of whoever happened to come into our line of sight next.

We were thoroughly bedraggled when we finally emerged from the water. Shaking like dogs, we attempted to rid ourselves of excess water, sloshing with each step. Looking down at myself, I couldn't help but laugh, but I also felt a bit of anxiety over my appearance as well. I needed to go back to school and retrieve my book bag that was still hanging in my locker. How on earth was I going to do that, looking as I was?! There was no way I could even ride the bus home!

My hair was hanging in dirty hanks, mud covered my clothing, my jeans were so sodden I had to hold them up to keep them from falling off with the extra weight acquired during our roll in the stream. And, I was missing a shoe. A quick search of the stream did recover my shoe, and after pounding it on the rock ledge I was able to dislodge some of the mud that had invaded it. We'd managed to miraculously find it buried in the mud, but it wasn't wearable by any means, not without a good hosing off.

After some discussion, I decided that I would try to sneak back into school. Using the door we escaped from, I might be able to reach my locker without being seen. It was possible if we could get there before the bell sounded since that part of the school was generally empty except during lunch. The original plan had been for us to arrive as the bell sounded, and blending in with all the other students pouring out of their classrooms, but our current bedraggled state no longer made that plan viable.

Driving up, Larry and Michelle waited in the car while I made my way to the door. After a quick glance through the glass, and seeing no one around, I quickly opened it and scuttled through, making a beeline straight for my locker. Head down. Eyes on the floor. Right hand holding up my drooping pants. Leaving a trail of water and flecks of mud behind me, with my one shoe sloshing. I walked headfirst into a rather large human being. Stopping dead, I slowly looked up, briefly stopping at the dark smudge made by my forehead, until my eyes reached the top of the 6 ft 7 dean's eyes.

Having nothing good to say about this situation, I slowly looked back down again until my eyes found the ground. I took two short, shuffling steps to the right, and at once began my methodical retreat towards my locker.

Sure at any moment there would be a call for me to stop, I made my slow, stoical way to my locker, braced for a call that never came. Reaching it, I spun the combination, quickly retrieved my bag, and turned around to make my return trip. Never taking my eyes from the floor I retraced my steps, walking slowly by the dean yet again, who was still standing in the exact same spot where I had last left him, and out the door, without ever looking back or up.

Not a single word was spoken by either of us. I do not know to this day if he was in shock about my appearance, and my complete lack of any excitement, and so, had let it go. Or if his brain simply could not process what he was seeing, leaving him unable to act. I think my actions may have surprised him as much as my appearance and so he let me go without a word. Mostly, I believe, because he just didn't want to know what had occurred to put me in such a state.

However it happened, I made good my escape, and for once, without any dire consequences.

 ## I didn't have any plans anyway

The school year had ended, and the beginnings of summer was creeping just around the corner. While most of my friends were looking forward to those long, lazy days eagerly, I was dreading the close confinement of my father's house. The only bright side was that I, and several of my friends, had flunked Driver's Ed and we were all going to be taking summer classes together. At least, I had that to look forward to.

I was still given my daily ten-minute walk out of the house; if I wasn't in trouble for something, it was the only highlight of my existence until summer school started. I couldn't go far, but it allowed me a break from the oppression of constant surveillance. My father, strictly enforcing the time, set a kitchen timer each time I left the house. If I was not in the door by the time the bell went off, I would lose even that. For each minute I was late, I would lose one day of freedom, such as it was.

One hot summer day, my father decided he could trust me enough to run to the store a few blocks away to pick up some things for the house. Now, I don't believe it had anything to do with trust and more to do with the fact it was hot and he didn't want to go himself. I was informed this would count as my daily free time while he handed me the cash, a short grocery list and given 15 minutes to return. An impossible task.

"But Dad, the store is like 5 - 6 minutes away if I walk fast. Plus the time it will take me to get everything in the store, go through checkout and then return." I protested, "I need more time than that."

"If you're quick you can make it," he responded, "and you should be happy that I'm giving you extra time away from the house." Giving me no allowances for delays and no choice but to go.

It wasn't miserably hot, but it was July in the Midwest hot. You couldn't fry eggs on the sidewalk, but the idea of running to the store or even walking very fast had little appeal. I took off in something more than a stroll, but less than a jog, making it there in about 5 minutes, which pleased me until I walked in and saw the lengths of the checkout lines. This could be bad.

I quickly went through the store gathering up the milk, bread, lunch meat and chips that were on the list and stepped into line. I impatiently danced from foot to foot, but there was nothing I could do to hurry the line along. If I left without the groceries, I would be in trouble for returning empty handed and he probably wouldn't believe I had actually gotten this far. If I continued to wait, I would be in trouble for not arriving at home in the time given to me. I was damned if I waited, damned if I didn't. Either way, I was going to be in trouble.

I watched the clock on the wall tick down, as the deadline came and went while the line moved forward with glacial slowness. Finally reaching the head of the line I paid for the groceries. Walking out the door, I decided, fuck it, I'm already late, I'm not running.

Arriving back at the house with groceries in hand, my father confronted me. "You're 10 minutes late."

Well, gee, thanks for stating the obvious, but what could I do except to acknowledge it? "Yes, I am." Continuing my walk into the kitchen and leaving my father standing in the dining room. He stood there quietly while I put everything away, calling me back when I was finished.

Sitting at the head of the table as if pronouncing some great judgment on my behavior, he announced, "I've been thinking about what your punishment should be for being so late. You'll be grounded to the house for the next two weeks."

"Okay," yielding to the inevitable. "Can I go to my room now?"

"Three weeks then." Beginning to look upset.

"Alright." Now I was becoming confused. I hadn't protested or gotten upset. This was something new.

"If you're going to have that attitude a month then." Pushing himself up from the table, hands braced before him as he leaned towards me.

"Fine," I screamed back at him, truly upset at this point.

His face blooming red, my father shouted back "You're going to be stuck in your room for the next year for that."

"Great!" I yelled back.

"You better get comfortable in that room of yours," becoming completely unhinged in his anger, "because that's where you're going to be sitting until you turn 18!"

"Whatever," I screamed back, "it's not like I'd made any plans that far in advance anyway!", and ran from the room to sit in my chair beside the window. And there I sat by myself, as the day turned to evening, until my stepmother returned from work.

Quiet words were exchanged between the two of them, too low for me to hear, but I assumed it was about me. I could see the two of them in the living room and their eyes often drifting towards me during their conversation. I was beyond caring at that moment. There was no life here beyond existing. No amount of good behavior ever offset anything my father deemed worthy of punishment. No leniency was given for when I did exactly what I was told, or how much I helped around the house, or for the good grades I had earned or any of the times I was perfectly well behaved.

My father had it in his mind that I was a bad kid who he would break and remake in his own image, and nothing I ever did or said altered that perception for him. Good behavior went without comment because it was expected. Exceptional behavior, he congratulated himself for since it obviously had to be his stern parenting techniques were working. Anything less than perfect was immediately and punitively reprimanded. I had walked willingly into hell and had no idea where the exit was.

It's worth noting, as all of this was going on I had also begun to suffer some malady of unknown origin. I started having sharp pains that ran across my abdomen and up my left side. It felt like someone was eviscerating me with a burning knife. Sometimes it would last for hours, and during those times, I would curl up into a ball wishing to die as I waited for the pain to pass. Along with the pain, there were bouts of nausea, headaches, and sometimes body tremors. I suffered from insomnia, weight loss, and a general feeling of exhaustion all the time.

My father did take me to see a doctor about it. After two months of tests, blood work and even a CAT scan, the doctor reported that other than a developing ulcer, he could find nothing physically wrong with me. His only explanation for my condition was that it was caused by excessive stress, to which my father responded, "She's 15, how much stress could she have?!" Then dismissed the entire thing out of hand. The idea that living with him under the rules he'd laid down may have been causing me physical injury was simply not something he was willing to entertain. In the end, he decided it was nothing more than a ploy to get my way, and thereafter ignored the entire situation.

Waiting in my chair, beginning to feel the first twinges of discomfort of another oncoming round of pain as my parents decided my fate, I realized there was nothing I could do about any of it. Nothing would make a difference, not what I did, not what I said, not how I behaved. I was in a hopeless, no-win situation. All I could do was sit there, staring out the window.

Eventually, my stepmother walked into my room and sat down on my bed. "I've talked to your father," giving into a small sigh, "I've convinced him to drop your grounding back down to two weeks, and he has agreed, provided you apologize for your behavior."

Sitting there quietly in the twilight of my room, I thought about it. I could mouth the words and be done with it. Life would go on pretty much as it always had if I did. I could say the words to make him happy, appeasing whatever slight it was he thought I had given him. It would cost me nothing, and gain me my freedom in a few weeks' time. Provided, of course, that I did nothing else to raise my father's ire.

"No," I responded, turning back towards the window.

My stepmother's shocked face alone may have been worth that one word, watching her from the corner of my eye. She sat there, staring at me for a long pause, unsure what to say next. "You only have to say you are sorry." Earnestly leaning forward as she said it, with a quick glimpse back at my father, still standing in the other room watching us from the doorway.

"No." I no longer had any desire to negotiate for my freedom, when there was truly no freedom to be gained. Every small concession from either of them was coming at too high a price for me to willingly pay any longer. Ten minutes of freedom was not worth what it was costing me.

"But you have to!" she insisted.

"No, I do not." Turning back to the window, staring out at the same monotonous view.

Becoming very flustered, she repeated, "But you have to!"

"No," turning back to meet her eyes, I smiled at her. "I do

not have to do anything. I can sit here and do nothing until I am 18."

She sat there for a few more minutes while I ignored her. I said nothing else, what else was there to say? They could punish me and they could take away pretty much anything they wanted, and I couldn't do anything about it. My life was in their hands, like it or not, for another 2 years. But, I didn't have to participate anymore either. I could choose to simply do nothing, and that I could live with. I was choosing my path now, not them. This was freedom. By making a choice, even if that choice meant I lost everything, it was still mine to make.

She eventually went away when I would no longer respond to her and nothing she said evoked a response. I could hear them arguing later that night, but I no longer cared. There was nothing else that could be taken from me since everything was already gone by their actions. But I could sit and do nothing, giving no concessions for his behavior or apologies for mine, and that was a choice I could live with.

 ## Vaseline in a police station

As summer progressed, I still had something to look forward to, summer school. Like a joyous reunion, I greeted my friends as we started Drivers Ed. I had never been so happy to flunk a class in my life. Along with all the people I did know, there was one I hadn't seen around school before. He had a shy smile and dark black hair, often smelling lightly of clove, from the cigarettes he smoked. He caught my eye, and as fate would have it, I caught his.

To this day, whenever I hear the song "*The Summer of 69*" my memories of him come flooding back. Looking for all the world like a young James Dean, holding himself in a proud slouch, white t-shirt blazing in the sun, a cigarette hanging from the side of his mouth.

Seeking each other out in our limited free time during class breaks, and hanging out before and after class while we waited to be picked up, our interest in each other peaked. And all was well, until one day after class it was my father who came for me, and he noticed the young man I was standing with. Displeased could not begin to describe the look on my father's face, nor could I fail to notice the look of panic on the face of my new interest.

As soon as I entered the car, the interrogation began. "Do you know that boy?"

"Yeah, he's in my driver's ed class."

"What is his name?" beginning to get himself worked up.

Well, I knew damn good and well what his name was, but I was reluctant to share after seeing his reaction. "Um, maybe David or Darren, something like that."

"How long have you been talking to him?"

"Just a few times." Knowing with absolute certainty this was someone my father distinctly disliked, "You know, he's just around."

"You will not speak to him again," slapping the steering wheel for emphasis, "not before, during or after class. Do you understand me? Not a word will pass between the two of you again. You will avoid him, and if he tries to speak to you, you will walk away. Do I make myself clear?!"

Now, if anything could have increased my interest in him, this was it. Not that I would share that tidbit with my father. "Yes Dad," was my response to his demands, but not anything near to what my actual intentions were.

The following day, I approached a somewhat apprehensive looking David, "So," he began with some hesitation, "was that your dad?"

"Yeah, I guess you guys have met before?"

"Um, yeah," looking at everything but me, "he arrested me a few years ago. It was really stupid and I got into a lot of trouble over it which is why I was sent away for a while. I'm just now getting back in town."

"Did you hurt anyone?"

"No." Finally looking at me for the first time, and sighed, "But I can understand if you wouldn't want to talk to me anymore, considering who your dad is."

"Did anyone get hurt by what you did?" I was very much interested in this (now) almost irresistible young man.

"No, it was dumb, but no, no one was hurt."

"Then don't worry about it," smiling at him. "If there is one thing I love in this life, it's doing things that would send my Dad into convulsions. If you're still interested, so am I."

He was. From that moment on, we actively sought out each other's company, while hating the fact we had so little of it. We didn't live far from each other, but I couldn't leave my house, and he was most certainly not welcome in mine. Slowly, a plan began to form. During the day, I was watched constantly. But at night, everyone else in the house slept upstairs, while my room was on the main floor. Right next to the back door. I knew from my frequent bouts of insomnia it was a rare occurrence that anyone would come downstairs during the night. And if they did, other than a quick peek in my room, no one really checked on me at night. A few pillows would take care of that if anyone did wander downstairs. No problem.

There was a park between our two houses, only a few blocks away for each of us, and easy enough to reach without anyone seeing either of us if we were careful. Setting our plan in motion, we would slip away in the dead of night and wait for each other at the bandstand for the rest of that summer. Most nights, both of us were able to sneak out of our houses, and those were good nights for both of us. From midnight until dawn we were free to be with each other. We often talked about our lives and all that had happened to us. How our lives had been connected and about what the future might bring.

We whispered the words "I love you" for the first time to one another while laying naked under the stars. He was my first love, felt both fierce and bright, as I reveled in the newness of it. The more time we spent together, the more time we wanted, and we began to take chances. Meeting more often and earlier in the night, we were no longer careful and, a week before my birthday, we were caught.

While laying in each others' arms in the bandstand, we saw headlights moving through the park. With the park closed to traffic each night, we knew it couldn't be just a random car. When the searchlights flipped on, we knew we were in trouble. Dressing quickly, we attempted to hide in the shadows of the bandstand. But, as another vehicle entered the search we knew we would soon be seen. With a lack of good options, we decided to make a run for the trees, hoping luck and the cover of darkness would let us slip by unnoticed. It was a very big park, one of the biggest in the area, with multiple trails through the wooded areas and much of it completely untended and left to run wild. I'd spent a great deal of my childhood in this park and on those trails when I lived with my mother. I knew if we could get to one of them we wouldn't be caught. But to get to any of the trails, we had to cross both a large empty space and the road to reach them.

Together we crouched, waiting in the shadows until the second squad car rounded the far curve, and off we ran. Running as low and as fast as we could, a third car showed up and spotted us. We froze for an instant, trapped by the bright spotlight, and then bolted once more. No longer caring that we'd been seen, we ran. Unfortunately, not in the same direction. I was heading for a trail I knew. A small jump down would take us away from anyone who didn't know it was there, but David headed the wrong way. We had drifted too far away from each other by the time I noticed him no longer at my side. I started to go back, but it was too late. We made it almost to the tree line, almost, but almost is never enough.

I was roughly stopped by a cop I tried to dodge past,

losing sight of David in the attempt. hoping he had gotten away even I had not. With a tight grip on my upper arm, I was escorted to the squad car and forced inside. The door slammed firmly shut behind me. I was caught and there was no getting away.

From the window, I could see the other squad cars up the road, while my two captors stood outside the squad car talking, doing an occasional indifferent sweep of the area. Eventually, I saw the other cars on the move again, with their spotlights now dark. Maybe they'd caught him, maybe he'd gotten away. Perhaps they'd given up since it was likely I was the one they were actually looking for. David would have been nothing more than collateral damage.

As soon as the cop slid into the squad car he began with his questions, "Name?"

"Sally," saying the first name that popped into my head. Just because I'd been caught didn't mean I had to make it easy for them to figure out who I was.

"Sally?" Turning to look at me and shaking his head, "I see. Last name?" Now I couldn't be sure, it was dark and I'd met a lot of my father's friends over the years, but by his reaction, it began to confirm my suspicion he knew exactly who I was.

"Harrison," I replied anyway.

"Age?"

"Eighteen."

While I suspected he knew who I was, I was willing to play along for as long as he was.

"Uh huh, and your birthday?"

After a bit of quick math in my head, I answered, "May 5th, 1967."

At this point, he turned to look at me and said, "Okay Lisa, why don't we cut the crap. I know who you are. Mind telling me why you were out here tonight and not at home like you should have been?"

"Out for a stroll. It's lovely this time of night, isn't it?" While that part of the game was over, I had no intentions of giving up anything they didn't already know. Such as David's name or what we were actually doing. And, while I'm sure he had figured out the latter, I desperately continued to hope they wouldn't the former.

"And the boy in the other squad car? What exactly do you think he was doing in the park?" Oh, poor David, he hadn't gotten away either.

"Out for a walk too, I guess." I truly felt bad for him, but there was nothing more I could do to try and help him. Hopefully, things would go a little better for him than they probably were for me. But I somehow doubted that too.

On the long drive back to the police station, I decided I should do some questioning on my own and find out how this had happened. "So, how did you find me?"

"What do you mean?"

"Well, you weren't just randomly searching, so you had to know about where to look for me. Who called this in, my Dad?" I doubted very much David's parents could have gotten this kind of police response. It had to have been my dad who set this whole thing in motion.

"I don't know what you are talking about." Looking back at me in the mirror.

Sitting quietly for a bit and I went over my options. I could sit quietly for the rest of the trip, I could become truly obnoxious and start flailing around the backseat, or I could start a repetitive patter that most adults, eventually, crush under. I chose option C. I might not get anywhere. But it was better than doing nothing, and no amount of flailing was going to help the situation.

"It had to be my dad you see, otherwise there wouldn't have been any cops in the park this time of night unless someone sent them, so you were sent by someone, and that someone had to have been my dad because he is the only option that makes any sense. If you were after someone else you wouldn't have stopped your search just because you found me, they would have continued the search even if you found me because that's what you do, since the search was called off as soon as I was found it then means you were after me, and the only person who could have sent so many would have been my dad, so you might as well admit that it was him because you and I both know that that's the truth. You must have owed my dad a big favor to get this many out here at once, they must have pulled every squad car in the area to do this kind of search, probably even leaving many other areas without anyone patrolling since there are only so many cars for any particular area at night. I mean how many squad cars run at night? It's a small enough town so what? Maybe 6 total at night? Which means you had to commit at least half of your patrol force for the sole purpose of finding me for a friend. But I guess that whole buddy-buddy system works really well for you guys, I wonder how this will be written up in your daily reports? Incompetent cop loses wayward daughter and turns the nightly patrol upside down to retrieve her? Or will you just skim over all of that to cover each others' asses? Just in case you do something stupid and need a favor later on?"

And on and on I went, for blocks at a time. Pausing on occasion for breath, but keeping up the circular logic of the situation until I could see his knuckles turn white on the steering wheel, and his breath coming faster with each passing minute of my tirade. Several times, I could see him wanting to jump in and say something. With each additional verbal round that I made, it became harder for him to stop himself. I knew if I kept it up and had enough time, he would eventually say something if only to make me shut up.

"So, how big a favor do you owe my dad to set this kind of thing up?" I began again, when he turned around, looking flustered and uncomfortable.

"Enough!" Practically roaring at me.

"Why?" Smiling now, knowing I'd gotten to him.

"As soon as we get to the police station, you will be calling your father and we will get this all settled as soon as he comes to get you."

"So, it was my father."

"He's waiting at home for you to call, and as soon as we are out of this car you will be calling him to come get you." Turning back around, he continued driving back to the station.

Well, that answered that question. It had been my father, but why he was awake this time of the night was beyond me. Maybe he'd gotten up for something to drink, and then decided to check on me since he was there. As to where to find me, it was possible that he had found the note that David sent me setting up our next meeting, hidden under the mattress in my room. Not a great hiding spot, but I didn't have many to choose from.

The rest of the ride was quiet. I had the information I wanted, and there was no point in continuing to upset him for no good reason.

When we arrived at the station, I was escorted into the squad room, and there sat David in the cage. It was a small one, basically just big enough for a few people to sit while being processed. He looked absolutely miserable. But, when he saw me, he gave me a brief smile, which I returned. I started walking in his direction since I assumed they would put me in there as well. But no, they didn't want me anywhere near him. They pulled me towards a desk and ordered me to sit quietly. Leaving me there unattended, the cop who had taken me into custody went to talk with a few of the others already there.

A few minutes later, a different cop came over to me and said, "Okay, it's time to make your one phone call."

"Okay," I agreed cheerfully, "I'd like to call my mother please."

"No." came the firm response, "You will be calling your father."

"No," I replied equally firm.

"What do you mean, no," a puzzled expression spreading across his face, "Your father is waiting for your call right now. This is your only option to get out of here."

"No." There is power in a simple refusal. A lesson I had learned very well living with my father.

And there we sat in a stalemate. He could not physically force me to make the phone call, and I refused to bend to his demands. He paced in front of me for a bit, unsure how to proceed. Falling back on habitual behavior that had always worked in the past, he tried again, "You need to call your Father."

"No." Shaking my head, "I will make a phone call for someone else to bail me out, but I will not call my Father."

"The only phone call you are allowed to make is to your Father," came his response, "if you don't call him, you're going to be sitting here a very long time." With that, he walked away. Assuming, I'm sure, after sitting there for a while with no other options, I would eventually change my mind.

Sitting in the chair waiting was, in fact, quite boring. I was seated too far away from David to talk to him, and when I got up to move closer I was stopped. At the same time, I also realized as long as I didn't go near David or the door, they would pretty much let me wander around as I pleased.

At first, I was content to just randomly move around. But, at some point in my circuit, I decided to engage in some harmless prankery. In my boredom, I'd made a mental inventory of what I had in my pockets: a couple of marbles, a few notes from my friends, a piece of string, a rubber band and a tube of lip balm Vaseline. With a smile to myself, I decided the last item held some promise.

Scanning the room, making sure that no one was watching me closely, I sat down at one of the desks. Sitting quietly as I was, I aroused no interest from anyone in the room. As their attention drifted elsewhere I began to Vaseline all the items on the desk, including the phone. I moved from desk to desk, not making any sudden movements. I would sit and rock in the chair for a few minutes until they lost interest in me, then begin the process yet again. Pens, pencils, drawer handles and even the chair seats once I got up were all likely targets.

Whatever had been left out for me to casually run my fingers over was fair game.

Vaseline is great stuff. A little goes a long way, it's not water soluble, and once you get it on you, it spreads easily to whatever else you touch. I was about halfway through my circuit when someone sat down at a desk I had so lovingly treated. The reaction was worth every bit of trouble I got into over it.

He sat down in his chair that had been slimed, picked up the phone and put it to his ear. As soon as it connected, he could feel it. Immediately slamming down the phone, he began rubbing at the now covered ear. As he rubbed, he put his other hand down on a row of pencils that had been similarly treated. With a yelp, he jumped out of his chair, pointing in my direction, yelling "Stop her!" to the room in general.

Since I was just sitting calmly in a chair, they couldn't at first, see what the problem was, looking back and forth at us in confusion. As the laughter bubbled up, I couldn't stop myself. It was just too funny. Watching with glee, as he continued to smear Vaseline all over his face in an attempt to get it off, and his, as yet unnoticed, shiny pants gleaming in the fluorescent lights.

With my laughter giving me away, the other cops began to realize something was definitely not right. Several of them moved closer to me while others approached the desks I had sat at. A quick search of my person turned up the lip balm, and as they went from desk to desk they realized what I had done. It didn't take long to connect the lip balm with what had been done to their desks and chairs. Less than pleased did not begin to describe their reaction. I do believe I may have seen at least one smirk among them, but the overall feel of the room was one of pissed frustration.

None of them were quite sure what to do with me since this was supposed to be one of those 'scared straight' moments for me. The plan had been to arrest me, put some fear in me of what might happen and threats of dire consequences if I didn't do as I was told. By my actions, they could clearly see that I was not scared and this was not working. They were now in a dilemma. This had been done as a favor to my father to help get a wayward daughter back on the straight and narrow. Instead, they had someone on their hands that wasn't playing by the expected rules, and they had no idea what to do about it. They couldn't just release me, and I refused to call my father. The plan had never been to truly arrest me, and the question of what to do with me became a pressing issue that they had no immediate answer for.

I was grabbed up by one of the officers and hauled over to a phone hanging on the wall. He punched in a number and began to talk, "Dave, I have your daughter here, she's become a problem and something needs to be done." I could hear my father's voice, but not his words. The cop on the phone nodded a few times, then handed the phone to me.

As soon as the phone was to my ear, my father's voice became very clear, "I wake up in the middle of the night and find you gone, and now you've been arrested. If you want to get out of this mess, you had better come back to me on hands and knees begging for my forgiveness. Apologize for everything you've done, and swear to me you will never, *ever*, do this again."

I sat there for a few minutes in silence and let his words roll over my mind, "Your offer is not acceptable." and hung up the phone. Turning to look at the room, I asked, "Now what?"

From the reaction of everyone around me, I knew I had done an excellent job of stirring up the anthill. The cop in front of me stood in open-mouthed astonishment, clearly unsure what to do now. "What did you do?" he demanded.

"I did not accept his offer," I replied, "so you will either need to arrest me, or let me make another phone call for someone else to come get me."

Poor David sat in the cage throughout this entire series of

events. I wasn't sure how much he'd seen or what was going to happen to him, but I did hope his family was more forgiving than mine. He could see that I'd caused some kind of commotion, but had no idea what it was, nor had I seen him make any phone calls for anyone to come get him either. It was possible that they'd been called before I arrived or even one of the officers made the call for him and he was simply waiting for them to show up.

A few more frantic phone calls were made. Most likely, several of them to my father. I was then taken from the room, down the hallway and put into an interrogation room. I was told in no uncertain terms I was to sit down, shut up and wait, someone would be there for me in a bit. I wasn't sure what all this meant, but I was pretty sure it wasn't going to be my father walking through the door anytime soon.

There wasn't much to do, they had taken away everything I had in my pockets before escorting me to the room to prevent any further mischief on my part. I took a seat in the chair facing the door and settled in to wait, with nothing to entertain me but the ticking of the clock hanging in a cage on the wall. By this point in my life, I had acquired excellent waiting skills; months of sitting in my chair at my father's house had taught me that.

In less than an hour, a new person arrived. It was Dennis, another juvenile liaison officer, and a frequent visitor to my father's house over the years, looking less than pleased with the entire situation.

"I get woken up in the middle of the night and told to come down to the police station because there was a juvenile here for me to deal with. I walk in and find out it's you Lisa. What do you have to say for yourself?!"

"Good morning?" I responded with a smile. I didn't have anything against Dennis. He wasn't a bad guy and had never done anything for me to dislike him, but at this point, there wasn't much I could say one way or the other. I might as well go forward with a smile. I wasn't sure what the worst they could do to me was, but at that point, I was pretty sure whatever it was it couldn't be worse than living with my father.

Dennis paced around the room, shaking his head at me while he did so. Clearly, trying to figure out what to say to me. Eventually, he sat in the chair opposite of me and said, "You could do as your father has asked, and we can just put this whole situation behind us."

"No, Dennis," wondering what he would do with my refusal, I still had a vague hope I could call my mother if I pushed hard enough, "I will call anyone but him. It's late enough in the morning now that my mother should be awake. I will call her if you let me."

He sat there for a bit looking at me, then got up and left the room. I suspect to this day that my father stood outside the room waiting for me to crumble under enough pressure. Even now, I do not know what went on outside, or what deals were made that day concerning my future. I sat quietly for quite a while, and when Dennis returned, he was looking less than happy with the situation. It appeared my fate had been decided, and calling my mother was not among the options to be given to me.

I was placed in foster care that morning, in an emergency 21-day placement program. It was used as a cooling off period in the hopes of reuniting a child with their family at the end of the program. There are counselors, caseworkers, and a whole team of people whose sole job is to facilitate the child in once again returning home. If that is not possible, then begins the process to find an acceptable placement for them. In the end, I did not go home to my father, nor to my mother's. Instead, I spent the remainder of my adolescence stuck in the foster care system.

## WHEN EVERYTHING CHANGED...

## Interlude One
## Stuck in the System

Going into foster care was very different from anything I'd experienced before. Some families were better, and others were, I can't say worse than living with my father, but it definitely wasn't an improvement from living with him.

During the emergency placement process, the parents of a few of my friends came forward saying they would take me in when they learned of my situation. Each was rejected, primarily due to my father's objections. I even attempted to contact my mother, asking her to take me back, but she had a new life, with a new boyfriend, and she was reluctant to disrupt the new life she started building after my sister and I left her.

By the end of the day, I was placed in an emergency program called EMRY. My new home a happy place to be, in comparison to my father's house. By the rules of the program, I couldn't leave their home and could only have one friend come to visit on a prescribed schedule. Even though there was no more freedom of movement within their home than I had had with my father, it was a different kind of confinement. There was no malice behind it. Francis and Wanda were cheerful, friendly women who loved children and did their best for them, even in these bad situations. They genuinely cared and that made all the difference in the world to me. I caused them no trouble and did not try to even bend the rules. I was happy and relieved in a way I did not then have the words for, and they declared me a wonderful child.

In the beginning, as the courts attempted reconciliation with my father, he was attempting to have me committed to a psychiatric facility. With the help of a psychiatrist, my father had me diagnosed as schizophrenic with delusions of grandeur. I did not hear voices, I'd done nothing to hurt myself or others, nor did I believe I had a special destiny. But I do believe my father was desperate to prove that everything that had gone wrong with me had nothing to do with him, and everything to do with being unlucky enough to have a disturbed child. By proving I was "crazy", he could exonerate himself without feeling any guilt or responsibility for what had occurred.

I stood alone in the courtroom and watched as my stepmother took the stand, pronouncing there was something terribly wrong with me. Insisting nothing affected how I acted, and every punishment they imposed rolled off me like water on a duck. My father, telling the courts I was deeply disturbed, and how he felt it would be best for everyone that I was placed somewhere where I couldn't interact with the world. They played the parts of the anguished parents very well. Telling the courts of their love for me and how hard they tried to help turn me from the dangerous path I had chosen for myself. All that they had sacrificed in their valiant attempts to save me.

I was very lucky I did not end up in an institution, heavily medicated for the rest of my days. A fate only narrowly avoided when two other counselors from my father's psychiatrist's office disagreed with his diagnosis and stood up for me in court. Instead, I was placed in the foster care system. As part of a compromise deal, I was ordered to attend counseling sessions for the remainder of my time in the system. It was a compromise I could live with. The two counselors who stood up for me that day in court still have my eternal gratitude, without them I may very well never have seen the light of day again that wasn't behind a set of bars.

My last day in the EMRY program was a sad one for me. I had enjoyed my time with them, and I was a bit fearful about where I would go next. From here on out, my life was entirely in the hands of the courts, and I could only hope for the best. For the next two years, I would be stuck in a system that I had very little say over where I lived or with whom I lived, by a court that had no care or concern for me personally. My life, yet again, was out of my control.

## Life with Eula

I arrived at Eula's house 21 days after entering foster care, following my case worker up the stairs to enter this newest stranger's house. I didn't know what to expect. My heart beating in my chest I waited to meet my newest "mother" I stood quietly in the hallway with my caseworker outside her parlor. In the house behind me I could hear voices and laughter drifting through the air, and an occasional glimpse of the body attached to those voices. Looking around the large house, I thought to myself, maybe I could fit in here.

Knocking on the parlor door, my caseworker entered, leaving me to stand alone while I waited for them to call me in. A short time later, I heard my caseworker call our for me to join them. I shyly shuffled in, looking down at my shoes, hands fidgeting in front of me. When I heard Eula say, "Look up at me child, let me see you."

Slowly raising my head, I saw Eula for the first time, sitting in her chair, smiling at me. Giving me a nod when our eyes met, she raised her arms and said, "Come here child, it's going to be okay now." I walked into her hug, tears in my eyes, feeling as if I had come home. And perhaps, maybe I was, finally home.

She owned a huge house next to the library that was always filled to capacity with the girls she fostered. Living with her was like coming home after a long absence. She loved each of us and we all loved her in return, welcoming us as we arrived like a long lost daughter.

Under her care, I was allowed to have a life again. Friends were welcome to visit and I was allowed to roam, within reason, with a freedom I'd not had before in my life. Always before, even with the absolute freedom while living with my mother, I had my sister to care for and worry about. With my father, I'd had no life to speak of at all. For the first time in my life, I had something resembling normalcy, and I savored every moment of it.

On warm evenings, we would all gather around her outside on the porch and share stories. She would listen to us talk about school, the boys we liked, and our lives in general, smiling indulgently at each of us as we talked. She accepted us for who we were, giving us unconditional love, no matter what our situation may have been prior to moving in with her. "A clean slate", she declared, to each of us coming into her home. What happened in the past was the past. From here on out, we would only be judged by how we acted now, both privileges and punishments based solely on our present behavior. I loved her dearly for that. I think everyone in her home did.

I spent time with my friends, hanging out after school, going to movies, grabbing something to eat at our favorite pizza place. I was able, for the first time, to ride to school openly with my friends, which to me was a very big deal. Michael owned a huge boat of a car, and we would all pile in, sometimes as many as 12 of us (in the days before seat belt laws or teen passenger restrictions) blasting Barroom Blitz as loud as his speakers could go every morning to school as we'd sing (scream) along to the music.

I did nothing that could have brought trouble to Eula. I did not drink, nor did I feel the need to get high. I no longer felt the need to escape the world I was in. I was happy and content exactly as I was. I studied hard and even helped my other foster sisters when they needed tutoring. I did my fair share around the house without complaint. I wanted Eula to be proud of me, and most of all, I did not ever want her to send me away.

 ## A Life Resumed

Many things changed when I began my life with Eula, and being able to date was one of them. Shortly after settling into her home, I pulled out a number I'd kept but never expected to call again. With nervous anticipation, I dialed the number, and heard his voice on the other side, "Hi Billy, it's me, Lisa."

"Lisa?" Hearing confusion in his voice, I wasn't all that surprised all things considered. We hadn't talked since the end of the school year, and I don't believe he ever expected to hear from me again.

"Yeah, it's me," wondering if he was even interested in seeing me again. It'd been months since we last saw each other, who knew, he may have gotten a girlfriend during the intervening time. "I'm not living with my father anymore. I've been put in foster care."

"Oh wow," came his surprised response, "is that a good thing?"

I started to laugh, "Oh yeah, for now anyway, it is a very good thing." I hesitated for a second, and then plunged ahead, "Would you like to hang out sometime? My foster mother is okay with me going out with friends," another small hesitation, then a final a rush of words, "or even go on a date."

"No shit?!" Sounding both surprised and pleased by this turn of events, "Well, what are you doing tonight?"

"Well..." drawing out my words, "I think I'm going out with this guy named Billy. I'm just waiting for him to ask."

"Lisa, would you like to go out with me tonight?"

"I would love to go out on a date with you tonight..." hesitating a heartbeat before continuing, "But you'll have to meet Eula before we can go out. She has a rule about meeting anyone I leave with before I go anywhere."

"Not a problem," without any hesitation on his part, "just tell me when and where, and I'll be there. I've missed you."

"I've missed you too," happier than I thought I would be

to hear this, "I can't wait to see you again."

After making all the arrangements on the phone with Billy on the particulars of when and where I hung up the phone and went in search of Eula. I found her sitting in her front parlor, a few of my sisters scattered around the room as well. When we weren't otherwise busy with chores, homework, or social activities, we usually gathered around her wherever she was. Finding an empty space, I sat down, listening to my sisters take turns recounting whatever tale they had for the day to share, usually about school, sometimes a boy. And, as always, Eula listened attentively, or at least, she gave an excellent performance if she wasn't.

During a break in conversation, I nervously told Eula about Billy.

She smiled in reassurance, patting my hand as she gazed at me with a knowing look. While I knew what the dating rules were, this was the first time I'd asked to go out with anyone since my arrival.

"Child, as long as I get to meet him and approve of this young man, you are free to go out with him tonight."

"Oh, thank you Eula!" I said, almost in tears as I jumped up to hug her. After so much confinement at my father's, her trust in me was as wonderful as an unexpected gift after a disappointing Christmas.

She leaned over and patting my cheek, giving me a smile, "Go on now and get ready for your date, just bring him to meet me when he arrives."

I raced upstairs to my room, a tiny closest like space, but I loved it because it was mine, with a door I could shut and I didn't have to share with anyone. As big as Eula's house was, most of my foster sisters shared a room. Even I did the first two weeks, but when she had offered me this tiny space, I jumped at the chance to take it.

I started going through my closet, pulling out random bits of clothing, then discarding them on the bed after a quick check in the mirror. As my closet emptied and my bed began to overflow, I started laughing at myself for the mess I was creating. Why I wondered, was I so concerned about what I wore? Sinking slowly to sit on the edge of my bed I realized, this was my first real date, ever.

I had male friends I hung out with, I had sneaked out of my house in the middle of the night and risked everything to see a boy, I'd even had sex, but I'd never, up to this moment, ever been allowed to go out on a date, and I was excited. I felt giddy, nervous, happy, distressed, a whole range of emotions that I had no idea what to do with as I sat laughing on my bed wondering what to do when I heard a knock on my door. Without waiting for a response, one of my sisters popped her head through the door.

"You okay girl?" Shannon asked.

"I have a date tonight and I have absolutely no idea what to wear." trying to talk through my giggles.

Eying the growing mound of clothing on my bed, she dryly replied, "Yeah, I can see that." Making a motion to indicate she wanted to come in, she slipped through the door at my nod of approval as I scooted back.

It really was a very small room, and already crowded with the scattered remains of my closet tangled everywhere. With another person in it, it was becoming downright claustrophobic. Shannon slowly inched her way in, distrustfully eying the piles of clothing. The contents of my bed gave the distinct impression of imminent collapse, needing only a small push to create further chaos. After assuring herself that she would not be immediately buried under this mountainous heap, she began to gingerly pick her way through my clothes, asking me questions as she did.

Slowly getting my giggles under control, I told her of our plans for the night. Nodding in all the right places while I rambled, she began to cautiously remove various items, handing them to me until a complete outfit emerged from the chaos that was my bed. "Here you go, wear this." With gratitude, I smiled my thanks for her help. Looking around one last time, she said, "Just relax, it's all going to be fine." Giving her head a final shake, she slipped back out the door.

Once again alone, I looked over the mess I had created in my frenzy. Sighing at what I'd done, I began returning everything to the now empty closet, restoring some sense of order, and giving myself enough space to change my clothes without falling on my face. Showing up for my very first date with a black eye was not the look I was going for.

With my room restored to order, and dressed in the outfit Shannon picked out for me, I went back downstairs to sit with Eula and the rest of my sisters until Billy showed up. Shannon, the ever helpful fashion consultant, had already related to everyone in the room my bout of closet insanity before I'd arrived. Slightly red-faced for my prior freak-out, I sat down and endured their good-natured teasing as I watched the time, nervously waiting for Billy to arrive. Creeping doubts entered my head, which I did my best to conceal from both myself and my sisters, not wanting to fuel the fire of their laughter any more than I already had.

But right on time, I watched his car pull up in front of the house, and with a great deal of relief, I went to the door to meet him. He looked good standing there in the doorway. He wasn't but a few inches taller than I was, but he had a compact strength from his military training, and a confident way to his walk that added to his overall stature. I'd always enjoyed just watching him move even when he wasn't aware of it, maybe, especially when he wasn't aware of it.

As soon as I opened the door he greeted me with a kiss and a smile, and possibly with a little of the nervousness I was feeling as well. Taking his hand, I led him into the parlor to meet Eula. As soon as I made the introductions she shooed everyone, including me, out the door. She wanted a few minutes to talk to this young man alone. I stood outside her door, shifting from foot to foot, wondering what was being said on the other side. My sisters crowded around me, offering reassurances that she did this with every boy who walked through the door, don't sweat it.

After some indeterminate amount of time, somewhere between forever and eternity, the door opened and Billy stepped out smiling at me, "Are you ready to go?" he asked.

Yes, yes I was, more than I could say. I was ready for this, my very first date, but before I could leave I had to go back to Eula one last time. I walked into her parlor, leaned over and kissed her on her cheek, "Thank you, Eula, for everything."

She smiled back at me, and I think she really understood. Without having to explain anything, she understood. "Go have fun child, but be a good girl and home before midnight."

Midnight? Absolutely I would be home by then and no, I could not even imagine doing anything to disappoint this wonderful woman. With giddy joy, I left the house with Billy, almost skipping to his car, babbling in my happiness as he did his best not to laugh at me. A fight he lost with himself before we even reached his car.

I didn't care, I was happy, and I could see he was equally happy for me.

He took me out to dinner, where we sat and talked, catching up on each other's lives. I told him how I ended up in foster care. He told me about AIT, explaining he was on hold for a few months. He'd been in a car accident shortly after returning from AIT and was waiting for medical discharge. He would be leaving for active duty as soon as he was completely healed.

He asked for Washington State as his station of choice because of a song, and had gotten it. It might have been '*America*' by Jefferson Starship but after all these years, I truly can't remember. I teased him about making life choices based on music, but I had also found it very endearing. There were worse reasons for doing something.

After dinner, we went out driving around in his car with no particular destination in mind and eventually ended up down by the river. We sat next to each other on the riverbank holding hands in the warmth of an early fall evening. The stars were bright as the river rolled calmly by, and we enjoyed the quiet of each others company. There was no hurry, no worry about what my father would do or say if I was seen in the company of a young man. I felt a contentment I hadn't known before, and I loved it.

Discussing our futures, it brought us back to our present. He would be leaving before very much longer, a few months at most. And, as much as we enjoyed each others company, serious dating didn't make a lot of sense to either of us. I had two years of school left and he would soon be leaving. When he left, I would not be able to visit. As a foster kid, I was confined to the state, and it would be a year or more before he would be able to come back again on leave. So it was decided, we would go out whenever we were able to, but there would be no commitment for it to be more.

I was not disappointed by this decision. Living with Eula opened up a whole new range of options I'd never had the opportunity to enjoy before. I was looking forward to spending more time with Billy, but I also liked the idea of not being confined by anything or anyone, even with something as simple as going steady. I was now ready to explore my new freedom, wherever it led me. To date, to meet new people without fear of harsh consequences, to engage in adolescent activities that always before. been denied to me. A new type of normalcy was opening up to me that I'd never had with either of my parents, and I intended to savor every moment of it for as long as it lasted.

## An Extra Ticket

Ginny had been my best friend since the first day of junior high. Both of our last names started with the same letter putting us next to each other in every class we shared, which were many. She was a devoutly antisocial person. In every class, when not paying attention to the teacher, she had her nose in a book, refusing to pay attention to the rest of the world around her. It wasn't that she hated any one particular person; she just seemed to hate everyone equally. Being a ravenous reader myself, I could understand the appeal of a good book, I carried one with me at all times throughout my day, so whenever the opportunity to read presented itself I would have one with me. But, unlike Ginny, I also enjoyed the social aspect of life. So I decided, with her being my almost constant companion in class, she could be my perfect new friend. She did not, at first, share my enthusiasm in this decision.

I began with a simple "Hi." in homeroom on the second day of school, which she completely ignored. By third hour I got a glance up from her book as I talked to her. As fifth hour rolled around, I was able to persuade her into a short verbal exchange, and by the end of school, she was willing to put down her book to talk to me. I considered this a great victory in my pursuit of friendship, and as we parted ways for the day, expressed how I was looking forward to seeing her again tomorrow. Her eye roll did nothing to deter me at all.

By the end of the week, we were talking at the beginning of every class and walking together to our shared classes, our conversations centered around books we enjoyed. She had a great love of Louis L'Amour, while I had a preference for Sci-Fi. As the days progressed, we began to slowly venture off beyond the topics of books and classes, and into the realm of our personal lives and history, and that is when our friendship truly began.

We eventually began to add other people to our little group of two. Others like us, who loved books, were socially awkward, had few friends, and did exceptionally well in class. In other words, the geeks. Most of us shared a common background of poverty, divorce, and absent parenting. For the first time, I had friends who understood my life and the isolation that had surrounded all of us faded as we became close friends.

These were the friends who helped me through the rough times living with my mother and stuck by me through the dark times with my father. Their friendship never wavered, and it was their support that sustained me when I didn't think I could go on anymore. This little group of nerds, geeks, and artists with Ginny, always, as my closest friend. She was the one I could always turn to, no matter what, and who I always tried to include in whatever it was I was doing.

By the time we all reached senior high, we had another small group of guys who had attached themselves to us. Hanging out within our circle, yet slightly apart. We mixed freely and often got together for any number of things. Sometimes, dating and pairing off, but always friends first and with never any hostility if things didn't work out. It worked out very well for all of us.

During my junior year, I was invited to Homecoming by Michael, one of the guys from our little satellite group, and I was more than thrilled to go. I'd missed every dance and social event my previous year while living with my father and Eula was more than happy to let me attend. But, after accepting Michael's invitation, I found out Ginny had not been invited by anyone, and I didn't want to go without her.

Fretting at the idea of Ginny sitting at home alone while I was at the dance with Michael, I came up with what I thought was a brilliant idea, Michael could take us both. He could have two dates for Homecoming instead of one, wouldn't that be fun? During lunch, after discussing it with Ginny, we approached him with my brilliant plan. At first, he was resistant to the idea, but I think the idea of taking two dates had a certain appeal to the male in him, and he finally agreed.

Once he finally conceded to our idea, he obligingly went to buy the three tickets for all of us. And there we encountered a snag to our plan. You could only buy tickets in pairs, not individually. After a great deal of arguing, in the end, poor Michael gave in and bought four tickets.

A week before the dance, my fashion consulting sister,

Shannon, had a bad breakup with her boyfriend and she was heartbroken. Honestly, she may have been more upset about the timing of the breakup than of the actual breakup itself. Her dress had been hanging in the closet for over a month, and now she would be sitting at home while everyone else in the house would be going to Homecoming. Sitting at the end of my bed, talking about how she didn't want to sit at Eula's alone while everyone else had dates and plans, my mind started turning back to the spare ticket Michael had. He'd already agreed to take two, perhaps he could be persuaded into taking three.

That evening, with both Ginny and Michael coming to visit me, I gave them my proposal. With a slight widening of the eyes, he thought it over and decided, sure why not?! Shannon, who'd been quietly sitting in the background began jumping up and down from his first nod of acceptance. She bounced down to Michael, giving him a big kiss, happy she wasn't going to be sitting at home alone, while the rest of us went to the dance. Ginny and I found the whole thing amazingly funny, giving her random encouragement to continue the show. Michael, on the other hand, stood slightly dazed as Shannon bounced all around him in her happiness. Stopping often to give him random hugs and kisses in her excitement. He was starting to resemble a doe in the headlights and beginning to wonder what he had gotten himself into.

The Saturday before Homecoming, everyone in our little group gathered at Ginny's to hang out and make our plans for the big dance. There were animated discussions going back and forth from each of the couples on what to wear and if we were going to go to the after-party at the theater sponsored by the school. All the small details that take up so much of a teenager's social life, especially when connected to a big school dance.

All of us, that is, except Katie. She dropped out of school earlier in the year, and while she did have a boyfriend, he was not in school either. He was older and graduated a few years before and (I believe) going to a tech school for a business degree. As the day went on we all started to feel bad for Katie. While the rest of us were in animated discussion over the upcoming dance, she sat there quietly with nothing to contribute.

Sitting next to Ginny, I leaned over and began a quiet

conversation with her. What did she think about us also inviting Katie to go with us? After so often being left out because of my father, it hurt me to see her sit there, the only one of us not going. Michael would have to get another set of tickets, but he might be willing. He was already beginning to enjoy the idea of taking three with him, would not four be even better?

Reaching an agreement, the two of us stood up and joined Michael on the couch, sitting to either side of him.

"I have an idea." I began.

"We think it's a great idea," Ginny added.

"We've been thinking about poor Katie."

"And how she's the only one not going to Homecoming."

"It's really sad how she's the only one, don't you think?" Smiling up at him, trying to be as persuasive as I could.

At this point, it began to dawn on Michael what we were talking about, and a mild look of panic started to spread across his features. He'd started this venture with one date to Homecoming and somehow ended up with three. Now we were asking for yet another to be invited.

"I know she would love to go with us," Ginny chimed in.

"And think of the impression it would make as you walked in with all of us."

"You'll be the talk of the school."

"Wouldn't it be fun for Katie to be with us?" Both Ginny and I now smiling up at him, holding him in place with our attention.

"I uh, yeah huh, I uh," stuttering over the words. "A ticket!" he finally spit out, "I'd have to get another set of tickets!"

"No problem," I replied reasonably, "they still have them for sale."

"It wouldn't be a problem, would it?" questioned Ginny.

"You wouldn't want to leave her out, would you?" I countered.

Michael, swiveling back and forth between the two of us with our rapid fire questioning, knew he was trapped and there was only one option to keep us happy. With a strangled roar, he stood up and yelled across the room to Katie, "So, do you want to come to the dance with us or not?!"

"Yes I do!" Jumping up and clapping her hands, smiling the whole time. It was settled, Katie would be coming with us.

On Monday morning, Michael once again shuffled up to the Homecoming booth asking to buy yet another set of tickets, getting him an odd look from the ticket seller.

"Didn't you already buy two sets last week?" came the confused question. "Did you lose a set?"

"No," Michael sighed, "I just need another set."

"I see," which he clearly didn't, "but it's your money."

As Michael turned with the additional tickets our growing little group gave a cheer as we ran up to surround him. With a roll of his eyes, he looked at each of us and said with a laugh, "What have you guys talked me into?"

Walking together to our classes the discussion then turned to the extra ticket, it would be a shame to let that one go to waste.

"Oh, now wait one minute," Michael cried out, "I agreed to add Katie to the group. I don't ever remember agreeing to add anyone else."

"But Michael," I reasonably stated, "you already have the extra ticket, we might as well use it."

Throwing his hands up into the air, he started mumbling to himself as he walked away from us, "Didn't think I'd get one date to Homecoming, now I have four, and now that I have four they want to add a fifth because of an extra ticket, just can't let it go to waste. Oh, no! That would just be silly to let an extra ticket go to waste. Of course, it makes sense to take *five girls* to Homecoming, normal as anything..." leaving the rest of his conversation with himself unheard as he moved further away from us.

By lunchtime, and after much debate, we decided to ask Tammy if she'd like to go with us. She wasn't a regular in our group, but she was friendly and I'd known her through family association for years, our parents had been friends since our early childhood. She didn't have a boyfriend at the moment and we heard mention she would love to go if she had someone to go with.

Since I was closest to her, it was decided that I would be the one to ask her. Going over to the table she normally had lunch at, I sat down next to her, "Hey Tammy, I heard you'd like to go to Homecoming but don't have a date to go with."

"Yeah," giving me a confused look, "why you ask?"

"Well, Michael is taking a group of us and we have an extra ticket, would you like to come with us?"

With a startled laugh, she thought about it for a minute,

"Sure, why the hell not?!" And as simple as that, Michael now had a fifth date for Homecoming.

The day of Homecoming we all gathered at Katie's house. Neither Ginny nor I could afford dresses for the dance, and she had offered us some of hers. For some unknown reason, she had a large collection of them, all stored neatly in a box. After we arrived, we started going through the dresses she had available and each of us was able to find something we could wear. All were long, formal dresses, and to a certain degree, we all matched one another, which pleased all of us.

Two hours before the dance Michael showed up, with a corsage for each of us. He decided to heroically roll with the whole situation, and each of us in return was deeply pleased. As part of the Homecoming tradition, dinner with your date was often part of the deal, and after passing out all of our flowers, he informed us he was taking us out for dinner as well. With a flurry of excited activity, we all finished getting ready, and in no time at all, we were ready to go.

Arriving at Pizza Works, a very popular pizza place in town, the looks began as people from school started to realize that we were all with Michael and dressed for the dance. Walking to our table, a general hush came over the place as everyone stared in wonder, alongside a brief flare of jealousy from some of the guys. It didn't last long, but we knew we'd made an impression during our entrance. Sitting down at our table, we were all enjoying our moment of notoriety. But, that was nothing compared to what we were to experience later that night when we walked into the dance.

We swept into the school gym, with Michael in the center, and with a flourish, he presented all of his tickets, receiving awed amazement in return. Now, Michael wasn't a bad looking guy, but it wasn't like he was the captain of the football team. Nor had he ever been known as a chick magnet in the past. He was just your average, if slightly, unnoticeable guy around school. Nothing special about him. Now, he was showing up with five dates for the dance, when most guys were lucky to have one.

Down we walked, into the dance, heads turning and conversation buzzing all about us, and each of us, in turn, getting a little thrill from the attention. None of us had ever been considered popular or the topic of anyone's general gossip. Now, we were at the center of it all. The concentrated attention didn't last long though; there were too many other distractions. People to gossip about, dancing to be done, socializing to engage in. But people lingered as they walked past our table, and looks were given when we went out on the dance floor.

Halfway through our evening, as we were talking, someone came up with the idea of dedicating a song to Michael. It had been done a few times throughout the evening for other people, mostly slow songs for some couple or another. After a few songs were bandied around, we went up to the DJ and requested, '*I'm just a Gigolo*' by David Lee Roth. For us, it nicely summed up the general feeling of the evening. As soon as the DJ announced our dedication we hauled Michael out onto the dance floor, laughing as we surrounded him, each of us giving him kisses as we swirled around him in turn. Making a long and lasting impression on his reputation at school.

Even the photographer found the situation amusing, as he tried to stage all of us for our Homecoming photo. He placed Michael in a throne-like chair at the center, while the rest of us clustered around him, for all the world looking like demonically smiling angels up to no good.

It may have been one of the best nights in Michael's life up to that point. He was now the envy of the same people who wouldn't have noticed him before. His status grew as the evening went on and him as the hot topic of conversation. For a brief shining moment, we achieved legendary status in the annals of adolescences. We made an impression that couldn't easily be forgotten. And through no lack of effort on the part of others in our school, Michael managed a feat that was never replicated during the rest of our time there. This small group of geeks and misfits had our moment of adulation and envy, and we revealed in this new-found position among our peers, fleeting as it was.

 ## Lisa's a Girl!

Once I was out of my father's house and beginning to enjoy the freedoms that came from living with Eula, I started to spend more time with my guy friends. Hanging out at their houses, running around with them, and even, on occasion, going out on dates with them. And it seemed to work out for everyone. I never made any effort to hide who I was dating at any given time, and by unspoken agreement, whenever I was with all of them, I played no favorites and treated everyone the same.

This found me, one afternoon, hanging out at Joe's house along with Ky, Willie and a few other friends of Joe's waiting out the rain for us to go find something better to do. Sprawled out in a loose semi-circle around the room, the guys, at first, were all very aware of my presence. Jokes were made at my expense, which I often turned back on them. With laughter and the occasional red face, we harassed each other mercilessly as the rain continued to beat at the window throughout the afternoon.

But as the afternoon progressed and the shadows darkened outside, the guys began to notice my presence less and less as the conversation drifted towards guy talk. Enjoying this moment of accidental inclusion in something that is normally outside the purview of mixed company, I decided to sit back and no longer call any attention to myself at all. Before long, the guys were deep into their conversation of woes in dealing with the opposite sex. The follies of women and their general confusion in dealing with girls on just about every level.

Quietly in the corner, I sat listening to their endless plight of misunderstanding. Which over the years I have noticed, seems to be a common theme on any subject involving the opposite sex, no matter what the age. They woefully commiserated on the terror of asking a girl out, and worst of all, getting turned down. Deconstructing conversations, desperately trying to figure out the real meaning of what was said and if it really meant what the words implied. The coy, flirty behavior that drove them all past insanity as they wondered if it meant a girl liked them or was just playing with them.

My presence was now completely forgotten, as their circle tightened in mutual bewilderment. Leaning forward in their earnest pleading of can someone, anyone, please explain what the hell was going on in the minds of women. Shaking my head often, I smiled to myself as I listened to their stories. I wasn't because I found it funny, but because I found it sad. The miscommunication on both sides of the dating rituals, and the absurdity that it brings for everyone. The almost constant comedy of errors that even as we grow older never entirely leaves us as we try to figure out what is meant, from what we say to each other. I'd watched these guys, who always looked so confident while out in mixed company, were as clueless as their counterparts. And now, thinking they were alone among themselves, they showed they were just as confused and unsure as the girls they pursued. It was enough to make you cry if you didn't laugh first.

With nods of agreement and each with their own story to tell of the mysteries of dating and relationships, they earnestly shared yet another tale of misadventure. I felt for these guys and how when dealing with girls nothing was ever as it seemed. That for every rule they seemed to have figured out another girl would shatter, leaving them as clueless as a priest in a brothel.

As the conversation escalated and the words became more animated, with large gestures made to accent a point, I found myself constantly on the verge of giggles. Try as I might, and with my hand often clasped firmly over my mouth to keep it contained, I eventually could hold it in no more. I began to giggle. Speaking up for the first time in over an hour, I tried to offer them a bit of insight that they all seemed so desperate to have. Not, at first, paying attention to who was speaking, there were a few nods of understanding, until it began to penetrate who exactly was speaking. My giggles quickly escalated to uncontrollable laughter, I couldn't stop. Looks of horror and surprise rippled through the room, my presence was once again remembered.

Quickly pulling apart, they leaned back with nervous shuffling and the occasional pink face, looking at each other with quiet guilt. Shifting uncomfortably, they darted glances at each other, then at me, then down at the floor, in a repeated pattern as words began to form, then fail, as each of them tried to find some avenue of escape from what I'd witnessed. When Ky, with a look of surprised epiphany, etched on his face, suddenly blurted out, "Oh my god! Lisa's a girl!"

Rocking with unconstrained laughter, shaking my head with the blatantly obvious statement, the guys shifted uncomfortably around me, caught between embarrassment and amusement. I gave in completely to my glee at that point, sliding to the floor rocking and holding my belly, as red in the face as they were, if for different reasons. Watching me laugh and rock on the floor, the tension of the room dissipated as first one, then another began to laugh, all nodding in agreement that yes, I was most certainly a girl.

 ## Meeting by Accident

Whenever Billy wasn't working at Pizza Works or otherwise busy, he would often pick me up after school and take me home to Eula's. Sometimes, we would stop to get something to eat or hang out with friends. Other times, he'd take me straight home and we'd sit on the porch outside the house and talk for a while. It was a pleasant routine we both enjoyed.

On one of those days, as we were pulling away from the school in the rush of vehicles from every other student trying to exit at the same time, traffic came to a sudden, and complete, stop. A few cars ahead of us, two vehicles had collided and locked bumpers. We sat there a few minutes gawking with the rest when Billy began to laugh after recognizing one of the guys trying to split the two cars up.

"Hey, sit here a minute and I'll be right back," jumping out to join the growing group of people surrounding the two cars.

I sat there for a few minutes, but quickly becoming bored, decided to get out and join everyone else. It wasn't like we were going anywhere until they got those cars moved anyway. I turned off Billy's car, grabbed his car keys and hopped out to follow Billy.

As I approached, I could hear the rising tide of laughter and insults being issued back and forth between the occupants of the two cars. While others yelled advice that wasn't being listened to, they tried to figure out how to get the two cars separated. It appeared that one car was slightly higher than the other, and bumper from the front vehicle had slid neat as you please under the other. No true damage had been done to either vehicle, but the bumper edges had locked and they were now stuck.

After my brief inspection, I walked over to Billy already deep in conversation with one of the occupants of the second car. I stood to the side, looking over the crowd of people approaching the cars. Listening with half an ear to their conversation that mostly consisted of insults, every once in a while I would laugh to myself, at some well worded verbal barb.

After a bit, Billy turned and waved me closer to introduce me to his friend. "Lisa, I'd like to introduce you to one of my oldest friends, Nev." While making a face at his oldest friend and rolling his eyes, he announced, "Nev, this is Lisa, my sometimes girlfriend, when she has time for me," Turning to me with a good-natured wink and grin.

I leaned around Billy to get a better look at this oldest friend, and gave him a slight wave, "Nice to meet you."

"Yeah, you too," first, giving Billy a sly grin, he turned back to me and asked, "How long have you known him," pointing to Billy in an offhand way.

"About a year or so now."

"And I'm just now getting to meet you?" Making an accusing face at Billy, "He always did try to hide the pretty ones from me."

"Hey now," Billy cried out with mock indignation, "just because we're friends doesn't mean I trust you!"

"Oh, you wound me with your distrust." Making hurt noises while patting his chest, he turned back towards me, "Only believe half of what he says to you about me, even if it is all true."

In the background of our conversation, the car separation was still ongoing, keeping a small part of my attention, watching with amusement. Someone had climbed onto the hood of the back car and started jumping up and down. It wasn't effective, but it was entertaining. Eventually, they somehow managed to lift the second car enough to pull the first car away, and our conversation came to a stop. With a last wave towards Nev, we left the milling chaos. Returning to Billy's car we joined the mass exodus with all the other sightseers.

Once again on the move, Billy took me straight home to Eula's, the conjoined car delay had eaten up all the time we had before he was supposed to go to work. I didn't mind. I had homework to do and, honestly, the show we'd gotten was worth the disruption to our original plan.

Sitting in my room later in the evening doing my homework, I heard one of my sister's calling up the back stairs that I had a phone call. In Eula's house, there was only one phone for all of us, located in the front stairwell.

Hurrying down, I reached the phone while several of my sisters sat close at hand, and answered, "Hello?"

"Uh, hi...is this Lisa?"

"Yes?" I had no idea who it was on the phone.

"Umm, you remember the guy you met by accident this afternoon?"

"Yes?" Now beginning to form a clue of who I was talking to, but had no idea how he had gotten this number.

"Yeah, well," he began, "I ran into Billy again today and he gave me your number."

"Oh?" a little surprised at his statement. "And why did he do that?"

"So I could ask you out this Friday night on a date?" came his hopeful reply.

At first, I wasn't sure what to say. I'd gone out on a few other dates besides Billy, but I'd never actually been set up for one by him, and I wasn't sure how I should respond. Nev was a good looking guy, seemed funny and I didn't have any objection to going out on a date with someone else. But, I did want to make sure that Billy wouldn't be offended either. I had no intention of disrupting some bro-code between the two of them.

"Umm, tell you what, call me back tomorrow and I'll let you know if I'm busy or not on Friday." hedging my bets with him.

"Or Saturday," jumping past my possible objection, "I'm free on Saturday too if that works for you."

Starting to laugh at his persistence, I could feel myself warm up to his pursuit of a date with me. "Call me tomorrow and I'll let you know. Talk to you then."

"Sure, sounds great. Talk to you tomorrow."

Walking slowly back up to my room, I thought over the situation. It wasn't as if I hadn't dated within friends before. Billy and I both agreed we had no exclusivity on each other, and I was much too lazy to sneak around trying to keep them from finding out about one another. I decided if Billy had no objections, then it could be fun.

Picking me up from school the following day, I related to Billy the phone call I had received from Nev, and him asking me out for a date on Friday. He seemed a little surprised, but not upset by this turn of events, and offered no objections. And so, the pattern was set for the rest of my stay at Eula's. On Friday nights, I would go out with Nev, and on Saturday nights, I would go out with Billy. There was a bit of teasing by my sisters, more I think from jealousy than for any other reason, but life is too short to worry about what others think of you. And, it's just too much fun to not indulge when given a chance.

 ## Free Pizza

On a warm Saturday afternoon, Ginny, Michael, Tina, Joe and I decided to spend our time out creek walking. Quincy has many large parks and several of them have waterways that run through them. The creeks in most of the parks were no more than knee-high, the banks a mix of sand and shale rocks, surrounded by old growth trees and often not a road or a car anywhere in sight.

Sometimes we'd pack a picnic, and other times we'd just go exploring to see what new things we could find. On this day, we opted for exploring. We were feeling especially rowdy that day, and along with the walking, there was a great deal of pushing, chasing and particularly, falling. By the time we exited the park, we were all thoroughly wet, tired and covered in mud from head to toes, and feeling high spirited from a time well spent doing nothing but enjoying the day.

Walking home, food, it was decided, was in order, and pizza was what we wanted. I was duly elected to order for us since Billy was working at Pizza Works that day. While everyone else descended down to the basement shower, I called in our order. Making the specific request to have Billy, and only him, deliver our pizza. Stressing several times we were more than willing to wait longer if he was already out with another order.

Hanging up, I followed everyone else down into the basement. It wasn't what you could call a finished basement, but what it did have was a shower, which was a generous assessment of the arrangements. It had a shower head in the ceiling with no walls or curtains around it and a small 4x4 area of concrete with a drain for the water next to the stairs. The rest of the basement being nothing more than dirt floors and exposed foundations. To get to the basement, you had to open a trapdoor set in the bathroom floor. On a good day, you could get your shower in before the door decided to slam shut at random moments for no apparent reason, leaving you in semi-darkness for the rest of your shower.

Peeling off layers of clothing as I went, I arrived naked, if still modestly covered in layers of mud, sticks, and leaves. I happily joined the rest of the group in flushing ourselves clean with gusto. With a great deal of laughter, we attempted to extract the muck both from ourselves and from each other, getting to those places not easily reached with friendly enthusiasm. Pushing and shoving for space under the falling water, often splattering each other in the process, streaks of mud ran down the frequently clogged drain, as bits of leaves and rock smothered the opening. It was a messy procedure for getting clean, but more fun than showering alone would have been.

Happily mud-free, aside from the small bits still clinging to my toes that I chose to ignore, I extracted myself from the squirm of bodies and headed back upstairs to dry off and wait for Billy's arrival, and most importantly for everyone else, the pizza. Standing naked in the middle of the dining room, drying my hair, I finally heard the much anticipated knock at the door. Grabbing David's wallet as I dropped my towel to the floor, I headed to the door wearing nothing but a wicked grin, feeling sure I was going to brighten Billy's day.

Flinging the door open, I realized that my surprise was indeed going to be a completely unexpected sight for the stranger before me. Looking up from the pizza just as the door completed its opening arc, the poor pizza boy stood in open-mouthed, stunned silence, gaping like a fish out of water. A creeping red blush that began somewhere below his shirt line, quickly inched its way upwards towards his hairline, as his stammering gradually became audible to the human ear.

Figuring it was now much too late to do anything about the naked situation, I decided to brazen it out, "How much do I owe you?" Asking as casually as I could.

"I.... umm... it's...," blushing a furious red, he looked back down at the pizza box, "...it's... yeah... pizza...."

"Yes? How much?" Helpfully prompted him again.

"Pizza... yeah... I uh...." looking back down to the pizza as if it was going to somehow magically give him the power of recovered speech, "it's.... pizza.... ahhhhh..."

Beginning to really enjoy this moment, and doing my best not to laugh at his squirming distress, I stood there as if answering the door naked was the most natural thing in the world, and inquired once more, "Sweetie, how much do I owe you?"

As the pizza boy once again reached for speech, Michael, a giant of a man at 6' ft. 4", followed by everyone else, emerged from the basement. All as naked as the day they were born and dripping wet, they clustered around Michael like satellites around a planet, initially unaware of the disturbance at the door as the banter from the basement continued. When Michael walked around the table to get a clear view of the door, he saw immediately that whoever it was, it wasn't Billy, and this person was, without a doubt, was in a great deal of distress. With a good nature roar, he called out, "Lisa! Stop teasing that poor boy and get us our pizza! I'm hungry!"

Alarmed by Micheal's bellow, panic seemed to settle into the already discombobulated pizza boy like a fat man settles into his favorite chair. He started to visibly shake, and the red tone of his face was quickly bleached out to a sickly white. His discomfort had now grown to full-blown panic as he took in the additional approaching nakedness.

Looking down once more to the pizza in his hand as if it was his only source of salvation, he attempted one last time to complete the ritual exchange of money for food that had been so rudely interrupted by my nakedness. As his eyes drifted upwards, away from the warm comfort of the familiar box, he lost all semblance of control. Unable to form words he finally thrust the box at me and bolted to his car without another sound.

Laughing so hard I almost dropped the pizza, I turned back to face everyone after firmly shutting the door, I announced with a wicked smile on my face, "Hey everyone! Free Pizza!"


P.S.....Later that night, an unexpected knock sounded at the door. Our tongue-tied pizza boy had returned to the scene of the crime. This time, armed with beer and pizza and eager to redeem himself in our eyes. He may have been a bit disappointed at our now not-naked state, a state that he had spent an entire afternoon recovering from, but if so, he wisely chose to keep it to himself.

# IT'LL FEEL BETTER WHEN IT QUITS HURTING

 ## A Living Canvas

Boredom has often played a leading role in my choice of activities over the years. When confronted with the options of sitting around and doing nothing, and doing something stupid, but harmless, stupid often wins. This was also true for most of my friends, and during one boring afternoon of nothing to do and no money to go anywhere, Ginny and I turned our attention to Michael, the only other person currently in her house with us.

Ginny and Michael had become something of a couple over the course of the school year. At times, somewhat reluctantly, but for the most part, it seemed to work for them. It was as if one day they both looked around and decided, "yeah, this one will do". It wasn't a great or epic love, nor was it fraught with the usual high school hormonal roller coaster careening out of control. It was more like watching two people who, in trudging away in tandem for so long, had eventually fallen into lockstep with each other and never stopped.

This resulted in my often being with the two of them, not as a third wheel, but just a part of the dynamics of their relationship. I'd been friends with both of them separately, I was the one who first brought them together, and now, I was simply there as part of the package.

Sitting on opposite ends of the couch with our legs stretched towards the middle, we were, for whatever the reason, discussing the process of creating a hickey, something Ginny decided she needed to learn. Trying to describe the mechanics of it, our eyes drifted more and more often to Michael sitting in the recliner watching TV, completely oblivious to his impending inclusion into our conversation as a test dummy.

With sly conspiratorial grins, we left the couch and approached Michael. Slowly, pulling his attention away from the bright flashing lights of the TV, he started to show some concern as we drew closer to him. Perhaps it was our identical grins or maybe he was becoming more attuned to our moods and self-preservation had kicked in. "Yes?" he inquired.

"You wouldn't mind taking your shirt off would you?" I asked, giving him my best innocent look.

"I guess not..." pausing in mid-removal, he gave us both a worried look, "Why?" Feeling that maybe, just maybe, this wasn't his best course of action.

"I just want to show Ginny something." With a big grin from me and a giggle from Ginny, he began to strongly suspect things might not work out well for him. Giving us both a questioning stare, he sat there half in/half out of his shirt, perfectly poised to go either direction, waiting for a clearer explanation.

"A hickey. Ginny wants to learn how to give a hickey." I replied as Ginny made come along motions towards his shirt.

Pushing himself back a bit in his chair, he looked from one to the other, and with a sigh said, "I'm not getting out of this, am I?"

Laughing at his distress Ginny shook her head, "Nope." and sat down on the arm of the chair next to him, while I descended to occupy the other.

Once again resigned to his fate, he settled back, knowing there wasn't much he could do to stop us short of jumping up and running from the house. "Alright, alright, but just a few, okay? And keep it below the collar, please?" Stripping off his shirt, he accepted his fate.

Leaned over his chest, I said to Ginny, "Watch what I do." Nodding in agreement, she peered closely as I began to suck on his chest. The resulting hickey was small, round, red and about the size of a dime.

Gesturing to the other side of his chest, I said, "Now you try."

Giving it her best shot, she gave him a faint pink mark that disappeared within minutes. Getting a bit uncomfortable, Michael asked, "Are you guys done yet?"

Shaking my head in the negative, I once again began creating another hickey to show her how it was done. Taking turns back and forth, and giving her tips on how to make them last, it slowly turned into a game. As we continued, we began to create patterns out of the dark dots that emerged from our attention. Trying to outdo each other in creativity, darkness of color and symmetrical roundness, we quickly covered most of his upper body. As space began to run out, we insistently demanded that he flip over so that his back could also be offered up for our entertainment.

With a great deal of bitching, he complied. The resulting masterpiece of body art was a sight to behold; covering every available inch of his upper body from neckline to waistline with connect-the-dots images. There were smiley faces and star patterns, squares, and even our initials were impressed into his skin for all to see, well, if he took his shirt off anyway. Then, finally satisfied with our handiwork, we stopped and stepped back to admire our creation.

Looking down at himself, he exclaimed in horror, "I'm not going to be able to take my shirt off for weeks!"

And all was fine until Michael dressed out for gym, the following day. Being reluctant to change his shirt in the locker room, he elected to remain in the shirt he'd worn to school that day. His gym teacher, seeing he had not "dressed out" appropriately, ordered him to change before leaving the locker room.

With a great deal of reluctance, Michael lifted his shirt to make the change demanded by the gym teacher, who was standing by to ensure compliance. Lifting his shirt for all the world to see the attention to detail we had bestowed upon him, his gym teacher freaked out as his classmates whooted their approval.

"Michael," he demanded, "please come with me to my office." Turning his back on the entire scene, he retreated into his office to wait for poor, poor Michael.

What followed was an hour long interrogation by several different members of the school staff. All of whom were absolutely convinced that this had occurred that day, during school hours. Each came at him, demanding to know what time it had happened, during what class it had happened in, and most importantly, why it had happened at all.

Doggedly, he continued to tell the same story. It had not happened that day, it had happened the night before. And, as to why it had happened, well, who can really know why girls do anything?

Eventually, he gave up our names and we were called down to the office, to be separated and questioned individually. The theory being, if we didn't have each other to back up our stories, we would eventually "come clean" with the truth they had decided upon already.

# IT'LL FEEL BETTER WHEN IT QUITS HURTING  135

As I was called into the dean's office, a bit confused since no one bothered to tell me why I was called down, I was directed to sit in a chair and asked, "Where and when exactly did the incident occur in school today?"

Now, completely confused, I responded, "What incident?"

"One of your classmates, Michael, I believe his name is, was seen during gym class to have been covered in marks. Marks he finally admitted came from you."

The light, now dawning, I started laughing, "You mean you're talking about all the hickey's we put on Michael last night?"

Becoming uncomfortable with my response, he stiffened up in disapproval, as is so often the case when you don't comply with another person's expectations of behavior. He began again, "It must have happened during school hours since no other teacher reported seeing these on the young man!" Giving me a look that said HA! Explain that! Sure at this point that I would now give him the answer he was expecting.

Shaking my head while trying not to laugh, I again tried to explain what had actually happened. "It happened last night, not at school. It took several hours and two bottles of juice to accomplish that work of art, and we haven't even been *in* school that long yet today. And the reason no other teacher saw what the gym teacher did is because we were most careful to keep all of them inside the shirt line so they *couldn't* be seen casually by a random person."

Sitting quietly at his desk while drumming his fingers, he continued to stare at me for a few more moments. Seeming to make up his mind, he got up and walked to the door, turning to me right before he left saying, "Stay here, don't move."

So I sat, quietly, and did not move while I waited for him, or anyone for that matter, to return. The wait was not long, maybe 10 minutes when both the dean and another school member walked back in and stood staring at me from the door as if unsure how to proceed. Looking out, I could see both Ginny and David, likewise sitting at a desk, in various locations around the office. Looking at each of us in turn, the dean cleared his throat, and with a look that could only be called disgust, said, "Both of your friends tell the exact same story."

I nodded and waited for him to continue, not knowing what else to say about the matter.

"Since we cannot prove that it happened on school grounds, there doesn't appear to be much we can do about it. And, as long as that young man keeps his shirt on, it's not even considered a distraction. So, we will let you all go *this* time, but as a warning," now shaking his finger at each of us to make his point, "*don't* let this happen *again*!"

Head down, I got up from my seat and, joined by my friends, we walked towards the door, exchanging sly glances while trying not to laugh and further incite the adults in the office. Walking quickly away until we were far enough away they could not hear us, we all broke down laughing, tears streaming down our faces as we looked from one to the other, over the entire situation.

Finally getting his laughter under control, Michael turned to look at us, as we continued to stifle our giggles, doing his best imitation of exasperation at our behavior. Eventually gaining our undivided attention, he glared accusingly as he spoke, "*SEE*! I told you this was a *BAD* idea!"

 ## Pick me! Pick me!

For the past several months, my date flipping was working out well with both Billy and Nev. If there were ever any issues between the two of them because of it, they never chose to share it with me. And I, being considerate, never talked about the other unless he brought the subject up first. But, on one occasion, the three of us found ourselves all going to the same party on a Sunday night.

The two of them, independently, decided to drop by Eula's at around the same time, both with the intention of asking if I'd like to go with him. The three of us sat on the porch while they took turns presenting their particular argument as to why I should pick him to go out with that night.

"You've had more overall dates with him. It's only fair to give me this one." Attempted Nev.

"You've known me longer." Countered Billy.

"I'm better looking."

"Oh, not even, have you looked in the mirror? I'm waaaay better looking than you."

And so it went, back and forth, as I laughed harder at each attempt that became more outrageous with each round.

Standing up in an exaggerated stance, "How can you turn this down?" Billy said with a wink and a nod.

"How could you say no to this?" Nev giving me his best eager puppy face.

"I have a car," Billy said slyly, playing his trump card.

"Damn, I was planning on riding with you tonight."

"Okay, okay, " I managed around my giggles, "it's not fair for me to pick one over the other, why don't we all just go together as friends?"

Each of them stopped in their antics, eying each other up and down, and with some form of unspoken agreement, they both shrugged.

"Sure." said one.

"Why not." said the other.

It was settled. We would all go together, as friends. While neither was entirely happy with the decision, both were willing to accept it, and I was just as happy not having to decide between the two of them.

At dusk, they pulled up outside my house. Approaching the car, Nev got out of the passenger seat, and stood holding the door for me so I could sit in front, in an unspoken gesture of "no hard feelings". I smiled my thanks as I got in the car, happy that neither had decided to become pissy over my decision.

In an empty store parking lot, we joined a growing group of partiers waiting to caravan to our final destination. A dozen different strains of music could be heard from multiple locations as people lounged on their cars, danced, and mingled, with shouts of greetings, good-natured heckling, and laughter occasionally pushing the musical pandemonium into the background. Exiting the car, I could feel the almost festival excitement from everyone. It was electric and growing with each new car that arrived.

It was the middle of fall, the air was crisp without being uncomfortable, and everyone was looking forward to what was probably the last big outdoor party of the season. With a full moon and clear skies, it was a perfect night for a bonfire in the middle of nowhere.

Waiting by the car to find out the location of the party, I noticed through the swirling activity a tall lanky blonde pausing at each group for a few minutes. With generally easterly pointing gestures and an exchange of cash, he would then move on. Coming closer to us, he had a vaguely familiar face, his long stringy hair, the blue half-moon sunglasses resting on his nose tugged at my memories. By the time he reached the car next to us, I realized he could have been a dead ringer for Tom Petty! And, in this, his doppelganger's most current gig, was the money taker and event planner for the evening. Once he reached our group, I could see that Tom Petty was also very drunk. His exaggerated movements and slightly slurred speech gave him away almost instantly.

"Okay, everyone," he announced when he was close, "pony up." Vaguely staring at each of us as he swayed, as if he was having trouble keeping track of who or even how many of us he was talking to.

As the guys were handing over their money he stopped,

and looking at me, said, "And what about you?"

"Oh, I'm not drinking," waving my soda in front of him.

"Uh huh," swaying slightly, "so you're sober?"

"Yeah."

"Oh good!" With drunken joy he began reaching into his pockets, pulling out crumpled bits of cash and change, "Can you tell me how much this is?" Dumping it all into my hands.

"Uh, sure, no problem." Struggling to restore order out the hodgepodge of currency, trying not to lose any of it in my sorting.

While my attention was diverted with the counting, Tom wandered away in search of new arrivals. The guys asked if I knew who he was, and I told them, honestly, not a clue. After a bit of effort, I did manage to restore order to the chaos that he had given me and began to wonder what I should do with it. I could no longer see Tom or any of his group and didn't want to go looking for him in case he came back. Then I began to wonder, as drunk as he was, would he even remember he had given me all this cash? My counting told me I was holding several hundred dollars for him. The last thing I wanted was to be the cause of a mob scene due to lack of alcohol funds for the impending party.

I decided the best course of action was to send each of the boys out to see if they could find him while I stayed next to the car in case he came back. Hiding the money in various pockets, I settled in to wait for any of the three to show back up. After a seemingly longish wait, I once again saw Tom wandering through the crowd and ran to catch up with him.

"Hey, Tom!" Not knowing what else to call him, but needing to attract his attention before he disappeared again. In the slow motion of a tipsy drunk, he turned in my direction, "Yes?" He asked as I began to pull the wads of cash out of my pockets. His startled expression almost caused me to drop what I had already pulled out as the giggles hit me watching his reaction.

"You missing something?" I asked.

"Damn! I was wondering what I'd done with that!" Clearly relieved with the return of the cash. "Do you know how much is there?"

Still laughing, I nodded, "Yeah, more than enough to get everyone here good 'n drunk."

"Outstanding!" Laughing along with me, "Let's get this party started then." Climbing up on the nearest vehicle he bellowed out, "Alright everyone, head on out to the farm, we are now good to go!"

Turning to walk away, I reached out to grab him before he could slip away, "Aren't you forgetting something?" Waving the cash under his nose.

"Oh yeah, can't do anything without that, good call." Holding out his hands, he stared around at the sudden activity he had created by his announcement.

"I have a better idea." Reaching to unzip his leather jacket, I started to transfer the money directly from my pockets into his. "This way you'll have a harder time misplacing it. Now, hand me the rest you've collected," holding my hand out again.

Complacently, he handed me the rest he'd been holding in his hand. Giving him a firm command, "Stay!" I began smoothing out the crumpled bills, arranged them by denomination, and added that to his pockets as well. "Now, try not to lose it!" I scolded while wagging my finger at him.

"Promise, promise," holding his hands up to me in contrition.

Returning to the car, both Nev and Billy had already returned and were ready to go. As I got in the car, Billy gave me a questioning look. "

All taken care of, the money's back with Tom."

"I swear Lisa, I don't know what it is with you," Billy sighed, pulling out to follow the rest of the cars already heading out, "but even total strangers trust you."

"It's my honest face." Trying my best to give him an innocent look and failing miserably.

"Nope, that's definitely not it." Looking over his shoulder at Nev, "It's got to be the red hair."

"Yep, that's got to be it," tugging at a lock of my hair from the backseat, "what else could it be?"


Heading out to the edge of town, with a string of cars, both in front and behind us, we turned off onto a dirt road almost hidden by encroaching trees and brush. To call it a road was actually a generous term, there were no signs or indications of much traffic. Only two vaguely seen ruts for the tires to follow into the night. But trusting the people before us, we confidently left the main road as the others had before us.

Rolling up, we could hear music. Glancing over, as I

stepped from the car, I could see people already dancing around the fire, their shadows thrown out into the night. Walking closer we noticed other groups sitting around bails of hay, or lying on blankets they had brought. I was amazed at the numbers of people there, at least, double the amount that had been waiting in the parking lot. It was obvious that many of them had been there for a while, getting everything up for the rest of us.

We were greeted with solo cups of beer as soon as we walked into the glow of the bonfire, which the guys gladly accepted. I attempted to wave mine away, only to receive a confused look for my troubles as she continued to try and give me a cup. After several minutes trying to explain I wasn't drinking, I gave in and accepted the cup. Not to drink, but as my only form of defense against her drunk, but friendly insistence.

Joining the revelers, most already well lubricated, we began to mingle. I knew a lot of the people here, but this was a large crowd, and not just my classmates from school, but from the smaller surrounding towns as well. Even in the days before social media and cell phones, word of mouth could travel far and with amazing speed, bringing out a surprising assortment of people.

I hoped as I looked around the crowd and the already almost empty keg, that poor drunk Tom remembered not only where I had stashed the cash, but also how to find us in his heavily intoxicated state. The possibility of a small riot was not out of the question if he failed to arrive. But, in short order, a lone truck pulled up, its bed filled with beer and a triumphant Tom behind the wheel. Pulling up to the cheers of the crowd, he jumped from the cab with a quick bow to the group before him. Grinning happily, he announced "Let's Party!", and began to tap the keg closest to him.

It was an almost surreal evening. Despite the agreement we made for us to go just as friends, the inhibitions against it receded as the solo cups stacked up. Whenever Billy or Nev found themselves alone with me, neither seemed to be able to resist sneaking in a kiss or some bit of affection. Having as much fun with it as they were, I indulged each of them in their sly inclinations.

Pulled first by one and then the other to join in the dancing near the bonfire until I couldn't breathe, and collapsing wherever I was to catch my breath. They vied for my attention. Each trying to outdo the other in some form or fashion, while trying to pretend they were doing nothing of the sort. I laughed at each of them in their antics, enjoying the attention their friendly rivalry brought. If I had been forced to choose between the two of them that night, I don't believe I could have done so.

As the moon climbed high in the night, the activity below it slowly began to wind down. People began to remove sleeping bags from their vehicles, setting them up around the embers of the fire. Others, like myself, made ready to leave. Nev would be staying behind while Billy would be taking me back to town. Walking slowly back to the car, Nev ran up behind me. Sweeping me up in his arms, and shooting a wicked grin towards Billy, he leaned over and gave me a kiss good-night. Settling me back on my feet, he said, "Have a good night you guys." With a mock salute to Billy, he casually sauntered back to join the remaining group.

Arriving back at Eula's, instead of leaning over to give me a kiss good-night as he normally did, he got out of the car and came around to my side. As soon as I emerged, he enfolded me in an embrace with a kiss to rival Nev's. Laughing as he put me back on my feet, "Just couldn't let Nev outdo you, could you?"

"Nope." with a laugh as well, "See you tomorrow."

"Yes, yes, you will."

 ## Another Sad Ending

My time with Eula may have been the happiest of my adolescence. I had love, acceptance, and stability, I had freedom laced with reasonable rules that kept me safe without feeling confined. I excelled in my classes and caused no problems for anyone. And, as it turned out, it was my doing so well that caused my exile from Eula's home. My father kept tabs on me after entering the foster system, we had no personal contact, but as a juvenile officer, he had close contacts with those in control of my life and was not pleased with my good behavior. I believe he took it as a personal affront that I did not self-destruct under the benign guidance of Eula's home and began to take steps for my removal from the area where I could be seen by his peers.

After only three short months with Eula, a caseworker came one day to say that I was being moved to another foster home out of town. Eula protested, saying she had not requested a removal, pointing out how well I was doing under her care. With no remorse, the caseworker stated that the paperwork had already been processed. I had 24 hours to pack my things before I would be taken to another home. She informed us there had been concerns raised about me remaining in town, and it had been determined that placement outside of Quincy was in the best interest of everyone. At that moment, I knew that "everyone" was my father, and somehow he had pulled enough strings to orchestrate my removal.

Eula cried when I left her the following day, and so did I. But there was nothing she could do to stop me being taken away, nor did I blame her for what was happening to me. She was as helpless as I in this situation.

# AND SO THE ROLLERCOASTER SWOOPS AGAIN

And now, for what's behind family #3

My next foster home was nothing like Eula's. It was not a welcoming place, and I believe to this day the family was in it only for the money (not an uncommon situation in foster care). There were seven other foster siblings in this home, two of them were my foster parent's actual children, and the distinction in treatment between us and them was as clear as glass. There were two sets of rules in that house: one for the foster children that were harsh and restrictive, and a benign tolerance for almost anything with the others. I often wondered if this was just the luck of the draw, or if my father had somehow personally picked the worst people he could find to place me with.

There were many small things to serve as a reminder we were not a family and it was, in fact, a cash business for them. Each person was responsible for providing for themselves everything from toilet paper to laundry soap. If we didn't have the money, we either went without or we could take out a "loan" from our foster mother. It had to be paid back, with interest added, at the beginning of the month when we received our monthly allotment from the state.

There was a massive whiteboard on one kitchen wall with the house rules, of which there were many. It included when we were allowed to eat each meal. If you overslept or were delayed and missed that given hour, you went without until the next meal. We were not allowed to snack between meal times unless you bought the food yourself. Even that was kept by my foster mother to be doled out as she saw fit.

At meal times, each person's plate was filled with what my foster mother considered the appropriate amount of food. Only the boys were allowed to ask for more if they were hungry. Food, once again, became a major issue in my life while living with them. My foster mother, at some point near the beginning of my stay with them, decided I was bulimic. It was her only explanation for being so thin while eating what she considered large portions for a girl my age. I was often left hungry with the allotment I was given, yet not allowed to leave the table for an hour after each meal, to ensure that I did not go purge in the bathroom as she was convinced that I was doing. She took me to multiple doctors and a dentist to confirm her suspicions, none of them did, which frustrated her greatly.

When transferring to this new school, which was very small, my entire graduating class was only 17 people and it was a very hard adjustment to make. But after going over the credit criteria, I realized I had enough credits to graduate mid-semester. Confirming it with my school counselor, I submitted a request to my caseworker to allow me to graduate early and enter college. I was denied. I would have to remain in high school, taking mostly study hall classes for the next two years.

The loss of my friends, along with all that was comforting and familiar, was hard. I had lost my support network, the love of Eula, my home, and just about everything else that mattered to me, to be placed with people who didn't care and only saw me as an additional source of income. During my time with them, I was mostly confined to their home, to sit alone, counting down the days until I turned 18.

After the freedom of Eula's, it was a bitter pill to swallow.

##  My Kingdom for a Story

I would love to give you some great stories from this time. Unfortunately, there is only one. You can read it next. This may have been the single most boring time in my life, that included such highlights as sitting alone in my bed staring at the ceiling and learning 42 different ways to play solitaire.

Nauvoo is a very, very small town. It boasted only two restaurants, one primarily for the tourists who came through to see the Mormons, and a small diner frequented by the locals. It had a Catholic girls school, and while we saw them out on occasion, easily spotted by their uniforms, we rarely interacted with them. They might as well have lived on another planet for all that we acknowledged each other. There was a Casey's general store, and when they started offering pizza, it was greeted with the same awe as sending a rocket into space. Almost too good to be true.

My foster parents lived on one side of the house, and the foster children on the other. The stairwell marked the center point of the house, on our side, we had a den and next to it the kitchen. There were only two rooms, other than our own bedroom and the upstairs bathroom that we were allowed free access to. It was considered a privilege to be invited over to their side to watch TV, the only TV in the house I should add, as long as you didn't mind watching whatever they wanted. No choice was ever given in that respect.

It was a very lonely and isolating environment. We were expected to sit quietly, obey the rules and not cost them anything in time, money or effort. If it was something required by the state to provide for us, it was only grudgingly done, and with a great deal of disapproval. We were nothing more than cash cows to them, kept fed and housed only for as long as the money continued coming in.

I missed my friends and the life I'd had at Eula's. I was so incredibly bored I missed homework because at least then I would have something to do to occupy my time. My school schedule consisted of history, English, gym, and art. The other four periods I sat in a study hall spending most of my day staring at the ceiling or reading a book until my art teacher took pity on me.

When she found out how I was spending my days, she offered me the chance to come to her classroom instead of study hall. She encouraged me to spend as much time as I wanted on my projects, and gave me a great deal of individual attention that I appreciated. My artistic abilities that were better than average before, now took on new dimensions, expanding under her tutelage. In exchange, I helped her whenever she needed it. I was happy to help get the other students' artwork ready for shows, cleaning up after some messy project, even on occasion, helping other students with their art, becoming something of a teacher's aide.

This was my new normal. Few interactions with the outside world, days of boredom and solitude, sometimes commiserated with Carla, another foster sister who shared the house for a brief period of time with me who I had known while still living in Quincy. But shortly after my arrival, there was a confrontation between her and our foster mother that resulted in her being moved to a juvenile institution. A place similar to jail without having to actually commit a crime and where you could be held until you reached adulthood with little recourse to get out. Horror stories of this place were often passed from foster sibling to foster sibling, incidents of abuse, rape, and neglect, told like camp stories around a fire, both to scare and educate each other on the hazards of being in the system. This incident encouraged me to keep my head down, my mouth shut and try to draw as little attention to myself as possible in a house full of people.

But on one occasion, attention was brought to me, and that was never a good thing. Shortly after my arrival in Nauvoo, my friends back in Quincy decided to help me buy a class ring for my senior year. To help me with this, they began sending me small amounts of cash that I would stash in my jewelry box after I received it. I didn't mention it to my foster parents, keeping the money hidden from everyone, or so I thought anyway. One day after returning home from school, we were informed that everyone had to remain in the family room until a full search of the house had been done. My foster mother claimed that money had been stolen from her, in the exact amount I had saved upstairs in my room, and the until the money was found we were to remain in the room.

I knew at that moment, someone had found my hidden stash of cash, and I had no choice but to tell them about it. My foster mother immediately demanded I hand it over to her to "replace" her missing money. I refused. As the situation escalated, I demanded they call my caseworker to help settle this dispute. My foster mother insisted I hand over all my money, along with any other valuable item I may have in my possession, to compensate her for being stolen from. I stood my ground and refused to let them take what little I had left. Like a Mexican standoff, we were at an impasse, and I wasn't going to be sent away because she was greedy when I could prove the money was mine. As we waited for the caseworker to show up, each of us backed into our respective corners glaring at each other. Not another word was passed between us as the clock ticked in an otherwise silent house.

As soon as my caseworker showed up, my foster mother began insisting money, "she had been saving" was missing from her room. After she ran down all the reasons she was sure I had taken the money, she stated she wanted me locked up for theft, after they had taken everything of value from me for compensation. My caseworker then turned to me and without asking for my side, she insisted I return the money. Refusing yet again, I informed her I could prove the money was mine. With a surprised look on both of their faces, she asked how, and I gladly explained. Each time someone had sent me money they had included the amount they had sent, and I had kept every letter I had received since moving into the house. I also offered them the phone number of each friend who had sent me money, and they would confirm how much had been sent, without any coaching from me. Since I had not been allowed to use the phone or in any way communicate with them throughout this entire incident, it would be an independent confirmation.

Following me up to my room, I found all the letters and the money I had hidden. I then matched the money up with each of the letters, the amounts came out the same. Returning downstairs, my caseworker told my foster parents she believed it was just a coincidence the money my foster mother said was missing and the amount of cash I had was the same. I was then told that each time I received any cash from anyone, I was to inform my caseworker of the amount, then have it verified by my foster parents to prevent another incident like this one.

I believe, after everything was settled, my caseworker was sure that my foster mother had tried to steal the money from me, thinking there would be no way to prove it was mine. But, there was also no way to prove that she hadn't had money taken from her by someone else either, so she let the matter lie and considered this a closed case. I followed my caseworker back to her car and requested that I be moved somewhere else, but as I had expected, she informed me there were no other available slots for me. I would simply have to make the best of my situation.

Interestingly, no other mention of the "missing money" was ever made. No one else was ever accused of taking it, nor was any other effort made to find it. It became a non-issue as soon as it was shown that the money was mine. I'm sure she thought she could bully me into giving her whatever she wanted without any fuss from me, out of fear of reprisals. I'm sure she was shocked things had not worked out, and she was most definitely not pleased with the results of her efforts. In dozens of small ways, for the rest of my time with them, she made sure that I knew it. And so, my time with them went. No good stories, no interesting times, just the day to day drudgery of getting from one moment to the next until I was able to leave them for good.

You need the bad days to remind you of all the good there is in life. Without them, life is meaningless. But, there are days when you have to stare up into the sky and ask yourself, does it always have to be my turn?

 ## Weekend at Laura's

As a foster child, one of the requirements is to go to court on occasion. It mostly consists of a lot of people shuffling paper in a courtroom, discussing you, while you sit quietly in a chair and are firmly ignored. There are usually caseworkers, counselors, perhaps a juvenile officer, a judge, sometimes your foster parents and a host of other people whose job mostly seems to be finding and handing over documents while nodding in agreement with whatever is being said. As the center of all this activity, you are only required to be there, as your future is discussed and planned out without any input. Progress goals are created that must be accomplished, but you're never asked if it's something you want or need.

A short while after I moved to Nauvoo, I was required to attend one of these hearings that can sometimes take all day. Not that you sit in court all day in front of the judge, but each of these people must be met with while they inform you of each new thing you must do while going over any prescribed goal you may have failed to achieve, to whatever level they required. It is a long, tedious, boring process that seems mostly designed for the generation of paperwork. My court appearances were always in Adams county since that was the point of origin for my induction into the system. My current foster parents had no desire to spend an entire day going through the court motions, emphatically telling me so on a number of occasions, as if somehow I'd done this for the sole purpose of inconveniencing them. I didn't want to go any more than they did and had less choice about it.

During all of this, I'd kept in contact with not only Billy while in my new foster home, but with his mother as well. Before being moved from Eula's house, I had, on several occasions, gone out to Billy's house on the edge of town and became acquainted with his mother, Laura. She was a tiny little extrovert at 4 ft, 10 inches. Always with a laugh or a smile for me when I was there that never failed to make me feel welcome. I loved going out to his house, and would often spend giant swaths of time with her. Sometimes, much to Billy's dismay. Together we would talk about him, sharing small stories that at times made him squirm as he quietly listened in the background to our talks. I felt genuine affection for this wonderful woman.

Laura would always have some kind thing to say while we talked and seemed to genuinely care about how I was doing in my new home. And always a sympathetic ear for my misery, even if she couldn't change the situation. The Shaffer's had allowed Billy to come up to visit me a few times. One of their few concessions to me, and made mostly I believe because it cost them nothing. And, he had, surprisingly, made a good impression on them. Not that he was a bad guy, it was more that they seldom approved of anyone. During one of these visits while we were discussing my upcoming court date, my foster mother, once again, voiced her displeasure at making the trip, and of the time that it would involve that could be better spent elsewhere. After she had wound down from her verbal barrage, Billy offered her a suggestion. Would it be feasible for him or his mother to be the ones to transport me to court instead?

This caused her to pause as she thought it over. "Have your mother call me, and I'll see what we can work out."

Over the course of the next few weeks, calls were made back and forth between my foster mother, Laura, my caseworker and several others that were all involved in my "care". And, somehow, Laura, wonderful, persuasive Laura, somehow managed not only to get approval for her to transport me to court on Monday but received approval to keep me for the entire weekend prior to my court appearance. I was overjoyed at the outcome, and somewhere during this whole process, my affection for Laura became love. I loved this woman for all she'd done and tried to do for me; for listening with compassion, and making me feel like a part of her family.

That weekend, with Laura, was the one and only bright spot in my time with the Shaffer's. Laura and Billy arrived shortly after I returned from school on Friday, and after a short verbal exchange along with all my transport papers, we quickly made our exit. On the way back to Quincy I sat in the back of her car with Billy, bubbling with happiness and babbled almost non-stop for the entire trip. Laura laughed at my ramblings, while Billy did his best to keep up with the predominantly one-sided conversation. Giving an occasional nod, or a one syllable acknowledgment, which was about all he could edge into the conversation.

Once we arrived at their home, Billy and I slipped away for some quiet time just to ourselves, with Laura's unspoken approval. I'd missed Billy more than I expected, given the casual nature of our relationship. He too felt the same way. He would be leaving very soon for active duty and had orders for the base in Washington he requested. This would probably be the last time we would see each other before he left. It was a bittersweet weekend for both of us, as we both acknowledged for the first time how we truly felt about each other.

We laid next to each other in his bed for several hours, talking about everything that had happened, and what the future may bring for both of us. Laying there in the dark, Billy's responses started to become more mumbled as he slowly drifted off, but I was much too wound up to even think about sleep. Once I was sure he was good and truly asleep, I quietly slipped out of his arms and crept upstairs to join the rest of the family.

Laura was in the kitchen starting dinner and I stepped in to help her. Laura was not what you would call a good cook, and she knew it. Her food was often the butt of family jokes, and she would laugh right along with them. I gladly offered my own limited help. I had no ability for it either, but neither could I do any worse. Talking as we cooked, our conversation animated and full of teasing and laughter. Something I'd not had in a long time. Cooking was either something I did alone, badly, or quietly helping out in the kitchen if required, but not included in the social aspect of it.

After dinner was put in the oven, we remained in the kitchen, both to clean up our mess and to continue our conversation. As dinner time neared, Laura walked up to me and patting my belly, teasingly inquired, "Any babies in there?"

Laughing at her, "No Laura," shaking my head, "no babies in there."

Smiling indulgently, she pointed back to the basement door and said, "You should go wake Billy up for dinner, we'll be eating soon."

It was a wonderful weekend. My days were filled with

time shared with Billy's family and my friends who came out to visit. My nights were spent in Billy's arms, with Laura's benign approval.

On Sunday night, while Billy and I sat together in his room, he proposed to me. He acknowledged all the difficulties. I had another year and a half before I would turn 18, he would be leaving soon, he knew we wouldn't be able to see each other again for almost a year, and he didn't care. He wanted me in his life, for the rest of his life. While he was talking, I realized, I wanted this too. For all the difficulties, for all the problems we would have to figure out, I wanted to be a part of his life, a part of his family, for the rest of my life as well.

We went upstairs and announced our intentions during dinner. Laura with a big smile welcomed me to the family, his stepfather Tom, who was often a quiet man, warmly expressed his happiness, and his younger brother paused in his eating to nod his agreement. I knew then, without a doubt, I wanted to forever be a part of this family, and felt tears forming in my eyes from their unconditional acceptance of me.

Monday morning arrived before I was ready for it, and Laura sat with me as I was shuffled from room to room. To be talked at, and have paperwork shoved in front of me to sign, whether I wanted to or not. My opinion, as always, was not wanted nor was it accepted. New rules were added while old objectives were removed. Input from a variety of sources was added to each new piece of paperwork, and a new set of goals I was to achieve were imposed. One new order that caught my eye was a requirement to write a letter once a week to my father for the rest of my time in foster care. It surprised me. I had not talked to him since entering the system, nor had he tried to contact me, but it was decided I needed to maintain contact with him. Each letter was to be reviewed by one of my foster parents and logged to ensure I complied. Interestingly enough, there was no similar order to write to my mom.

By afternoon, the tedious process was completed and I was free to leave. Laura took me back home and we spent a final few hours together before I was to be returned to the Shaffer's. All my friends came out to see me off after school, they made quite a crowd as we packed up my stuff into the van. With hugs and promises to come visit me soon given, I climbed into the car my heart heavy at the thought of another year with the Shaffer's. If it had been any way possible, I know that Laura would have kept me, and regretted having to return me to my foster parents, knowing what she was returning me to. But, like me, she had no choice in the matter.

It was a treasured memory in my life in foster care, a weekend where I felt what it was like to be a part of a family. To be accepted, loved and wanted.

# FOUR HOMES, THREE CITIES, TWO YEARS

## The Final Home

The constant push and pull of conflict within my foster home came to a head as the school year ended. I had few friends at this school, very little interaction with my foster family other than meal times, and spent most of my free time sitting alone playing solitaire. The idea of spending yet another year with this family began to wear on me and began to manifest itself in physical ways. I started to lose weight, which at 92 pounds, I could hardly afford to lose. An ulcer I developed while living with my father, once again flared up, spending most of my time nauseous and sick because of it. I was living in almost complete isolation in a house full of people, and I started to consider my options.

I could stick it out for another year with this family, I could run away and hope for the best, or I could contact my case worker and demand removal. None of these options were great, but I knew I couldn't stay where I was. I didn't know if I could disappear for a year without being caught, and I my hopes for college and a life beyond high school would no longer be possible if I did. Which left chancing a move to another foster family as my best option. It was a crap shoot, but one I was willing to make. During a very tense phone conversation with my case worker, I made it clear to her, either move me within a week or I disappear. I would not continue living with this family under any circumstances.

Within five days, I had a new foster family, in yet another town. They were better than the last family, but they weren't great either. They also had two children of their own, and like my last foster home, they were treated differently than the foster children. But they did, at least, attempt to make us feel welcome rather than just walking ATM's.

My foster father was a police officer, and often had the

most troubled kids placed with him, DCFS felt his background as an officer gave him an advantage in dealing with these types of kids. His home was often the last stop before being put in a juvenile facility. Which meant most of my foster siblings had issues and long records. I was considered an emergency placement, not put there because I'd caused trouble, but because I needed immediate placement and they had an opening.

I liked my foster father. He wasn't a bad guy and did his best for all of us when he was home. My foster mother, on the other hand, was quite honestly, insane. If I had to guess what was wrong with her, I'd say she was bipolar with paranoia. Life with just her was a series of unpredictable expectations. There was very little consistency and it caused a great deal of frustration for everyone in the house. My foster father was sympathetic to our plight, but he rarely interfered unless he felt it would cause physical harm to one of us.

I remained there for the rest of my time in foster care. Things were not always great, but they were still better than where I escaped from. My foster mother's insanity often drove the rest of us crazy as she issued demands, then changing her mind midway through. Granting permission for something, then rescinding it as you're walking out the door. It made making any type of plans almost impossible. But still, it was better than the Shaffer's where there were never any plans to make. I spent my last year there making plans for my future. I would not remain in this system, not even for college. I wanted out. I took jobs babysitting and other odd jobs, saving my money like a miser for the day I turned 18 and I could run away with Billy.

Life in foster care is like living in a nightmare you fight to wake up from. But, no matter how much you scream, you are in it until the end. Reality was whatever you were told it was, there is no control, and it's always unpredictable. At times, it's terrifying, as you are pushed around by forces beyond your control. You hope for the best, brace for the worst and know that nothing you do in the end is going to change anything. But, on occasion, there are interludes of happiness, brief moments of something going right, giving you a fleeting interlude of joy to just revel in the moment.

 ## Ghost in the House

I spent my senior year in Hamilton which was a bit bigger than my previous school. I was given the option to take several classes for college credits, which I signed up for. I gained a bit of freedom and even acquired a consistent babysitting job. During it all, I held to the hope of escape with Billy in less than a year's time.

I'd resumed using drugs while with the Shaffer's, predominantly pot, to cope with all the stress in the meantime. I remained an honor roll student, studied hard, saved my money and looked to my future while dealing with my present. I was not an addict, I could take or leave any drug without any issues, and when things were good I had no desire to use anything. It was only during times of depression, stress, and helplessness would I turn to drugs as a coping tool. For the better part of three years I'd been living in environments that kept me in an almost constant state of anxiety, and however hard I tried, I could not alleviate all the ramifications of it. Stress can manifest itself in many different ways and sometimes can cause unexpected results.

For many years I suffered from sleep disorders, ranging from insomnia to sleepwalking brought on by excessive stress or anxiety. It started while living with my father, and on one occasion, I slipped out of the house in the middle of the night. I was returned to my father by a police officer who found me walking down the street in my nightgown. In this sleepwalking state, I was completely unaware of what I was doing, and I would remain non-verbal throughout the episode. While I was compliant when moved, I gave no sign of recognition or awareness to my surroundings. Unless I was caught, I would have no idea that I would leave my bed during the night to wander freely wherever my sleeping mind chose to go. How often I wandered was unknown, since I was rarely caught, it's possible it could have been a nightly experience or only something that happened every blue moon, and I had no way of knowing either way.

Shortly after moving in with the Faulkner's, odd things began to happen. At first, it was small items moved to unusual locations, then bigger things that were harder to explain. My foster family began to joke uneasily about a ghost in the house. Even I joined in, at first completely unaware I was, in fact, said ghost. I knew intellectually I would, on occasion, go for a stroll in my sleep, but in the same way that people know their eye color. It's information you have, but don't think about unless asked.

My midnight strolls didn't appear to be an every night thing but occurred often enough to become an issue with everyone in the house. During one night's foray, I took every one of my foster sister's bras and panties from her room and hid them in my foster brother's bottom dresser drawer. Even in sleep, it seemed I had a sense of humor, as my foster brother in red-faced chagrin, protested his innocence when they were discovered in his possession. He was something of a chauvinist, in both word and deed, so to be found with all of her under-things caused him to squirm endlessly with our teasing. This was not outside the realm of possibility of something he could have done simply to torment her, and we all knew it.

On another occasion, I took every can out of the cabinets and built some kind of patterned structure with them on the kitchen floor. It was as impressive as it was disconcerting for everyone, as we all stood in the kitchen doorway looking over my handiwork. The sprawl of cans took up the entire area, some stacked as many as six high, making grouping displays out of the colors and sizes. The longer this went on, the more discord it began to sow among everyone in the house as things came up missing, moved or placed in patterns throughout the house. No one ever saw or heard anything, and no one seemed to be exempt from my odd excursions, including me.

After several months, I did begin to suspect I was the one causing all the mischief. But since I hadn't been caught, there wasn't any proof. I assumed that if it was me, as I became more comfortable living with them, the incidents would eventually taper off naturally, as they had always done in the past. Similar happenings occurred while living with the Shaffer's, but not on this level of flamboyance, and it had stopped after a few months. While living with them, the stress was higher, and it was insomnia that I predominately struggled with, sometimes going several days in a row without actual sleep.

Then one night, the mystery of the ghost in the house was solved. My foster father, after working late one night was sitting in the living room watching some TV in the dark before going to bed. When out of the corner of his eye he saw movement in the hallway. He glanced over, but seeing nothing in the dark, went back to watching TV, discounting it as shadows and moonlight from the window.

Sitting there in the dark, he slowly became more convinced he was being watched. Calling out a few times, "Is anyone there?" into the motionless dark, feeling the weight of someone watching but unable to pinpoint from where. Getting no response or flicker of movement, he decided it was just his imagination playing tricks on him. The lateness of the night, the quiet of the house, and the TV throwing odd shadows in its bright movement. With a dismissive head shake, he settled back in to finish his show, chiding himself for jumping at nothing. When once again, he saw movement from the hallway, but this time, moonlight picked up the outline of a figure standing silently next to the stairs, staring straight ahead without movement.

As he told us this story the following day, he said it was one of the most disconcerting moments of his life. At the sight of this shadowy figure, he leaped out of the chair, demanding to know who it was. Confiding to us, that for one brief moment, he really did almost believe he was seeing an actual ghost. Reaching over, he flipped on the light, as brightness flooded the room it became immediately obvious it was not some otherworldly specter, but me.

"What on earth are you doing Lisa?!" he demanded, beginning to stride up to me, stopping dead after only a few short steps. I had not moved, nor even looked in his direction during all of this. He cautiously took another step in my direction, "Lisa?" Getting a good look at my face for the first time, which held no expression nor any recognition to my surroundings. He said it was like looking into the eyes of the dead, and it stopped him cold.

Unsure of what to do at this point, he continued to stand several feet from me when slowly, as if in slow motion, my forward gaze turned and settled on him. "Lisa?" he hesitantly inquired again, "Are you alright?". Once again, there was no flickering of awareness to my movements, only the unnerving dead stare now looking through him. Taking another hesitant step towards me, "Lisa?" he realized I was not awake at all. He'd heard of sleepwalking before, but the reality of it was much different than what was portrayed in movies and television. This was not amusing or comedic. This was downright terrifying.

After several minutes, I torpidly shifted my gaze straight ahead once more. "Lisa?" trying, yet again, to elicit some kind of response while taking a step closer to me. In my sleepwalking state, I do not know if I was aware of him other than as an obstacle to whatever mischief my sleeping mind had planned, but his presence had disrupted that night's endeavor completely. Without any acknowledgment of his existence, I turned quietly as a ghost and walked back down the hallway. Following slowly behind me, he watched as I entered my room and laid back down without a sign I had ever emerged from my room. Shaking his head, he returned to the living room, now at least, satisfied with an answer to what had been happening in the house since my arrival.

The following day was an interesting one, as he recounted the night before in vivid detail, to me and everyone else in the house. When asked if this had ever happened before, I did relate the story of being returned to my father's house after being found walking down the street. "Why on earth didn't you tell us about this before?" my foster mother demanded.

"Because," shrugging my shoulders, "I wasn't sure if it was me. It could have been someone else playing a practical joke or something on everyone. No one ever saw me and I had no recollection of doing it."

"But you knew you'd done this in the past."

"In a way, yes," I hesitantly admitted, "but never to my knowledge to this extent, and how could I know for sure if I never remembered what I'd done?"

Showing some concern for my distress, my foster father asked, "Do you know what causes you to do this?"

"Stress," I replied. "This is my fourth foster home in less than two years, new people, new surroundings... " shrugging my shoulders, "it could have been caused by any or all of those of those things." After a short pause, I hopefully added, "On the bright side, in theory, as I become more comfortable here the less it should happen."

True to my word, after a few more months of sporadic

activity, I did settle down and ceased my midnight wanderings. Much to the relief of everyone in the house, including myself.

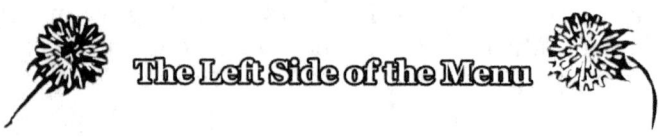

## The Left Side of the Menu

With less than a year left until my 18th birthday, I'd been busily planning my escape with Billy. With great enthusiasm, whenever he called, we talked about getting married, the things we would do together, and how he would take his month's leave in August to help me make all the arrangements for my departure. I started looking into colleges in the Washington area, pestered my school guidance counselor into helping me find scholarships and continued to save my money for the big move.

At the height of this, all of my hopes and plans were crashed in the space of a single phone call.

"Hey sweetie," I excitedly said into the phone, "how have things been?"

"Lisa, you should probably sit down." Came his troubling response.

"Is something wrong?"

"I uhhhh...," followed by a long silence.

"What's wrong?" Starting to become worried, he didn't sound right, he sounded scared.

"Oh shit! I don't know how else to say this," he responded angrily, "I got married yesterday."

I sank slowly to the floor, my entire world dissolving in that one sentence. "You what?"

"I got married yesterday," he sighed, "I didn't know how to tell you."

Well, that was obvious. "Why did you get married?" Completely confused by what I was hearing, it made absolutely no sense whatsoever.

"Remember me telling you about Ali? How she had been showing me around?"

"Yes..." feeling my stomach clench and getting a bit nauseous.

"Well... I got her pregnant." He finished in a rush, "We were told either we had to get married or get out of the army. She's in my unit and we weren't supposed to fraternize... and

I really fucked up."

"Yeah, you could say that." In silence, we both sat there on the phone, for I don't know how long, but it seemed like just this side of forever, as my life seemed to stretch out and snap in that moment.

"I am so sorry Lisa," he began to plead, "You have to understand, I am so sorry I did this to you, to us, but I didn't have a choice."

"Uh huh," my mind tried fitting all the broken pieces back together. It was failing miserably in its task. I had no words for what I was feeling. It was beyond heartbreak. It was my whole world collapsing. It was the loss of hope and all the faith I had put into him.

"You understand why I had to marry her, right?"

"Yeah, sure, I understand." I didn't, but it was done and nothing could change it, so why draw it out?

"I still love you," he whispered into the phone as if somehow that would make everything all better.

"I love you too, Billy," beginning to cry.

"Please don't," he begged, "I am so sorry, please don't cry."

"Yeah, okay," trying to hold it in, knowing it wouldn't last, "I guess I should let you go. Um, I guess congratulations on getting married and having a kid and stuff," Groping for something to say, but not having a single idea in the world what I was supposed to say in a situation like this.

"Yeah," equally as awkward, "thanks. Umm... yeah, I guess I should let you go and get back to her, she doesn't know I'm calling you."

"Okay. Well... goodbye."

"Good-bye" after a short hesitation, "I love you, Lisa."

"Love you too Billy. Good-bye." As I hung up, I continued to sit there for the longest time staring at the phone. I had no idea what I was going to do now. For the first time since our engagement, I felt completely alone. I could hear my foster family all around me but didn't want to face any of them or explain what had happened. I didn't want to be in this house anymore. I didn't want to be stuck in foster care surrounded by people I didn't much care for and who didn't give a shit about me. I didn't want to be alone.

I wiped the tears from my eyes and getting my emotions under control enough to walk up the stairs I hollered out to the house I was going for a walk, not even waiting for a reply before stepping out the door. I didn't know where I was going. I just felt the need to be moving, to get away, to be anywhere but where I was. I randomly picked a direction and started moving. Some aimless time later, I found myself close to Chris's house. He was new to the school, and I was one of his only friends. The few times I'd been there his family had warmly welcomed me and made me feel at home. Remembering those feelings of inclusion, I turned towards his house.

As I stepped up to the door, I could feel the tears beginning to run down my cheeks again and couldn't stop them this time. I knocked and waited for a response, feeling like an idiot, standing there with tears in my eyes. I almost turned away when the door opened and his mother emerged. Taking one look at me, she quickly stepped aside, waving at me while saying, "Come in sweetie, come in." As I stepped across the threshold, she turned and yelled, "Chris, Lisa's here!"

I stood dejectedly in the living room waiting for him to come out of his room, not sure what to say to anyone. His mother came up and slipped her arm over my shoulder and said, "What's wrong honey? Do you want to talk about it?" I shook my head, but hugged her back, thanking her quietly for her concern.

As Chris walked out of his room, he knew instantly something was wrong and held out his arms to me. Slipping away from his mother, I gratefully walked into the hug he was offering me. With his arm still around me, he gently turned me around, and we slowly walked together into his room and sat down on his bed. He didn't ask any questions, he just sat with me while I cried. Eventually, the tears slowed down and I was able to tell him what had happened. One of the traits I loved about him was his uncanny ability to listen, not to offer advice or solutions, but to truly listen without judgment or comment. I appreciated that trait in him more than ever right now.

After I had no more words to say, he went out and spoke to his mother. She invited me to stay for dinner, offering me a viable excuse to remain away from my foster home for just a while longer, which I gratefully accepted. I called them and told them of my invite. My foster father, who had answered the phone, gave me permission with little question as to why I had so suddenly left. Nor did he ask why I was at Chris's house, and I felt relieved not having to provide one.

Walking back into his room to wait for dinner, Chris pulled out a bag of weed. With a small smile, he said, "I can't fix what's wrong, but I can help you forget for a little while." And, at that moment, that was good enough for me.

He lit some incense, put on some Pink Floyd, rolled a joint and we proceeded to get as high as kites. We laid side by side on his bed, listening to the music, neither of us really talking, and I let everything just wash and roll over me. Laying there in the dark, listening to Blue Skies, I let it all go. The anger, the sadness, the loss, I let all of it go, this wasn't the end as much as it may have felt that way. My life was not over, only changed. And there we stayed, quietly in our own thoughts, until Chris's mother called us to dinner.

Dinner was a boisterous affair, as it often was in his household. I did my best to join in, to forget all that was happening and maintain the mellow resignation I'd come to terms with earlier. As a nice side effect, the rolling nausea I'd been experiencing since receiving Billy's phone call had subsided, and I was not only able to eat, but actually enjoy the food. After dinner, we all helped clear the table and clean up before Chris and I headed back to his room to smoke another joint and forget the world for just a bit longer.

As evening approached, I knew I would have to be heading back home soon, and Chris offered to walk me home. But a few blocks later, we both began to feel the munchies. Even after the huge meal we'd eaten earlier in the evening, our stoner munchies couldn't be denied. Looking around and seeing how close Dairy Queen was, we decided to stop there before continuing on our journey.

Walking into the bright fluorescent light, blinking like moles as we tried to get our bearings in this shiny world. Laughing at each other, we tried to keep a straight face, but it only made it worse. We were much too distracted by each others giggling to concentrate for long on reading a menu. Every time we'd glance at each other we'd start laughing again, not for any particular reason, but unable to stop for more than a few seconds at a time.

After everyone in front of us had ordered, we continued to stare blankly at the menu board, trying to make sense of all the food offerings through our stifled giggles while we held each other up. "Do you know what you want?" asked the kid behind the counter, sending us back into gales of laughter, "Nope." shaking our heads while we swung back and forth from the effort. After a couple of minutes I started to poke at Chris, we really needed to either order something or get out. People were beginning to stare at us, inconspicuous we were not. He was a giant of a guy, 6'5 and probably 220 pounds, while I looked like a wisp of a child at 5'5 and all of 90 pounds. Our sizes exaggerated one another as we stood there, side by side. The sporadic laughter didn't help much either.

"Do you know what you want?" he asked me.

"Not a clue, food, whatever... I don't care." trying hard to keep my laughter contained. It was getting us nowhere and I really was hungry.

He straightened up and approached the counter, giving the menu one more vague glance, he announced with a wide sweeping gesture, "I'd like everything on the left side of the menu."

The kid behind the counter gave a start, "Excuse me?"

"The left side. I'd like one of everything on it." Glancing down at me and smiling.

"Right." His gaze darting back and forth between us, "One of everything. On the left side of the menu."

"Yep." grinning widely, "That's what we want."

"This is a joke, right?" he almost pleaded this time.

"Nope, just bring it out to us as you get it done."

Giving the kid a wink as he pulled out his wallet. "It's for here."

"Whatever." the kid said with a sigh, glancing at the board and ringing up the order. After several minutes his fingers stopped their dance across the keys, "That'll be..." (to be truthful I don't remember right now what the total came to, but I know that high double digits were quoted.)

Counting out bills and stacking them on the counter, Chris paid for everything and we walked over to a table by itself, next to a window, and waited. Hot dogs, chili dogs, chili-cheese dogs, hamburgers, cheeseburgers, double cheeseburgers, bacon cheeseburgers and still the food came, chicken sandwiches and fries, taking over the table next to ours as it was arriving faster than we could make it disappear

Finally bringing over one last tray, the counter kid announced, "That's it. Enjoy," walking away shaking his head at the two of us.

We sat there, sampling and eating until neither of us

could stomach anymore. We looked over the piles of paper trays, half eaten food, napkin wads and empty soda containers. In blissful bloating we leaned back from the table, amazed at the carnage we'd managed in our undertaking. It was truly an impressive sight. We sat there too heavy to move while full dark descended outside. I watched the streetlights go on and knew I was going to be in trouble, but for once I just didn't care. I was content to just sit among the wreckage of our meal and stare out the window. I didn't know what I was going to do anymore, but both the trouble I was going to be in and the problems of my life could wait for just a bit longer.

With reluctance, I finally announced, "I need to get home. I'm already in trouble no need to make it worse by waiting any longer." Nodding, he stood up first, taking me by the hand and pulling me to my feet as I groaned mournfully. I felt as gravid as a pregnant woman ready to pop. Hand in hand, we went out the door, slowly meandering in the general direction of my house. "You going to be okay?" he asked as we neared the house.

I took several more steps before replying, "Yeah," I said with a sigh, "I'll be okay."

I left him a block from my house to continue on by myself. I knew that for a while I would be sad, most likely angry for a while as well, but yes, I knew I would eventually be okay. It hurt and it sucked and I hated it, but this was not the end of the world, just the end of a relationship. Tomorrow I would start thinking about my new future, one without Billy in it, and decide what I was going to do. But that was for tomorrow. For right now, I was okay, and sometimes that's as good as it gets.

 ## Never Say Never

Saying never is like tempting the universe to make it so. You're going along, minding your own business, casually mention, "oh, I'd never do that" and Bam! like a double-dog dare, the universe conspires to arrange your life so the only reasonable option is doing what you once claimed would never happen.

I'd been babysitting for Steve and Dee since I had arrived at the Faulkner's. They were a fun couple I enjoyed spending time with, often arranging things so I could hang out at their house, even if they didn't need a babysitter.

We played Dirty Scrabble, where you get double points if you could create atrocious words or phrases, and triple points if you came up with something really original. We went bowling and I actually became pretty good at it. We played Trivial Pursuit for shots, a game I'm not sure I can recommend but always enjoyed. I don't recall anyone ever winning since the longer you played the drunker you got. Your ability to answer even simple questions, much less ones like, "What timepiece has a Gnomon in the middle?" (it's a sundial in case you're wondering), rapidly decreased in direct inverse proportion to the increasing amounts of alcohol you've imbibed.

But most days after they returned home from work we'd just hang out and listen to music and talk.

They were a safe haven away from judgment, sometimes allowing me to engage in much more trouble than I would have looked for on my own, but protected from discovery simply by them assuming the roles of "supervising adults". I'd never been a drinker. Alcohol was hard to find while drugs were everywhere. But, there were many evenings I returned home with a good buzz on, and no one the wiser, going straight to my room, with no more than a nod and a wave to anyone as I walked through the house.

At around the same time my world came crashing down around me with Billy, Steve's world suffered a similar fate.

Dee left the state to take a job a few months before, with the plan that Steve and her son would join her soon after. Once she had a place set up and got settled in, she would send for them. Instead, she drifted away. Within just a few short months she made the announcement she had found someone else. Neither Steve nor her son would be joining her after all.

Steve and I spent many evenings in commiseration after putting her son to bed. Drinking and listening to his extensive music collection, we talked about our mutual heartbreak. Impulsively, late one night during one of our conversations, I leaned over and kissed him. His first reaction was to push me away. He was not young, but a man in his late 40's and he knew the trouble that could occur if we were to continue. But he was as lonely as I was, and I was persuasive.

This was not an accident of alcohol, but something I'd been considering for a while. He was kind, affectionate in a distant way, and most of all, "safe". I was not a doe-eyed virgin, nor was I looking for a relationship. He was someone I could share my loneliness with who would not ask for more from me.

After his initial shock and his insistence that I didn't know what I was doing, I patiently explained that I did know what I wanted and why. I realize now I had an unfair advantage. He may have been older, but the loss of his wife and their life together had left him emotionally distressed and vulnerable to my affection. He was as lonely as I was, a mirror who reflected back his own loss and hurt, and each time we talked, the connection we had grew stronger. It wasn't that we both hadn't felt this, I'd just been the one to act on it. Without my prompting I don't believe it would have happened, he may have felt it, but I don't think he would have ever acted on it.

Gradually realizing I was truly serious, that his attention was not only wanted but encouraged, he began to return my affection. Slowly at first, as tentative as a virgin on her wedding night, he gave me every chance to change my mind, eventually giving in to me completely. Standing, he swept me up off my feet and carried me into his bedroom.

Late into the night while lying quietly in each other's arms I began to laugh, leaning up on his elbow, he looked down at me with a questioning stare.

"Do you remember about five months ago when Dee and

I were here in the bedroom talking while she was getting ready to go out with you for the evening?"

Shaking his head no, I continued, "I told Dee how much fun your waterbed was while I rocked and made waves. She started laughing and told me I could make as many waves on the bed as I wanted, but no sex in her bed was allowed." I started laughing again, realizing I had tempted the universe with my next statement, "Oh no Dee," giggling now as I continued with my little story, "I'd never have sex in your bed, promise." Turning to him now, I looked him in the eye, "I truly meant it at that time you know." Giving in to a few more giggles, I laid back down to stare at the ceiling, still nestled securely in his arms and thought about the universe's dirty trick on both of us.

Steve, beginning to laugh now as well, rolled over on his back to stare at the ceiling with me, "Oh god," shaking his head, he continued, "yeah, try not to say never again, it'll get you in trouble every time." Giving me a sighing half laugh, he rolled back towards me pulling me in close and nestling his head near my ear, he whispered, "Never, never, never again."

Since that night, I have very carefully not uttered the phrase, "Oh, I'd *never* do that." It's not that I have regretted my choices, but I do prefer my mischief to be of my own devising, not the universes.

##  Stuck on a Bridge

During my senior year, I reconnected with my first love, David. He was moved out of Quincy after our arrest and living with extended family about 2 hours from my current foster home. We started exchanging phone calls and letters, catching up with each other's lives and began building a new type of relationship as friends. I had worried he might have held some resentment for how things had turned out, and I'd been hesitant to find him. Only to find out all my worry was for nothing, easily slipping back into a friendship that had been interrupted.

At the end of my senior year, I invited David to come visit and go to Prom with me, which he happily agreed to. We hadn't seen each other since that disastrous night, and both of us were excited to see each other again after such a long separation.

Two weeks before Prom I received a phone call from David, he'd been in a motorcycle accident and wouldn't be able to make it down. I was disappointed, but understanding. Shit happens. The question now became, what to do? I'd already purchased the tickets, the dress and everything else that goes with a big dance. I still wanted to go, but everyone I knew already had a date and I wasn't sure I wanted to go alone.

The following week, while still debating what to do, my friend April had a bad breakup with her boyfriend and was now in a similar boat. All dressed up, and no one to go with. After giving her the time for the traditional rant & rave of a bad breakup, I offered to take her to Prom with me. I had an extra ticket, she had everything but a date to go with. She happily took me up on my offer, which left only one problem, a way to get to Prom since neither of us had a car available to us.

The last obstacle was overcome when Steve offered to let me use his car. It was an old red two-door stick shift with transmission problems, reverse didn't work at all and the clutch was touchy, but it was a car. But there was a problem with his generous offer, I'd never driven a stick shift in my life. I hadn't even had my license that long, for less than two months and hadn't driven much at all since I'd gotten it.

Sitting in Steve's living room explaining this to him, he tossed me the car keys, said put in the clutch when you want to shift gears and when the engine whines put it in the next higher gear, easy. Now go practice.

"Aren't you going to go with me?" I asked in surprise.

"Nope," shaking his head "I'm a horrible teacher and the best way to learn is by doing. Take it around the block a couple of times and you'll be fine."

I spent the next hour grinding gears and killing the engine repeatedly, as I lurched and died over and over again. But, after about an hour I seemed to have gotten the hang of it, or, at least, didn't kill it continuously. I figured I should, at least, be able to make it the half mile to the school without killing anyone and called it a day.

The night of Prom arrived with a great deal of chaos with everyone in my house trying to get ready for the dance at once. Every one of my foster siblings was going and the bathroom became a war zone, with everyone fighting over whose turn it was. I gave up early of having any chance of worming my way into that mess, so I packed up everything and went over to Steve's to get ready instead. He lived less than a block away and it would be so much easier to walk there in tennis shoes than in high heels and a long white dress.

Steve was surprised, but helpful, as he let me into the house. When I finally emerged all ready to go he complimented me on how I looked. It was, in a way, bittersweet. I had no parents to make a fuss over me, no posing for awkward photos in the hallway or any of the other activities that were going on all over town in a hundred homes. There aren't any photos of that evening, I didn't own a camera and Steve's had no film. But, I remember the beautiful white dress, with my hair pulled up and dotted with dozens of small pearls, and white stiletto heels. I felt beautiful, even if there's no photo evidence to back me up on it now.

With a grinding of gears, I left Steve's house and headed out to pick up April. My choppy driving smoothed out a bit as I became more comfortable with driving, but I was grateful for the almost empty streets of a small town.

Pulling to April's house, she was waiting for me on her porch, rushing down to greet me with gales of laughter as soon as the car came to a dying stop. I still hadn't gotten the hang of keeping the car running at a complete stop. I knew I was doing something wrong, but I had no idea what. By the time we reached the school, both of us were hysterical with laughter over my driving, convinced if we made it through the night without killing ourselves we'd call it a successful dance.

It was your standard Prom, streamers and glitter littered the gym, tables with candles and other shining centerpieces, dim lighting and a disco ball graced the center of the dance floor to complete the effect. The music was set at wall thumping levels and milling teenagers danced with various degrees of success, and the general hum of voices pervaded the air. It was wonderful.

As the dance neared its end April and I discussed going to the after-Prom being held across the bridge in Keokuk and brokered the odds of my driving abilities getting us there and back without disaster. We threw caution to the wind and decided to go for broke and make the attempt.

Exiting the gym and returning to the car, we encountered our first hurdle to leaving. I'd forgotten reverse didn't work and we were stuck facing an embankment with no option of going forward to get out. As we stood laughing outside of the car discussing how to get out of there, a couple of guys nearby overheard us and offered to push the car out for us. Graciously, we accepted their help. Climbing in and putting it in neutral they gave us a push, and after only killing it two or three times we roared off into the night, waving our thanks.

In the next town over, Willy a friend of mine from Quincy had moved there with his father during the school year. With some time to kill before the after-Prom we decided to stop in, and if possible, take him with us for the remainder of the evening. Letting ourselves in, I waved a greeting to his dad who was watching TV in the living room and announced we were stealing his son for the night before heading upstairs to his bedroom.

We found Willy fast asleep in bed, peacefully unaware of our impending invasion. We pounced on the bed yelling his name to wake him, while jumping up and down and rocking the bed, scaring the crap out of him with our abrupt and sudden onslaught. Dragging the covers from him and shushing his protests, I informed him we were taking him to the after prom. As soon as his eyes were open and tracking, I went to his closet looking for something appropriate for him to wear. Dawn and I had already changed at the school into more casual clothes, so no tux was required, just something clean.

After first protesting he was tired, he put his hands up in defeat at our insistence on him joining our fun and began to get dressed. Grumbling to himself, he pulled on clothes, glaring at us on occasion, but in short order, he was presentable enough for kidnapping. As soon as he was ready, we headed back downstairs and told his dad that we were stealing him for the night and would return him in the morning. After-Prom went until 6 a.m. if you could stay awake that long. With his dad's benign permission we left the house, Willy reluctantly in tow. Quietly resigned to his fate, knowing no help would be forthcoming from his dad, he docilely followed us to the car.

Everything was going well until we came to the T-intersection right before the bridge. It was on a slight uphill incline, and as soon as I came to a stop the car died. No one in the car had ever driven a stick shift, so none of us knew why it kept happening, but with dogged determination, I continued to start and roll the car as I tried to go forward. The uncontrolled laughter didn't help my driving skills at all, but eventually, mostly because I had rolled far enough downhill to find a level spot, I was able to get the car going again.

Just as we passed onto the bridge, with the music playing loudly and all of us joking about nothing was going to stop us now from reaching our destination, I saw bright flashing colored lights in the rear view mirror. Well, crap.

I pulled over to the side of the bridge and right on cue the car died, on yet another uphill slope. By the time the officer came to my window, I was almost delirious with laughter. No matter how hard I tried, I couldn't get it under control, it was just too much. I wasn't scared, none of us had been drinking or smoking anything illicit. I was simply a very bad driver, but I was a bad driver with a valid license. My concern wasn't even about getting a ticket, but how the hell I was going to get off the bridge without rolling back into Illinois and the more I thought about it, the funnier it seemed.

Tapping the window with his flashlight he inquired, "Have you been drinking?"

Shaking my head while my body vibrated with unconstrained laughter, I managed to stutter out, "Nu-n-no." I don't believe I was very convincing.

"Can you please get out of the car?" motioning me out with his flashlight. I luckily remembered to put the emergency brake on before exiting, because nothing says "I'm sober" like a rolling unmanned vehicle.

"I swear I haven't been drinking officer," wiping tears from my eyes, "I'm just a bad driver, this is the first time I've ever driven a stick shift and I'm having a few problems."

"I see," he said while looking at me and then shining his light inside the car, "and is this your car?"

"Um, no, it belongs to the guy I babysit for," finally getting my laughter under control, "he does know I have it if that's what you're worried about."

"Can anyone else drive a stick shift?"

"Um, nope, just me, sorta." Shrugging my shoulders, "I think I pretty much have the hang of it, except stopping, stopping seems to be a problem, the car keeps dying."

Looking me up and down, shaking his head, "You do know to keep the clutch in while coming to a stop, right?"

Giving him a look of astonished surprise, "That's the problem? That's what I've been doing wrong? I thought you only put in the clutch to shift the gears!"

"How did you learn to drive this car?"

"Steve tossed me the keys and said drive, put in the clutch when you shift gears and try not to crash," I responded with total sincerity.

Once again, shaking his head, "Do you know why I pulled you over?"

Actually, no I didn't. I had my lights on, I'd used my blinker while making the turn to get on the bridge and I wasn't speeding or swerving. Other than the malfunction at the stop sign, I hadn't done anything wrong. So I shook my head and spread my arms to invite him into telling me what had gotten me in this position.

"Back at the stop sign, your behavior looked suspicious while you sat there and started and killed the car for over 15 minutes while I watched you."

Thinking to myself, if that was the problem, why the hell didn't he come over then, but kept it to myself and instead replied, "Oh yeah, uphills. I'm having a problem with those too." Once more glancing at the bridge wondering how I was going to get going once he let me go.

Asking me for all my papers and drivers license, I also informed him I lived with the Faulkner's, his senior officer at the police station. He took everything back to his car and while doing whatever it is that they do in their squad car, another one pulled up, this one was from Iowa. Apparently, being stopped at the halfway mark between two states required the presence of both.

He pulled up behind the first squad car, looked over the scene and walked over to the first officer and had a quiet conversation about us.

Apparently satisfied with my story, we were told we could go and they walked back to his car to continue whatever conversation they had started while I climbed back into mine and attempted to leave. And an attempt was all it was.

There was, at least, a car length between me and the squad car behind me, but the slope I was parked on was steep, much higher than the small rise by the stop sign. I started the car, it began to roll, I panicked, put on the brake and killed the car. I tried again, and the same thing happened, each time inching slowly backward towards the squad car, and the more nervous I would become. After five such attempts and less than 4 feet between the cars, my legs were shaking so hard I could barely hold in the brake. In frustration, I turned off the car, put on the emergency brake and just sat there, with my head on the steering wheel, wondering what I should do next. I considered asking them to move out of the way so I could roll backward until I reached more level ground, but I wasn't sure how well that would be received. And so I continued to sit there hoping they would leave before I tried again.

After a couple of minutes, the officer walked back towards my car, "Is there a problem?"

Nodding my head, "I can't seem to go forward."

"Are you putting in the clutch while putting on the gas?" he asked.

"Uh, yeah, but it doesn't seem to be working for me right now."

"Well, try again, I'll walk you through it."

Nervously glancing back behind me, I started the car, "Okay, now hold the clutch and the gas and go." stepping back from the car as he said it.

Lurch and die. Try again. Lurch and die. Try again. Lurch and die. Yeah, this wasn't working, becoming more distressed each time.

Looking exasperated, he told me to just sit tight and he'd be right back while retreating to the other officer. After a short conference, they both walked back to the car, "Okay, here's what we're going to do, we're going to wait a short time until another officer can arrive and I'll drive you across the bridge to your after-Prom."

Well, this was an unexpected turn of events, "You can do that?

"I'll drive your car while the officer from Iowa will drive in front of us, and the other officer from Illinois I've called over will drive behind us. He'll bring me back here after we get you safely deposited at your destination."

Fair enough. "Sounds good, and thanks."

And so we sat there on the bridge, an Iowa cop in front of me, an Illinois cop behind me, while cars filled with other prom-goers passed us by. We waved at the people we recognized, once again laughing over the ridiculousness of the situation and settled in to wait for the other officer's arrival.

As soon as he arrived, the original officer who had started this whole chain of events approached the car and waved me over to the other seat and climbed in. Doing our best not to laugh, we watched him adjust the seats and mirrors and settle into the tiny car. Once he was done, he waved his arm out the window and we all preceded across the bridge, arriving at our location with my newly formed police escort.

We made quite the sight as we pulled up in front of my classmates all heading into the building, as they paused to check out what was occurring. After he pulled into a parking space (I had forgotten to tell him about the no reverse, and decided against telling him now), we all exited the vehicle. I walked over to the driver side, just as the officer shut the door, he gave me a small bow as he handed me the car keys, quickly retreating to the other squad car waiting for him.

Turning to go in I saw all of my peers staring at me in surprise and wonder, with a laugh, I gathered in my companions to join everyone else in the ongoing festivities. There really is nothing like arriving in style with a police escort.

 ## Graduation

Graduation was rapidly approaching, with finals to be passed, senior photos to be taken, and all the paraphernalia for the big event to be purchased and distributed accordingly. Among those items were invitations to be sent out. I invited many of my friends from Quincy, my mother, and even my youngest sister, but I drew the line at my father. I flatly refused to have him attend.

This caused a great deal of commotion as many individuals from my caseworker to my father himself tried to convince me that this was simply unacceptable. Pressure was brought on me to rescind my refusal and accept him with open arms on the day of my graduation. No, no, absolutely not, I would not budge and dug in my heels. If he was attending my graduation, I would not be, period.

The contention ended with a phone call between my father and me where I informed him he had done nothing to get me to this point and I would not allow him to play the part of the proud papa in front of everyone. Not once during my entire stay in foster care had he contacted me or even replied to the dozens of letters I'd been forced to write to him over the past two years. He was not going to show up now and try to bask in the glory of my accomplishment.

The phone call ended with a very terse, "You'll regret this decision. Maybe not now, but sometime in the future, you'll regret having made this choice."

I never have. In all the years between now and then, I still stand by my decision and have not felt one moment of regret over it.

Once the matter was settled, I eagerly fell into all the preparations that needed to be done before the big day. I happily opened RSVP's from everyone who sent them back and was even surprised when I received one from Nev. We hadn't spoken much since I left Quincy. He was sharing a house with several other people I knew, and I invited everyone there on the off chance any of them might want to come.

It was a glorious day, many of my friends showed up, along with my mother and her new husband. I wasn't class valedictorian, but I did graduate with high honors which pleased me greatly. We sweated through several speeches, music and all the trappings of tradition, and with great joy flung our hats in the air at the end. We all stood on the cusp of adulthood and it was exhilarating with the first recognition of adulthood.

There was a graduation party at my foster home. Primarily because their daughter also graduated, but none of us were forbidden from bringing our own guests as well. My guest list had dwindled by the time we left the school. Several of my friends carpooled and needed to get back to Quincy for various reasons, and my mother and her new husband left shortly after we returned to the Faulkner's. By evening, only Nev remained of the group I'd brought with me, and the two of us slipped out unnoticed by anyone to find a little time alone to talk.

We went for a walk, holding hands under the stars with no destination in mind. We ended up at the park not too far from my house and sat on the swings and continued our catching up.

He told me how great it was to see me, and how he had missed me, but didn't want to intrude when he heard Billy and I were engaged. He confessed meant to get in contact with me again when he heard of our breakup and his marriage to Ali, but after so long he wasn't sure if I would have been interested in seeing him again.

I let him know I was leaving the state in three months. I would be moving to Arizona with Cindy as soon as my birthday arrived, but if he was okay with that, I wouldn't mind his company. I had missed him in a vague way and it was good seeing him again. We always had fun when we went out and I had enjoyed our time together before I was moved out of Quincy.

I didn't want to be gone long from the Faulkner's, we had left easily enough, but I would be missed if we stayed out too much longer. We walked slowly back to the house and he kissed me good night at the door before leaving for home.

Sitting down on the front step where I could be seen if anyone was looking for me, I wanted a little time to think and reflect before going back into the mass of people still in the house.

Graduation.

I was now a high school graduate getting ready to start the next phase of my life. The next big step would have to wait for another three months. Graduate or not, the state was not going to let me go until I was officially 18, but freedom was not far away now.

It was time to put childish things aside. The drugs I'd been using to cope with the stress of my life were to be set aside while plans for my big move to Phoenix needed to be arranged. My life would soon be mine. I would be in charge of the choices I made and only I would be responsible to myself for getting things done. And I felt a thrill with the unchecked possibility of it all.

As I continued to sit there in the dark with the party slowly winding down behind me, I thought about my past and everything that had happened to get me to this point. Of the many friends I'd made who helped and sustained me through the years, I hoped we would not lose each other to the passage of time.

I thought of my parents and everything they had done. I'd forgiven my mother but knew that forgiveness for my father would be years coming, if ever.

My life hadn't been all bad, thinking back over my life and letting those random moments flow in a haphazard way.

I remembered a skinny-dipping picnic with another group of friends and falling asleep on a warm rock in the shade only to wake up with a sunburned ass when the shadows moved on while I slept. As badly as it hurt, I'm sure it was nothing compared to the guy next to me who had fallen asleep on his back. He was indescribably miserable for two weeks after that. Oh, we had laughed over that, miserable and sunburned as we were, the day spent playing in the waterfall had been worth it. Which, I reminded myself of each and every time I sat down for the next week.

I remembered my first lover, both of us virgins fumbling like the blind leading the blank, neither of us quite knowing what we were doing but gamely trying to figure it out. I thought about Steve, sweet and caring, and probably as scared as my first, if for very different reasons. I reflected back upon David and Billy, my two great loves up to this point in my life, and of the other lovers I'd taken over the years, missing each of them in turn.

I thought back on stolen kisses and slumber parties, stupid pranks and quiet moments of bliss that only comes from being content with the universe. I thought about the times I'd worked on my homework sitting in a bar with Ginny while we fed quarters into the jukebox. And, one year for Halloween when we dressed up as hookers with Michael as our pimp. And the time Ginny, LeeAnn and I all piled into Larry's beater car and he tried to teach us how to drive, stopping for ice cream and instead of eating it, smearing it all over each other's faces.

These were the good moments, the ones that make everything else worthwhile. They are the quiet interludes that aren't long enough for a story, but enough to keep you going when everything else in your life is a mess. They are the songs you sing loudly, and badly, in a car full of friends. The hand that reaches across to touch yours so you know you're not alone. It's giggling in the middle of the night with your best friend because one of you said something stupid. They aren't the big things, but a series of small things that let you know you are loved, that you have a place in this world and would be missed if you were gone.

As I stood up and prepared myself to go back inside, I knew I was ready for whatever happened next. I was ready to graduate into the next phase of my life, and I was eager to see what that would be.

**YOU'VE REACHED THE HALFWAY POINT! GO YOU!**

## The Great Escape

After two long years in foster care, I was, at last, able to implement my escape. It wasn't easy and my last three months was a busy time filled with paperwork and worry. I had hoops to jump through for the state to ensure my release, I had to prove I could provide for myself since the state could, if it wanted to, hold me until I was 25 for various reasons. Some foster kids chose to stay in for college or other reasons since the state would help support them until they were able to go out on their own, but I wanted nothing to do with any of that. I wanted out.

I didn't just want out of foster care, I wanted out of the state and as far away from their possible reach as I could reasonably attain. A few years before, Cindy, one of my close high school friends, moved to Phoenix with her mother. Throughout all of her moves and mine, we'd kept in touch, and as my 18th birthday approached we began making plans for me to move out there with her. When she was 16, she was emancipated by the courts, and now had a job, a live-in boyfriend and an apartment with a spare room. All I needed was to get from here to there, and I could start a whole new life.

With Cindy's help, I was able to prove employment in Phoenix at a restaurant her boyfriend owned called The Knock-Kneed Lobster Company. At first, I wasn't believed due to the name, but it well and truly existed, even though the job did not. It was only a ploy to help expedite my release. Cindy and I assumed as soon as I arrived in Phoenix and was settled in I would have plenty of time, and opportunity, to find a job and until then use my savings to live off of. I wasn't worried about finding work, I was worried about getting out from under DCFS as quickly as possible.

I continued with my steady babysitting job watching Steve's son. I also signed up for a JTPA program that gave summer employment to teens. I was chosen to participate in a program that sent me to the university in Macomb for three weeks and then back to Hamilton, to continue working for them the remainder of the summer. By summer's end, I'd managed to save up several thousand dollars for my move and to support myself until I was able to actually find work out there.

Over the summer, I started seeing Nev again. I wasn't looking for anything serious since I was leaving and he had no desire to leave the area, but I thought it would be a fun way to pass the time during the summer.

We saw each other when we had time, and I always had fun when we were together, but we kept it very casual by choice. He wasn't well liked by many of my friends, which caused some tension, but we weren't often with them so I didn't let it bother me too much.

But then, shortly before my birthday, I realized something was wrong with me. All my plans were set, I had a release date, I had money set aside and Cindy was on her way to Illinois in less than two weeks. All these things were fine, but I wasn't. I wasn't feeling well, I felt tired a lot, had been getting sick frequently and just didn't feel right. I began to get a sinking feeling in my stomach, I was pretty sure I knew what was wrong, but refused to believe it at first.

But believe it or not, I needed to know so I called my friend Willy and he came to get me on one of my off days and I went back to Warsaw with him. I told him of my suspicions and the good friend that he was, went to the store and picked up what I needed. Twenty minutes later, my suspicions were confirmed, I was pregnant.

Well, ain't that just a kick in the ass. I sat there silently thinking over my situation, trying hard to process everything. I'd been told by several doctors that due to my size and low body fat ratio I would have a very hard time conceiving if I ever wanted to have a child. But even so, I'd gone on the pill two years prior and had faithfully taken them every day, and now I was pregnant. I had certainly beaten the odds on this one.

Well, one thing was for sure, I would still be leaving for Phoenix. I would keep this information to myself and not let anyone know. I was not going to give the state any reason to keep me any longer. That decided, I moved on to what to do about Nev. Without a doubt, he was the father, and I felt he had the right to know, but I was not going to stay in the area, pregnant or not.

While I sat in contemplation, Willy had been making phone calls. I hadn't been paying much attention until he sat the phone down in its cradle and he came to sit down next to me.

"Have you decided what you are going to do?" he asked.

"I'm going to keep it. I suppose I'll need to tell Nev. I'm still leaving, I can't stay here."

"What about Nev?" acting a little nervous now.

"I don't know. I'll tell him, and if he wants to come with me, I'll invite him to come with us, but I'm not staying."

Becoming very serious Willy leaned towards me and took my hand, "You know none of us like him, there's something dark about him. We haven't said much before because you were leaving, but we're worried now."

Surprised, I looked over at him, "We?"

"I just got off the phone with Ky and Joe," he replied, "we have a proposal for you."

Now, over the years I had, in turn, dated each of these guys. We were all friends, often hung out together, and the three of them were close friends. The fact that I had dated each of them was not a secret, each of them knew about the other two. There were no hard feelings or jealousy over it, it was casual and I was always careful not to hurt any of their feelings. But I was somewhat confused on what this proposal could be.

"Okay?" And settled back on his bed to hear him out.

"None of us like him Lisa, we don't think he's good enough for you." Almost pleadingly, he continued. "We all know this baby is his, but we don't care. All three of us are going into the army and we'll be leaving soon, but the thing is," and here he hesitated for a minute, "we want you to pick one of us. Don't tell Nev, break it off with him, and pick one of us. We've all agreed, you marry whichever one of us you want, and the other two of us will help raise and support you and the baby."

It may have been the weirdest, and sweetest, marriage proposal I have ever gotten in my life, and I have had many over the years, twice from gay men. I was truly touched and felt tears falling from my eyes at how much they cared about me.

"Oh sweetie, I can't ask any of you to do that."

"It's okay," he exclaimed, "just pick one of us. We won't even interfere with your plans, just before you leave we'll go to the courthouse and you can marry whichever one of us you choose and the other two will stand as witnesses. Or, go ahead and leave for Phoenix and when we're finished with Basic and AIT, and get to our duty stations you can pick whichever one of us you want to live with. Or, stay in Phoenix and we'll each send you part of our paycheck to support you both. Just please, don't tell Nev, and we'll be there for you whatever you need."

I was speechless. I didn't have a single idea what to say to what he had offered. It was generous beyond imagining was without a doubt, but I didn't feel I could ask that of any of them. I cared about each of them, loved them in my own way and I knew each of them loved me in return. But, to have them dedicate their lives to me, and raising a child that wasn't theirs, wasn't something I could ask of any of them.

I started shaking my head, "I love you all for offering me this, but I can't. Nev deserves to know he has a child coming, and while I doubt he'll come out with me, I still can't ask you guys to support me."

Taking both of my hands in his, and looking into my eyes, "If you won't take our offer please, at least, don't tell him. There is something dark in him." Looking hard at me, pleading with me to understand, "We don't want to see you hurt. Think about what I've said, the offer from us is there and we'll be here for you. All you have to do is ask."

I didn't take them up on their offer. Even though they tried several more times, both individually and as a group, to convince me to accept their proposal before I left. I did tell Nev, and as I expected, he had no desire to leave with me but did spend the rest of my time in Hamilton trying to convince me to stay, but I would not be deterred.

I could not hide my pregnancy from my foster brothers, as much as I tried to do so, and I was a bit worried about it. I had a contentious relationship with one of them. We truly disliked each other, and all he had to do to ruin everything was to tell my foster parents. In the end, all my worry was for nothing. We may not have liked each other, but the silent, unspoken rules that govern all foster kids held more sway than his dislike of me.

The number one rule was "you never rat out a foster kid to the system". If it was discovered you had, there would be consequences that would make your continued stay in the system torturous. Information flowed from foster home to foster home, and narks were marked and their names passed on. You could not get away from it once it happened, there was no violence, but small and petty acts would be utilized to ensure a miserable existence for the remainder of your time. No one would have your back, you would be shunned and alone. It was as brutal as it was effective.

While we may fight and quarrel among ourselves, there was always a solid front when any member of authority was around. We would help conceal each other's small infractions, never took our personal grievances to our foster parents but self-regulated ourselves. Fighting, bickering, and even the occasional physical confrontation was allowed, as long as at the end of the day we had plausible deniability if asked.

My foster brothers helped me conceal my pregnancy. Without their help, I don't know if I could have escaped a critical look if either of my foster parents had given me one. They did their best to distract them when I had to share the same space as my foster parents, without being obvious about it. I may not have gotten along well with all of them, but I was grateful for their protection.

Even my newest foster sibling, who arrived unexpectedly in the middle of the night, helped. Coming home very late from babysitting, I noticed someone in the lower bunk of my bed. I figured another sister had arrived while I was away, and quietly got ready for bed without waking her. The next morning while getting ready for work, my sister rolled over in bed and asked in a deep voice, "So, how far along are you?"

Startled, I gave my newest foster sister a closer look and realized it was not as I had assumed a sister, but a brother. "Hey, sorry to startle you." Shifting up to lean on his elbow while we talked, "I got here really late last night. I guess they figured you wouldn't be home for a while and told me to stay in this room for the night until they got the other room set up for me."

Recovering from the shock of him in the other bed, I asked if he minded if I finished getting ready. Shaking his head no, I resumed brushing my hair. While putting on my makeup, I asked, "How did you know?"

"Oh, the baby," shrugging his shoulders, "pregnant women just look different that's all."

"Please don't say anything," I begged him, "my foster parents don't know and I want to keep it that way. I have less than three weeks until my 18th birthday."

"Hey, no problem," he responded, "I get ya. Your secret is safe with me." And so it was. During that short period of time, he and I became good friends. He was an emergency placement and only staying with the Faulkner's until they could figure out where to move him next. Then suddenly, without warning, he was moved before my release date while I was away from the house. I'd hoped to be able to keep in contact with him, but I never did find out where they sent him, and once I moved to Phoenix I doubt he would have had much luck in finding me. We never saw each other again. It happens a lot in foster care, you make a good friend and then one day, they're gone, never to be seen again.

My last week in foster care I was granted permission to leave the Faulkner's and stay with my mother. Before I left I said my final goodbyes, some harder than others. My foster siblings and parents, I left with mostly a nod of farewell, there were no tears. My foster brothers wished me luck on my travels. A few with a bit of envy for my successful escape from the system.

I visited the few friends I'd made in town, and we made promises to each other to keep in touch. We never did. I never heard from anyone I met while in foster care once I left.

Saying goodbye to Steve and his son was the hardest of my farewells. I'd become close to both of them. They had been a huge part of my life while there and I wished them both well. Dee had dropped off the map completely, leaving not only her husband, but her son, and it hurt them both deeply. Steve had stepped up, claiming his stepson as his own, and not abandoning him with the dissolution of their marriage. It was hard on both of them, but they had each other, and I hoped it was enough to get them through.

My week in Quincy was wonderful. All my friends visited often at Ginny's house, where I spent most of the week. Nev and I spent some time together, and he tried yet again to convince me to stay "for the sake of the baby" which I refused each time he brought it up. My three suitors also attempted to change my mind, both in turn individually, and together. I felt a gratitude I couldn't even begin to express, but even so, I continued to gently, but firmly, turn down their generous offer.

Cindy and I enthusiastically discussed our trip and the best routes to take and how much fun we were going to have once we arrived. I was excited. Almost bouncing off the walls in my wish to get moving, but I had one more court date to attend before I could leave. I wasn't worried, it was only a formality, but I was required to attend anyway.

The day of my birthday, I went to court and was released from foster care. I was an adult now, the state said so. I was now considered functional enough to be let loose on society with only the minimal supervision that all adults are constrained by. Somehow, on this magical day, all teenagers, who had needed close watching before are now deemed able to make life decisions on their own. After the cloistered existence I'd been living under for so many years, the anticipation of my newly gained freedom was almost intoxicating.

Later that day, my mother threw a party for me, and my friends kidnapped me later that evening and took me out to dinner, it was a large and noisy affair, and I felt wonderful. After dinner, we returned to Ginny's house to spend this last night together. but as the excitement wound down we broke off into little groups scattered around the house, sharing memories of our time together throughout our years of mischief and mutual support.

Many of my friends had paired up, and some of those pairings ended up in lasting relationships. Ginny and Michael married shortly after he returned from Basic training, and eventually had three children together. Tina and Ky were together for many years and had a son before ending their relationship. Even Cindy and Richard had a brief fling before the two of us headed back to Phoenix and her boyfriend. Others didn't last long, but we were, for the last time, all together.

All of my good friends, everyone I loved and who had loved me in return. I think we all knew that this was it, summer was ending. Some would be going to college, others into the military, a few would stay behind and find whatever work they could and begin their new adult lives. But, never again would we be like this, it was both frightening and exhilarating, and each of us felt it in our own way.

I kissed each of them goodbye, a few would be coming over to my mother's in the early morning light to see me off, but most would not. I didn't want the night to end, but I was also eager to begin my journey in the morning. A new life was waiting for me, for all of us, and as much as I wanted to hold on to each of these people who meant so much to me, growing up requires letting go.

 ## Two Kittens and a Toyota Truck

The morning dawned bright and beautiful, an auspicious, if deceiving, omen for our travels. Loading all my worldly possessions into the back of Cindy's Toyota, it didn't even take up all the space in that small truck bed. Mostly clothes, a beanbag chair, some household odds & ends collected over the past year, and a cooler of food my mother packed for our trip.

A small group was gathered in the driveway to see us off, but it wasn't the exuberant affair of the night before. This was it, I was truly leaving. The first of our group to not just leave home, but to go far beyond a quick road trip.

While saying my final goodbyes, Nev pulled me aside to make vague promises to keep in touch and maybe join me later, and I made reassuring noises back. I had no faith in him packing up and leaving his life here, but I didn't discourage him from the attempt. I did love him, and would not keep him from the babe I was carrying if he chose to come.

With final hugs, well-wishing and promises to call and keep in touch, Cindy and I climbed into the cab of the truck, taking with us two kittens we acquired while she was in town. I have no idea why we had gotten the kittens, but there was one for each of us, and it seemed like a great idea at the time.

By mid-afternoon, the bright blue skies had taken on a decidedly dark cast, with rolling clouds and falling temperatures. Looking back worriedly over all my possessions in cardboard boxes we stopped at the next convenience store hoping to buy a tarp. What we ended up with was a box of trash bags and a roll of duct tape.

As the wind whipped and the first drops of rain began to fall, the two of us climbed into the bed of the truck and began our attempt at covering everything. In hindsight, we probably would have been better off putting each of my boxes inside a trash bag and duct taping it closed. In reality, we tried to tape them all together to make a makeshift tarp that we duct taped to the sides of her truck. If given more time and less rain we may have succeeded in our endeavor. Mostly what we succeeded in making was a rain catcher that collected a great deal of water that eventually broke through the duct-taped seals and soaked everything at once, in one big splash.

Not to be deterred so early in our trip, once we applied the last bit of duct tape, we climbed back into the cab and continued on. Wet but resilient. The kittens were much less impressed with the quick soaking they'd gotten when the truck doors opened than we were, complaining loudly until they dried each other off, and giving us long suffering looks in the meantime.

Onward we traveled with the goal of making the entire 1400 mile trip in one go. We were young and decided we could switch off as needed when one of us became too tired to drive. Now that we were on our way, we wanted to get there as quickly as possible.

The farthest I'd traveled up to this point in my life was a few trips to Chicago taken over the years, but always with family. I'd never navigated using a map, and as co-pilot of this joint venture, it was my responsibility to get us there. Continuing west, the look of the land began to gradually change from lush farmland to scrub desert, so I knew I hadn't gotten us too far lost at any point along the way. The route was fairly straightforward, keep going west and if you reach the ocean you've gone too far. We only got turned around twice, and I was pleased.

By the time, we reached the toll road in New Mexico we were both getting that giddy feeling from being awake far too long, but still able to function reasonably well. Entering the toll road, another car joined us on our right as we headed out of the booth. As we started to pick up speed, so did they. Neither of us wanting to let the other car get ahead so by the time we were a bit more than halfway through, we'd reached speeds exceeding 90 mph with our impromptu race. We began communicating with the other car through pantomime and nearing the end of the toll road we motioned for each other to pull over at the next rest stop.

Once the turnoff was agreed to, Cindy revved up to slide in front of them, then rapidly downshifting to hit the exit before them, laughing at the fun our little race had brought. By the time the other car pulled into the rest area we were

# IT'LL FEEL BETTER WHEN IT QUITS HURTING

sitting on a picnic table playing with the kittens waiting for their arrival.

Two young, clean cut guys exited their car and gave us a look up and down before approaching. Neither of us had been able to get a good look at each other as we had raced back and forth on the road other than glimpses now and again as we passed by the other vehicle for brief moments. Both groups approved of what they saw.

Cindy and I, while waiting, had begun calculating how long we should wait at the rest stop before continuing. Our toll tickets were time stamped, and if we arrived too soon our illicit driving would have been obvious. By our best calculations, we figured we had, at least, a half hour to kill and this rest area seemed as good as any to waste it at.

Our cohorts quickly joined us, sitting down on the opposite side of the table with happy grins. Boxing in the kittens at the center of the table, they started to play with our fluffy companions. With only minor distractions from the kittens, we started to exchange information, where we were headed and why we were traveling. They were military heading back to San Diego from leave and been traveling for much longer than we had. They started their journey close to the east coast where they had been visiting their families. They weren't related but their families lived close enough to each other it made sense for them to travel together and share expenses.

After more inane small talk they offered to take us to dinner once we left the toll road, which we immediately accepted. None of us knew the area around Albuquerque, and this was a time before GPS or even cell phones, we were going to have to wing it. Our plan was a simple one, at the next exit that indicated there were restaurants we'd stop and eat at the first one we saw.

Back in our vehicles, we took off at a more sedate pace than we'd entered. Eventually leaving the toll road and getting back on the main highway, we followed behind them, keeping pace without trying to pass them. We rolled along for the better part of an hour, getting darker with every mile when we finally spotted a road sign with food logos. None of them were familiar to us, but we stuck with the plan and took the exit.

The first place we pulled into was a drive-through only, so we continued on, waving each other onward to the next one down the street. It looked like nothing special on the outside, a small place lit up with neon lights and your average southwest white stucco with terracotta trim. The guys were dressed in jeans and polo shirts, while Cindy and I, dressed for comfort, were rocking the sweatpants and t-shirts. Walking in, we realized that this was not anything approaching casual, we'd gone from drive-through to fine Italian dining.

With a shrug the guys gave an arm sweep towards the dining area, giving each of us a wicked grin, in turn, saying, "What the fuck, let's eat." To which we agreed, what the fuck.

The hostess gave us an odd look, but seated us in an out of the way table, brought us bread sticks, menus and left without a word. While looking over the menu the guys reassured us that dinner was on them. They invited us to dinner, and it was their treat. That relieved me greatly. Cindy had very little money and I was the one financing this trip from all the money I had been saving. I still had most of it, but since I had no idea how long it would be before I could find a job, I was trying to be careful with every cent.

It was a wonderful meal, the food was grand and the company entertaining. They told us stories of their adventures in the military and we gave brief histories of ourselves in exchange. The one thing we did not exchange was any contact information. We had vague details of each other's final locations, but nothing specific and no last names.

At the end of the meal, we headed back to our vehicles. Standing in the parking lot, we talked for a bit longer as we let the kittens out to wander before we headed off again. They were planning on stopping for the night in Flagstaff, and encouraged us to join them there and have breakfast with them in the morning before heading on our way. But with Phoenix being so close to Flagstaff, neither of us wanted to delay reaching our final destination, even if it was only for the night. As tired as both of us had been getting, the meal and the company had refreshed us enough to consider this last nonstop push.

Following each other for the remainder of their trip, we waved them a good journey at the Flagstaff exit. Continuing on into the night, alone in our travels. Honestly, there is nothing like the desert at night. The flat, endless vistas and the bright stars, free of street light pollution, and without another car in sight. It was beautiful. I stared out the window, soaking in the feel of my new home. We were less than an hour from Phoenix now and I was looking forward to the promise of everything it had to offer.

As we rolled into Phoenix and reached the main strip I was mesmerized. It was like entering a fairy tale, the whole of the city was lit up in sparkling wonder, even the mundane car lots had a magical glow to me. With wide eyes, I tried to grasp all that I saw. This was nothing like Quincy or even Chicago, this was a relatively new city by all standards, and it was as shiny as a tree at Christmas. Even at this late hour, the traffic was heavy by my standards, I had yet to see rush hour, and was impressed with the number of open shops and restaurants.

As we drove Cindy played tour guide, pointing out various places and things I should see, laughing at my awe. Eventually, we pulled off the main roads into a quieter, and darker, subdivision. She pulled into a parking space and announced, "We're home," with a grin.

Grabbing the kittens and a few small things we headed into the apartment she shared with her boyfriend. Talking excitedly about how much fun we were going to have and how much I was going to love it there, giddy with exhaustion. And all was right with the world until we walked through the door.

With a look of trapped guilt, Cindy's boyfriend disengaged himself from the intimate embrace of his companion. "Oh, uh, hi," he managed to sputter out, "I didn't expect you back until tomorrow."

While he continued to stutter out some excuse, Cindy was looking over the apartment, noting the boxes stacked in the corner and a lack of her possessions anywhere in evidence. "What's going on," she demanded, standing in the doorway with hands on her hips, her face taking on a red tinge.

"Oh, yeah," beginning to look sheepish, "I was going to tell you when got back, uh... we're breaking up."

Sitting down on the floor abruptly, she started to look around aimlessly, after a few moments she settled her gaze on him yet again, "Breaking up?"

"Well, yeah," looking more uncomfortable, "I hadn't planned on it this way, but while you were gone I met (insert name here, I can't remember after all this time, or his either for that matter) and we really hit it off. I didn't want to tell you while you were still gone, I wanted to do it in person, but you showed up early. This wasn't how I meant to do it."

"You are seriously breaking up with me?" Incredulously, she looked wildly around the apartment, "I've been gone for less than three weeks and you found someone else and moved her in?"

"Uh, yeah." Sheepishly replying, having no defense for his actions. Then in a placating attempt to soothe her, "But you and your friend can stay here a couple of days to figure out what you're going to do."

"And my job?"

"Oh yeah, that." Looking even more uncomfortable, if that was possible, he began to squirm, "I gave it to (what's her name) while you were gone. I was short-handed with you gone, and she's working out really well."

"Yeah, I'll bet she is," Cindy said, looking around once more. "Fine, give us the spare room and we'll talk about this more in the morning."

He nodded. Cindy and I picked up our few belongs, and walked into the agreed upon bedroom, she slammed the door behind us. "Well, fuck."

I could only nod in agreement, well fuck indeed.

 ## Looking for Living

My first week in Phoenix was not what I'd been expecting at all. I assumed we would settle in, and Cindy would go back to work while I found a job and only have to rely on my savings sparingly, as needed. As it turned out, without my little nest egg, we both would have been in a world of hurt.

The morning following our disastrous introduction, Cindy and her now ex-boyfriend had a huge fight while I hung out in the spare bedroom. It did not end well for either of them. Sweeping through the room, she gathered me up and announced we were going to Doug's. I had no idea who Doug was but figured going with her had to be better than sitting in an empty room with an unhappy ex in the house.

Doug turned out to be a jovial guy, a college student and soon to become a good friend, but neither of us knew it at the time. He listened as Cindy poured out our story to him and offered us a place to stay, but only for a week. He was living with his grandparents while he went to school and they would be back at the end of the week from vacation.

On our way to Doug's, we had stopped at a 7-11 and Cindy picked up a phone book sized advertisement called For Rent. I was amazed. It was nothing but apartments, flipping through page after page of places to live. Back home, you looked for apartments in the newspaper and there might be as many as a dozen available, but nothing compared to this book. Some places took up as much as a full page in advertising, even still, there were hundreds, if not thousands of places to choose from.

The book was broken down into sections. After first eliminating several surrounding cities that make up the conglomerate of "Phoenix", then taking out several locations they both considered too risky to live in, we were still left with a sizable amount of places to choose from. Doug, at first, tried to convince Cindy to consider the Mesa area so we could be closer to him. But eventually, she rejected the idea, thinking we'd have a better chance of finding work, etc in

Phoenix proper.

I counted out what was left of my savings, which had taken a hit in our travels, but if we were careful I hoped it would last long enough to get us through until we could find work. Next, we looked for cheap. Luckily, there was an index in the back that is broken down into bullet points, we needed cheap, pet-friendly, smoking, 2-bedroom, and hopefully, in a not too dismal section of town.

That giant collection of apartments was quickly whittled down to less than two dozen. After Doug left for class, we started on our search. The first couple of places were quickly rejected and one we didn't do more than drive past without stopping. It looked just this side of early crackhouse.

The first day of searching was a failure and dejectedly, we returned to Doug's. While looking for an apartment we couldn't look for work, since we had no idea what area of the city we would end up in and we hoped to find work somewhere close to wherever we eventually moved to.

After three days of searching, we found it. A small complex with less than 20 units, a spacious 2-bedroom, with a laundry facility, and a small pool as well. It was not gated and set up a bit like track housing, all one level with two lines of apartments with an ally like space dividing the two sections, backs facing each other. But the rent was cheap, the manager was nice, it was pet-friendly and we could move in right away. Bingo!

Once we secured the apartment it took us less than two hours to move in since all my stuff was already packed and all of Cindy's stuff had been packed up and waiting for her at her old apartment. It was simply a matter of loading up her truck and taking it all to our new place in one trip.

Milling around our partially emptied boxes wondering what to do with our things, our new apartment manager came knocking at our door with his German shepherd at his side. We hollered out our invite in as we continued poking through the boxes. Opening the door, he stopped and asked, "Can my Dick come in?"

This caused us to stop in our activities and look at him. "My dog," pointing down, "Dick, can he come in?"

"Uh, yeah?" Looking over to Cindy for confirmation, and her agreeing with a shrug of the shoulders.

"Yeah, I always like to ask if my Dick can come in if I have him with me," giving us a mischievous grin, "it's just polite you know. Oh, and you can call me Yo, everyone does."

Looking around the place he noticed an absence of furniture amidst the boxes, "Will you be needing any help with the rest of your stuff? I can get a couple of the guys around here to help you move anything heavy." Assuming there would be more coming, and it was only a lack of muscle that it wasn't already there.

"Nope," I replied. "This is it."

"If you're interested, there's a table and chairs, and a couch left over from the last tenants if you want them."

Absolutely, we wanted them, anything would be better than sitting on the floors all the time. Our current plan was to use the boxes flipped over on their sides as dressers, and a load of blankets to make up a pallet on the floor to sleep on. I had a few dishes, but it was an odd collection. I had a set of steak knives, but no silverware. A set of glasses, but no plates, we also had a few bowls and a cheap set of pots & pans, but no utensils or serving dishes. Cindy had almost nothing. She had moved into her boyfriend's right after moving out of her mom's place and had never acquired anything other than clothes, a set of outdoor folding chairs and a few other odds & ends.

After walking around the place for a few minutes, Yo offered to take us around to meet our new neighbors, and we agreed. It was an odd collection of people, but everyone was friendly, many were from out of state like me and no family in the area. We were told that everyone often got together for BBQ's and other get-togethers, and we were both looking forward to those.

Doug came by later in the evening with a small plant as a housewarming gift, and even more welcome, food for dinner. We spent our first evening sitting on the floor, listening to the radio, and enjoying the feeling of having a place of our own, as the neighbors we hadn't met earlier randomly stopped by to welcome us. A sense of peace swelled inside me. We had a place to live, and things were beginning to slowly fall into place. I enjoyed the friendliness of our new complex and felt content with the choice we made to move here.

There were a few inconveniences aside from the lack of furniture, with a limited amount of money, we had to choose between turning on the electric or the gas. We decided since everything was electric but the water heater, cold water was preferable to sitting in the dark. The other was, we only had one vehicle, and public transportation was outside of walking distance. We either needed to find jobs at the same place or work opposite shifts and hope for the best, but we assumed we could figure that out as we went. We couldn't afford phone service so if we needed to make a phone call, it was a two block walk to the nearest phone booth. Not horrible, but in the daytime heat, standing in a phone booth was melting hot. But we were no longer homeless, and that was good enough for now.

 ## My Guardian Angel

Settling into our new apartment, we began to realize the amount of water damage that had been inflicted to my clothes during our trip. Everything needed to be washed or it would be lost to mildew, and as an added surprise, there was a green goo over a large swath of my things as well. My mother had packed us food for our trip, and somehow a container of green Jell-O salad escaped the cooler, sliming whatever was near it as it oozed out.

Instead of taking days to get everything washed, since the laundry room was often busy and only had two washers, we decided to take it all to the laundry mat instead. Once again, Cindy's truck was loaded up with all my clothes and we headed out on a quest for washing machines. It was late when we arrived, but the place was open 24 hours and filled a comfortable amount of people even at this late hour, and more than enough open washers for everything. So we proceeded to feed clothes and quarters into the machines and settled in while we waited.

By the time we had everything done, were folding our clothes, the place had emptied of people. They'd been drifting out in ones and twos since our arrival, but no one had come in to replace those leaving.

Standing near the back of the building folding what was dry and checking on what was still damp, three guys walked in. We gave them a glance, then went back to what we were doing, we were almost finished and ready to get out of there. They didn't have any laundry with them, but there were vending machines near the front doors, maybe they stopped in for a soda or some such.

Looking us over, they saw we were alone. There was no one else was around either in the parking lot or in the building but us. In a small circle, they held a short conversation, often looking our way, separating when a decision seemed to have been made in regards to the two of us. With leering grins, they advanced towards us with nothing to stop them.

Cindy and I passed worried glances, there was no back door, no attendant to call for help. The area around us was empty, so even screaming would not likely bring anyone to our rescue. Yeah, we were in trouble and we knew it.

We slowly backed away from the table, and I grabbed one of the rolling baskets that the laundromat had. It wasn't much of a defense, but it was better than nothing if I could keep it between us, maybe it could buy us a little time.

The one in the lead pulled out a switchblade, grinning big while he did so. "So what do we have here?"

Neither of us replied. Trying to keep an eye on all of them, we backed ourselves into a corner. It was not the best option, but the front door was beyond reach, and at least where we were it would be harder for them to reach us. Clearly not impossible, but harder.

I think they wanted to bait us. To make us afraid, and they were enjoying our rising distress. They could have come at us faster, but continued their slow pursuit, fanning out as they advanced, making mock lunges as they came closer. With all of our concentration focused on the three in front of us, we paid no mind to the world outside of the ever tightening circle created by these three.

Less than a dozen steps from us, there was a sudden shift in our situation. In a blur of movement, the one in the center flew backward, followed quickly by the other two. Towering over the three of them like an avenging angel, our newly arrived protector slid in to stand between us and them, his friends circling around on either side, completing the barrier. "Out!" our protector shouted, "Get out now," pointing towards the front of the building.

Laying on the ground, the three sized up the new situation and decided it wasn't worth it. We were no longer the easy targets to terrorize that had emboldened them to action before. Scooting back out of reach, they quickly scrambled back up on their feet and bolted out the door.

One of our new companions followed them to the door, then leaning against the frame, watched the parking lot to make sure they had truly exited the area. When they no longer could be seen he turned to the guy who seemed to be in charge and nodded, walking slowly back towards us.

With a slight nod of the head and a grin, the man in charge said, "Hi, my name is Shawn."

At first, Cindy and I were too surprised to say anything. Our rescue was still sinking in, along with all the other possible outcomes of what might have occurred if they hadn't happened by. Wanting to both cry and laugh, I hesitantly held out my hand, "Hi, I'm Lisa."

Taking my hand warmly in his he replied, "Nice to meet you Lisa." raising an inquiring brow in Cindy's direction, she quickly said, "Cindy. My name is Cindy. Thanks," looking around at the other two, "for everything."

"Do you have much more to do?" Shawn asked.

"Ummm..." I looked around and noticed most of the remaining dryers had stopped, "just a few more things to get out of the dryer and we should be done. Thanks for your help, it seems we owe you a great deal."

"Naw," he said with a smile, "just a meal." giving both of us a wink.

Looking back over at his friends, they were restlessly pacing the laundromat ready to get back to wherever they had been delayed from by helping us. "Hey guys, go on without me, I'm going to stay with these two until they're done."

"You sure man?"

"Yeah, go on, I'll feel better staying here and making sure those guys don't decide to come back." With a casual wave from both of his companions, they strolled back out into the night.

Settling down into a chair, and propping his feet up on one of the washers where he could keep an eye on both us and the door he started talking. "A little late to be here all by yourselves."

"There were a lot more people here when we got here, they all left," Cindy said, stating the obvious.

Looking over at me, "So when's that baby due?"

Startled, I looked down, with the shirt that I was wearing I was surprised he could even tell I was pregnant. "Around April I think, I haven't seen a doctor yet."

"So, why isn't he here to help with the lifting and carrying?" Giving me a friendly smile.

"Oh," giving him an unsure glance, then turning back to folding my laundry, "he's back in Illinois, I just moved here earlier this week with Cindy."

"When's he going to arrive then?"

"I'm not sure if he is," I said with a shrug, "he may, but I don't know."

"Really, now?" looking interested, "Big fight or something before you left?"

"No," shaking my head, "nothing like that. I had plans to move here before the baby without him, and didn't change my plans afterward."

"A woman with a plan," once again giving me a quick grin, "I like that."

Laughing now, "Yeah, that's me, a woman with a plan. Not that it's worked out so well so far."

As Cindy and I folded and packed up all of our clothes, we continued with the bantering conversation, when Cindy asked, "Do you live around here?"

Laughing, and giving her a wink, "Yeah, you could say I live around here." Making it sound like some kind of private joke then waved away the question.

Putting the last items in our baskets, we glanced around the area once more to make sure we had everything all packed up. Jumping up and brushing us aside once we completed our inspection, he started carrying everything outside, stopping with a questioning glance at the parking lot, I pointed to the truck. He carried the remaining clothes out and loaded them in while Cindy and I double checked each of the dryers we had used to make sure nothing had been left behind. Reassured we hadn't forgotten anything we grabbed our purses and went out to join him outside standing by the truck.

"Would you like a lift home?" Cindy asked.

"Sure, why not." With a shrug, he slid in next to me on the passenger side.

"Where do you live?" she asked.

"Tell ya what," looking around me to her, "start heading to your house and I'll stop you when we're close."

"Okay?" Cindy and I gave him a look of confusion, but we were willing to go with it, he saved our asses after all, the least we could do is give him a ride.

Driving back to the apartment only a few miles away, we gave him our address, along with an invitation to join us in the morning for breakfast, which he readily agreed to. Less than a block from the apartment complex he told us to pull over. We looked around, but didn't see much of anything, and gave him another questioning look.

"Oh, don't worry, it's not too far from here and I'd hate

for you to go out of your way for me."

As Cindy slowed to a stop, he bounced out of the car with a wave and said, "See you guys in the morning." Turning, he walked away, quickly becoming lost in the shadows.

True to his word, Shawn showed up in the morning, happily joining us for breakfast. He was a friendly, easy-going guy with an infectious laugh, which had quickly put us at ease the night before and erased all lingering tensions from us during the meal.

After an extremely pleasant breakfast with our new friend, we started gathering our things to begin our job search. As we were heading out to the truck he stopped and asked, "Would you mind if I came back later tonight for a shower?"

I paused and looked at Cindy, this was an odd request, "I suppose so, but I'll warn you, there isn't any hot water. We haven't had the money to get it turned on yet. Is something wrong with yours?"

"Yeah, you could say that," laughing, "since I don't have one, you could say there's something wrong with it."

When both of us gave him a strange look, he continued with his explanation, "I live down in Cardboard City." Which answered the question for Cindy, but I was still clueless. She looked over at me and said, "He's homeless."

Ohhhhhh.

"Hey, don't sweat it, it's cool," seeing our concerned looks. "I'm homeless by choice. Except for the not having running water, it's not as bad as it sounds." Considering that the end of the conversation, he gave us a half salute and wandered off without another word.

## Sliding Down a Mountain

After securing a place to live and getting settled into my new life, Cindy and I went out one night with some of her friends. We didn't have much of a plan, mostly we just drove around randomly, talking, and occasionally singing along to the radio. Until that is, we reached the end point of a road leading up to the base of Camelback Mountain.

Stopping the car at the end of the road, we all piled out. Wandering around the area, we began speculating about how great the view would be from the top of that mountain. The idle talk slowly began to take on a serious note, and by the end of it, had become a decided plan. We were going to climb that mountain and see what there was to see.

Camelback is not actually a mountain, but it was high, steep and mountain-ish, the way up dotted with cactus, and no path to speak of. Not a single one of us were dressed for such an endeavor, but we couldn't let something as simple as common sense stop us, we were going up and that was that. In jeans and flip-flops, I began my ascent up the giant rock, doing my best to avoid cacti and slippery rocks in my upward flight.

Going up a mountain is easy, especially in the dark and not having a good clue of just how high up you are. You just keep putting one foot in front of the other as your hands find good holds along the way, pulling yourself up a little at a time until eventually, you reach the top.

And some indeterminate time later, we did eventually reach the top. Getting there, we stood high above the world and looked down at the city in front of us, all lit up like a jewel in the night. Turning around the other direction from which we came, there were fewer lights and mostly dark spaces. Looking down I started to get a real sense of just how high up we were, and how very far away the car was from us now. It looked like a child's toy from this distance, and now that we were up there, to get back to the car, we would have to go a long way down to reach the ground.

# IT'LL FEEL BETTER WHEN IT QUITS HURTING

Sitting down on an overhang near the edge, I really looked at the path we had vaguely created on our trek up, noticing for the first time exactly how steep a grade it was. With my legs hanging out over the side I started to feel some nervousness. Going up had seemed easy. Going back down, a fool's errand. Calling Cindy over, I said, "I think this wasn't the best idea we've ever had."

Looking down, she slowly nodded her agreement, sinking down beside me. Both of us just staring down over the edge with nothing more to say. Swinging my legs as they dangled over the abyss, I occasionally picked up a few small rocks, tossing them down the side to watch them careen around until they were lost to sight. I wondered if I were going to go the same way as the rocks on my way back down.

Eventually, the rest of the group grew tired of the view and wandered over to where we were sitting. One of the guys gave a soft, low whistle after looking over the edge. The front side of the mountain had more gradual grade than the backside we climbed up from. But, having no choice but to return the way we'd come to be anywhere near the car, we would have to go back down the same way.

Taking that first leap of faith, I slid off the rock I'd been sitting on and began my long slide down, quickly followed by everyone else. Going back down was not so much a matter of climbing, but more controlled sliding with a hint of not falling, as you push downward on your butt, holding onto rocks with your hands and using your feet to steer.

The problem with this position is the cacti that were so easily avoided on the way up, now, became a road hazard almost impossible to avoid. And, going down was a lot faster than going up. Gaining speed with our only moderately controlled descent, sliding this way and that, over rocks and with cries of agony occasionally piercing the air as someone else found yet another cactus.

My hair whipped around my face, laughing as I fell, knowing I was committed to this course of action and there was nothing to do but enjoy the ride down. Getting fleeting glimpses of my companions, I wondered if my face had the same look of fear and ecstasy as theirs did. We whooped and hollered all the long way down, this wasn't a time for words, only defiant shouts to the universe that we were alive.

By the time we reached the bottom, hands and feet, that were still in good shape at the top, now had a decidedly ragged and raw look to them. Jeans that were comfortable only a short time ago were now an agony of small cacti needles too small to remove but too big to sit comfortably on. A problem I solved by simply taking my pants off. Who cares about modesty when you are being jabbed by a thousand small needles every time your butt jiggled.

For a long moment, I stood looking back up the way we'd come, pantless, missing a shoe, my hands and feet bleeding lightly from dozens of small cuts and I felt good. I felt free for the very first time in my life. I'd done something I wanted to do, for no good reason other than because, knowing truly for the first time ever, there was not another person on earth who could punish me for it.

## IT'LL FEEL BETTER WHEN IT QUITS HURTING

 ## Drugs in the Oven

Several years ago, I was listening to Jeff Foxworthy and went into hysterics as he described his first apartment. He told of his leftover couch acquired by someone's abandonment, lawn chairs for seating, flipped over boxes as dressers, a pallet of blankets on the floor to sleep on, a giant spool for a coffee table, and in his case, a lava lamp and in mine a flashing warning light with no off-switch. Acquired on a late-night lark through the city and sat on our table as a centerpiece, and blinking nonstop for 6 months before the battery finally gave out.

My first apartment was all of that, and so much more. It wasn't just the jumble of furnishings for our apartment, often acquired by late night street raids of someone else's discarded junk, but the people we encountered who shared our complex with us. We were a very diverse group, with one common thread, a need for a cheap place to live in a not horrid neighborhood.

Yo, our apartment manager, held two side jobs, one legal, the other not so much. As Cindy and I discovered one evening when our oven died and we needed to cook dinner. I ran down to his place at the end of the row to ask if he would mind us using his and offered to share our meal with him in exchange.

He happily agreed, with a parting comment that he'd have to get all his drugs out of the oven before we started. Assuming he was just playing with me, I cheerfully agreed that would be a good idea before returning to my place.

But, true to his word, when Cindy and I returned, he was diligently removing an impressive amount of drugs and paraphernalia from his oven and making quite a pile on his table. Staring at him from the door, he waved us in before he continued to clear out the oven, double checking to make sure nothing had been left behind before announcing, "You're good to go! What's for dinner?"

He was an interesting person, colorful even. His other job

was a legal server for the courts, which he confided to us while we waited for dinner to cook, did not conflict at all with his other side business. It allowed him to meet people he wouldn't get a chance to otherwise. In fact, it often helped him gain new clients previously unknown to him.

The couple to the left of us ran an antique shop and often took me to auctions with them when I wasn't working or otherwise busy. They were a gregarious and friendly gay couple who never seemed to have a bad day and were obviously hopelessly in love with each other. I envied them sometimes because of it wishing there was someone in my life who loved me as much. When they found out I could sew, I was brought a seemingly endless supply of shirts with missing buttons, and they offered to pay me a dollar a button for each shirt repaired. I never inquired closely why so many buttons, sometimes an entire shirt row had been disconnected, but they always seemed happiest on those days.

Chuck and Janet lived to the right of us, and we stayed close friends until I left Phoenix for good several years later. No matter how often either of us moved we always stayed in touch. They had a fondness for cats, and their apartment was always full of them. They couldn't ever turn down a stray, eventually creating something of a cat sanctuary in the last place they lived before my last move in Phoenix. They were responsible hippies, laid back, but working. He was a house painter and Janet worked in an office. They weren't rich but managed comfortable easily enough.

One neighbor, who was something of a night owl, I did not meet until late one night when I decided to go for a swim. I did not use the pool during the day, with my pale skin and red hair, the desert sun could be brutal. But, any of us could swim whenever we wanted as long as we turned the lights off and locked the gate when we left. Letting myself in I saw a dark shape moving through the pool. Coming closer it resolved itself into a vaguely human form, stopping before me treading water. "Oh, hello." the shape said.

"Hi!" I replied, "Mind if a join you?"

"If you don't mind optional skinny-dipping, come on in," and flipped back towards the opposite end of the pool to continue with his laps.

Walking over to the cabana I turned on the pool lights. I've always enjoyed the sensation of swimming at night with only the dim luminescence created by the underwater lights. I doffed off my robe and began slowly swimming laps. I was far enough along in my pregnancy the buoyancy of the water was a sensual treat I enjoyed whenever possible. I wasn't so much concerned with exercise as much as freedom from gravity.

Occasionally, stopping midway between our laps, we'd exchange a few words while treading water. He was an odd fellow, in a mostly harmless kind of way, and Yo was less than a stone's throw from the pool so I felt safe enough.

On his final lap, he gave his farewell as he exited the pool, naked as the day he was born. It was at that moment I started taking much more literally what I'd previously taken as jokes. I wasn't shocked by his nakedness, but even after his telling me, I hadn't seriously considered his statement truthful. Who swims naked in a public pool? Apparently, he did.

Little things began to click into place for me, Yo's drugs, his nakedness, the broken buttons and all the other oddly truthful comments tossed around without a hint of concern or worry began altering my view of the world. I was slowly crossing over between the boundaries of hidden childhood into adult realities, and it was a bit shocking at times.

As children, and even as teenagers, the adult world shields and distances the young from the harsh realities of adulthood, as a way to protect them, but as we mature and venture out on our own, reality comes crashing in, sometimes in the most unexpected way that we're not prepared for. After spending our entire lives splashing around the kiddy pool, thinking this is all there is to life, we are suddenly thrown into the deep end to sink or swim as best we can.

In this new life, I was learning how to swim. It wasn't always pretty, but even a doggy paddle will keep you afloat as long as you don't give up.

 ## The Leaning Tent

During a blistering hot week, Doug, Shawn and I decided we needed to go camping in the mountains near Flagstaff. It was just the thing to escape the heat and the mounting tension in the apartment between me and Cindy.

I'd found work at McDonald's. It wasn't a great job, but it paid the bills, if very little else, now that my savings were completely depleted. Cindy had not yet found work, spending most of her days out, but I wasn't sure what she was doing other than running gas out of the truck. We'd been in the apartment for over a month and she claimed she wasn't having any luck finding a job. For all the time she claimed she was looking for one, it seemed unbelievable she hadn't found one yet. Aside from her continued unemployment, it had been a particularly stressful week that began with sending Cindy on a grocery run with the last of my money. We didn't have so much as a Kool-Aid packet left in the house, much less food at that point.

When she returned, she excitedly showed me what she'd purchased, cases of Ho-Ho's, Zinger's, Snowballs and other assorted Dolly Madison snacks. Speechless, I stared at the assorted sugar bombs and felt my anger at her rise to cardiac levels. Gleefully telling me how much she was able to purchase with the money I'd given her, thinking she had done good. I was livid, but for the sake of our friendship, I chose to say nothing. But, it didn't stop me from wondering how she survived this long without someone holding her hands and tying her shoelaces for her. And then I remembered, oh yeah, up to the point of moving in with me, she had a boyfriend that did all of this for her.

But, done was done, and it was all we had. For the rest of the week, we lived on nothing but sugar and water. To this day, I can't look at a Zinger in the eye without feeling slightly nauseous. When Doug showed up around day five of the sugar diet and found out what she did, he immediately left in a huff. Returning a short time later with bags full of food for me and my growing belly.

That was followed by a tense, low argument with Cindy in her room, which I could not hear, but could infer, from her demeanor, when they both emerged.

While Doug and I discussed getting away for a few days, Shawn showed up in his usual way, unannounced, unexpected, with a smile at the back door. He had made it a habit of coming around to check up on me whenever he found himself near our part of the city. Which meant I could see him two days or more in a row, followed by nothing for weeks.

He was a general contractor, and when he was low on funds would find a day laborer job, work until he had what he needed then wander away. If work or wandering put him near me, he'd stop by. It worked out well for both of us and his visits were always entertaining. Gradually, Doug was included in his group of friends along with me and Cindy.

With his arrival, we worked out a plan. Camping, somewhere in Flagstaff. Now, all we needed was a tent, camping supplies, food and for the weekend to arrive so we could leave. Talking to Yo he offered us his tent, and after making a quick trip to Cardboard City, we gathered the rest of our camping supplies from Shawn's personal living stash. Food, we decided, could be picked up along the way once we got up there, and Yo threw in a cooler to go along with the tent.

It was 120 degrees when we left Phoenix. We drove through the desert I'd to come to love so much, but now I was ready for a little cool air and a reprieve from the heat. We didn't have a destination in mind, figuring we could find a campsite easily enough from road signs and stop when one appealed to us. We weren't on a time schedule, had no particular place to be, it was the journey, not the destination that mattered. We stopped often along the way to admire the mountainside views, an interesting stream, or roadside attraction that caught our eye, enjoying the aimlessness of wandering.

We eventually found a small out of the way open campground. It wasn't a park, just a small 3-site inlet off the road indicated by a small sign pointing the way. There weren't any other campers when we arrived, so we had our pick of the place. There were fire pits outlined with rocks and a stack of firewood off to one side. The place was surrounded

## IT'LL FEEL BETTER WHEN IT QUITS HURTING 217

by pines and brush, giving us easy access to kindling to start a fire. It was screened from the road, giving us a feeling of privacy out in the middle of nowhere.

Unpacking the tent, which we hadn't seen in all its glory back at Yo's place, it was a huge circus tent affair, with no instructions, and I believe several missing pieces. No matter how hard we tried, the thing leaned over the fire the entire time, always just this side of falling over. By the time we had the tent up, we also realized we'd left the sleeping bags back in the city, and only the two ground covers that'd been rolled up in the tent for bedding. We didn't get too distressed, it was cool but pleasant, and we figured the three of us could share what we had. By nightfall, we began to fully understand our mistake.

It was pleasant in the mountains during the day, but when night fell, it got downright cold. After baking for months in a hundred plus degree heat, a plunge into the 50's had us shivering and blue. We cuddled like puppies for warmth inside the tent. I was lucky enough to be kept in the middle, but both the guys spent the whole night shivering and fighting over the top blanket.

The following morning, drinking coffee around the fire we discussed whether to stay or go. We had been freezing overnight, but with the coming of dawn, the air was already warming and the day was clear and beautiful. Forgetting our misery of the night before, we all decided one more night of freezing was worth it.

We went out exploring the area and later headed into town to see what cheap and/or free entertainment they had to offer. Mostly window shopping in their town square was all that was available, not even a movie theater could be found. But we enjoyed the bearable temperatures, the extraordinary views at every vista and, personally, I was just plain happy to be away from Cindy.

Returning to our leaning tower of tent, we realized for all the time we'd spent in town, none of us thought to stop and purchase any food at all. Sending the guys back into town, I stayed and cleaned up what little mess we'd made the night before, building up the fire in anticipation of dinner. With nothing else to do but wait, I brought out one of the ground covers to enjoy the fire and the quiet of the forest.

When I sent them into town I expected the guys to return with your standard camping food, hot dogs, marshmallows, soda and the like. What they returned with I wasn't sure if they were high or stupid, either fit at that point. They unpacked packaged microwavable burritos, cans of tuna, a small jar of mayo, a box of cereal, and a few other odds & ends such as a can opener.

Looking over this collection they procured and I wondered what the hell to do with it. None of it could easily be cooked over a fire. For the tuna, there were neither bowls, bread or silverware to mix to eat it with. While I looked over the food selection, the guys went looking for sticks to cook their burritos on, and I decided, tuna it is.

While I ate tuna from the can with my fingers, I spent my time laughing at them as they attempted to cook the burritos like hot dogs on sticks over the fire. After losing two to a fiery death, they then attempted to use flat rocks set inside the fire. Neither method proved useful, but in the end, they did manage to warm a few of them up enough to be considered edible, blackened edges aside. Watching them eat the burritos was almost as funny as watching the guys cook them. With no plates or utensils, they were forced to juggle the hot/cold food frequently back and forth between their hands to keep from burning themselves as they nibbled around the edges until reaching the cold center filling.

After our disastrously unfulfilling dinner, we built the fire back up and I offered each of them a part of my cover. Warmed by the blanket, their body heat and the blazing fire we had built up, we watched the stars come out, talking quietly late into the night. I knew then that I loved them both, my saviors, each in their own way, and I think they felt the same way towards me. Safely nestled between the two of them, warmed by their affection and the fire, I fell contently asleep thinking nothing could ever truly hurt me again.

 ## The Boys are Back

True to my word I kept in contact, as I was able to, with friends and family back home. And on occasion, I contacted Nev as well to let him know how the baby and I were doing. After I left town, he moved in with Ginny. She had a spare room and he helped out by paying rent after the place he'd been sharing had been lost. It was a friendly arrangement I approved of since it helped both of them out. It also gave Ginny some company with so many of our friends continuing to disperse all over the country and David in boot camp.

With each phone call, Nev continued to tell me how much he missed me and seemed to be changing his mind about coming out to live with us. I encouraged him to come if he truly wanted to be with me, but didn't insist on it either. I wanted him to come because he wanted to, not because he felt guilted into it.

As fate would have it, around the same time Nev was considering his big move out west, so was Richard for reasons of his own. Cindy being a large part of it. I asked Ginny to introduce Richard to Nev but left it up to them to go from there. Within a month of their introduction, they were on their way to Phoenix.

It was a happy/tense time waiting for them to arrive. Cindy still hadn't gotten a job, but it seemed she'd reconnected with her ex. I didn't know it at first but had my suspicions something was up, even if I didn't know who. I just never considered him as a contender after how he treated her after our arrival. The two of us were spending less and less time together, the ho-ho fiasco was still bitter for me, as was her not helping out with the bills.

And truthfully, she had reasons to be mad at me as well. On my way home from work, I'd gotten into an accident with her truck. Three pedestrians stepped out into traffic in the middle of the street, I slammed on my brakes, and so did the Harley in front of me. Unfortunately, motorcycles stop much faster than trucks. I only popped his back tire, the idiots were completely unharmed, and only I was ticketed. The causes of the accident legally weren't responsible, since pedestrians always have the right of way. Sadly, her little Toyota truck also took the brunt of the damage as well, with new fiberglass and crumple zones, the front end looked like an accordion. Unknown to me, she'd also let the insurance lapse, which made fixing the truck far outside of our current budget. It was still drivable, if barely, but I don't think she forgave me for it either.

Doug was also becoming increasingly anxious as the time of Nev's arrival approached. With less than a week before they were expected, Doug came to pick me up for the evening. We drove up to the peak of South Mountain, from there you can see all of Phoenix spread out in front of you like a sparkling string of jewels at night. It was one of our favorite places to go. It cost nothing, the view was spectacular, and his company was always enjoyable.

Finding a free picnic table we sat down, sitting next to each other staring out at the view. Several times, Doug started to say something, then stopped himself, only to continue to stare out straight ahead. I didn't press him. I figured when he found the words he would share them with me, and I settled back, in comfortable silence.

Eventually, he turned to me, "I want you to tell Nev not to come out."

"Huh?" was all I could say, why wouldn't he want Nev to come out?

"I, uh...." looking away for a few minutes, then turning back to me, "because I want you to be with me. I want us to be a family, you, me and the baby."

Now it was my turn to sit in silence. I knew I loved Doug, but I didn't know if I was **in** love with him. Then again, I didn't know if I was truly in love with Nev, either. I'd always had fun with him, but my mind kept turning back to my friends saying there was something dark in him. I didn't want to believe that, I did love him and I did want him to be a part of this baby's life. I could see a future for us together, even if it was a bit fuzzy around the edges.

"I don't know what to say." It was all I could manage as my mind darted around. I was confused and wondered why he waited so long to say anything to me.

"We could have a good life you and me," he began. "I only have two more years of college, and I'll be able to support you and the baby well when I'm done." Seeing my hesitation he pleaded, "Think about it, please."

"I'll think about it." And I did. What else could I say? I'd already turned down Willie, Ky, and Joe from a similar offer, and I loved them all as well. Not in love, but friendly. Maybe with more time, I'd know how I truly felt about Doug, but this was too fast and Nev was coming too soon to make a choice this big. I couldn't be unfair to Nev either, he was packing up his life to come here for me, how could I just tell him no when this was also his baby?

Long into the night, we sat on the picnic table, each wrapped up in our own thoughts. Eventually, I made a decision. It may not be the right decision, but it was the fair one. As much as I cared for Doug, I couldn't turn Nev away. Given more time, a different choice could have been made, but there wasn't enough time left and I made promises to Nev I couldn't break before I'd left Quincy if he ever decided to come out.

Explaining my reasoning to him, he said he understood, then made a promise to me as well, "I will always be here for you, no matter what. And if you ever change your mind, I'll be there in a heartbeat."

Nev and Richard arrived more or less on time a few days later, tired, broke, and excited to have finally made it to us. Richard's arrival was not the happy reunion with Cindy he'd been anticipating. For someone who had so avidly encouraged him to come join her, she was distant and distracted once he was here. Not long after their awkward homecoming, Cindy announced she would be going back with her ex-boyfriend and would be leaving us.

I had mixed feelings about it. After all the tension of late, I was relieved to see her go but felt increasingly bad for Richard. He moved halfway across the country for no other reason than he thought he loved her. Even Doug, who had been her closest friend in Phoenix, made no objections to her leaving our little group. He too was upset by many of her actions of late, enhanced by his growing loyalty to me.

With her leaving, Doug moved in with us on a part-time basis. Richard, despite his disappointment, decided to stay, mostly for financial reasons. Nev and I settled into a new domestic relationship, getting to really know each other for the first time. Even Shawn came around a bit more for a while and was well liked by the new arrivals in our house. And, for a while, life was everything I had hoped it would be.

## Interlude Two
## Here there be Monsters

Not all monsters live in books, not all boogeymen hide in closets, they often walk among us unnoticed in the guise of a human. They wear innocent faces, speaking sweet words, spinning tales, and creating glorious illusions. They can destroy worlds, leaving devastation in their wake, all without a moment of guilt.

If you manage to survive long enough to look back at the desolation your life has become, you may ask yourself, how did I allow this to happen? The answer is because it starts off small. Like someone testing the waters, they don't just dive in, but slowly probe the limits, getting a feel for the currents and the underlying wakes. It is slow and insidious, covered with apologies and flowers, blinding in subtle shifts, easy to dismiss, and binding in the whispered guilt of, how could I let this happen?

It happens because not all moments are bad, there are good times that cover the horrific. You lie to yourself in these good moments, saying "well, of course, it will never happen again." This is the roller-coaster. The savage ups and the gut wrenching downs, the twists that make your head spin, as you tell yourself over and over again, there has to be an end somewhere. You just have to hang on long enough to reach it.

I had been a strong person, I had survived a difficult life, I had coped with what had been done to me. But, as with anything built strong, microscopic cracks begin to form underneath it all. They cannot be seen on the surface, but they are there, and if enough pressure is applied, anything will shatter.

# JUST REMEMBER, IT'S GOING TO BE OKAY

## Moving On

Shortly after Cindy left us, we moved to a different part of the city. It was another two bedroom, in a slightly nicer and bigger apartment complex, closer to the highway which made it easier for Doug to commute, and closer to work for both Nev and Richard. I hated to leave the apartment I'd lived in since moving to Phoenix, but it made sense to do so, and sadly, I said goodbye to the many friends I'd made while there.

I was becoming big pregnant, and one morning while I was sleeping, Nev called my work telling them I was quitting. He was working nights and I was working days, and he didn't like us not having much time together, and this was his solution to the problem. I was a little upset he hadn't consulted me before calling, but he was persuasive. Carefully explaining to me that he was only looking out for my welfare and the baby's, and I forgave him.

Richard gained a new girlfriend, also named Lisa, who spent many nights with us and we all became friends. During those nights, Doug often slept in my room instead of on the couch since Nev worked overnights. If Nev happened to get home early he'd just push us over to make room. He never voiced any objections to our arrangements, and Doug was always the perfect gentleman.

Our domestic relationship often caused a few comments, with me living with three men, but it worked out well for all of us. I took care of the apartment, cooked all the meals, ran all the errands, and paid all the bills while the guys worked and we pooled all our money in mutual support.

We acquired both a TV and VCR along the way and started a tradition of "bad movie night". We'd troll the video rental stores looking for the worst pieces of cinematography that we could find, pop popcorn and invite all of our friends over to heckle and jeer at these masterpieces of the god-awful. It was cheap, fun entertainment we all enjoyed whenever we all had the same night off.

While my cooking skills were slowly improving, popping the popcorn was forbidden after my first failed attempt. I filled the bottom of the cooking pot with oil, added popcorn and proceeded to inadvertently set fire to it. When I lifted the lid, black rolling smoke poured out, quickly filling the entire apartment. The guys jumped to open all the windows and the door for good measure, and we all took turns standing outside telling our neighbors no fire, just a small popcorn incident until the smoke finally dispersed.

On yet another night I made a perfectly good cherry pie, leaving it in the fridge for Nev after work. Waking up the next morning and walking out into the common living area I smelled something not right. Not sure what it was I walked around the room searching for the source of the smell. During my search, both Richard and Doug woke up and proceeded to try and help identify the location of the smell. It covered the entire apartment making it hard to pinpoint, but eventually, we were drawn to the oven.

After returning home Nev had put my pie in the oven to warm it up, sat down and promptly fell asleep, forgetting all about it. After 6 hours on low heat, my beautiful pie had turned into blackened, bubbly tar, completely inedible and fork-proof. Both the pie and pan were a complete loss, taking more than two hours to cool down enough to even throw away.

Those were good days. We had very little money but we had each other and managed to have fun despite all the other difficulties. Sometimes, when the guys had the day off and we had some spare money, we'd pile into the car, fill the tank and pick a direction, going wherever a quarter tank would take us. Sometimes ending up in the mountains, other times in desert canyons exploring the area. Other days we'd explore the malls, parks and recreational areas scattered all over the conglomerate of Phoenix and it's surrounding cities.

Throughout this time, Nev started asking me to marry him. As happy as I was with him coming out to be with me, I wasn't sure if I was ready to be married, and I didn't know if it was Nev that I wanted to marry. My mother had been married multiple times over the years and I didn't want to repeat her mistakes. If I married, I wanted it to be forever.

But the bigger I got, the more persistent he became in his quest to marry me. It would be brought up at random moments, inserted into at least one conversation a day, no matter how tentative the thread between what we were talking about and this topic was. It was the only true blight during this time. Which is saying something, considering there were times without food, times when we all struggled to pay the bills, and many other small inconveniences that came with being young and poor in a big city.

In an ambush late one night, Nev gently woke me up, and whispered into my ear, "Marry me."

Barely awake, I rolled over and mumbled, "Sure."

"When?"

"Monday," I responded, promptly falling back to sleep. The next morning I woke up with a sinking feeling in my stomach. Was I dreaming about what I'd said last night or did I actually agreed to marry Nev in three days?

Nope. It was not a dream. Walking out into the common room everyone, including Nev, was sitting around the table. He was awake and busily including everyone in his plans for our upcoming wedding. Doug was going to be his best man, and they had decided in my absence that Lisa was the only option for my maid-of-honor. She was one of the two females I was friends with, and a more frequent visitor than Janet now that we were across town from her and Chuck. Lisa was called while I was still asleep and asked on my behalf, she had happily agreed.

Throughout all of this activity, Doug gave me several questioning glances, and I responded with only a resigned shrug. I had agreed, I'd even picked the day.

That I was half asleep didn't matter, I had accepted. I knew I wouldn't have if I'd been awake, but since I readily enough agreed in that state, maybe subconsciously, I'd decided I did intend to marry him. I just wasn't ready to admit it to myself.

At the end of three busy, frantically hectic days, Nev and I stood in our living room with our few close friends and said our vows.

Doug moved out shortly after our wedding, he didn't say why, but I knew. He continued to be a part of my life, but could no longer live with us now that I was married to Nev. Richard had gotten a slightly better paying job, and decided it was time to be out on his own. He could get a small studio even closer to his new job and be able to make it. With the loss of both of them, Nev and I decided it was time to look elsewhere to live as well. While looking we found a small apartment complex looking for a manager, free rent and utilities included with the job. We applied and were hired within days.

Our little group had broken up. I'd known all along it would not be forever, nothing ever is. But, it was a sad day for me on moving day, leaving the place we had all shared. We were all moving on.

 ## The Married Life

As we moved into our new apartment, Nev and I moved into our new life together as husband and wife. It was a smallish place made of cinder block, right off a busy street in a not too great part of town. It was only an 8-unit complex and didn't have the amenities I'd gotten used to while living in Phoenix, no pool, laundry area, playground or clubhouse. There was a small courtyard between the two buildings with an equally small lemon tree, but mostly it was gravel parking lot with a little bit of grass here and there, dotted with a palm tree or two.

The owner lived in Texas and needed someone to care for the place and I think he may have chosen us out of desperation. The previous apartment manager was a hoarder of Nth degree, leaving that apartment completely unlivable for the time being. There were issues with him skimming money from the owner and he'd let the place deteriorate at an accelerated rate through neglect. Refusing to fix even the simplest of problems for any of the tenants. Eventually, as the problems piled up, the tenants contacted the owner with their complaints. The owner, concerned with his investment, flew up to investigate the situation, which resulted in the previous manager being fired, and our being hired.

We moved into an empty unit on the second floor during the digging out. There was no way we could have safely lived in the apartment set aside for the manager until it was cleaned and fumigated. Along with cleaning out the manager's apartment, we were left with a long list of repairs that needed to be done and a small amount of petty cash in which to get it all done with. The owner was not what you could consider a generous man, he wanted to protect his investment, but wanted it done in the cheapest way possible.

We hired Chuck, of Chuck and Janet, to paint all the empty apartments. Hopefully improving their appeal to people, and help get them rented since less than half of the units were occupied. We also worked on the outside of the building, hoping an appealing exterior would bring more people interested in renting. But there was more work to do than was reasonable for me and Nev alone, even with Chuck doing all the painting. And, the petty cash was fairly petty. Not nearly enough to hire contractors to install the irrigation system the owner wanted for the grass or the many other small problems in each of the units.

Our solution came one day while heading to the home improvement store to pick up a few items. Pulling in, there was a man holding a sign, "Will work for Food". He wasn't dirty as many of the homeless were, he was sitting comfortably in a lawn chair, next to a toolbox. We slowed down to get a good look at him before proceeding on to the store where we discussed hiring him. Why not, we decided. He needed work and we needed help, and our experience with Shawn made us more amenable to the idea. We would have hired Shawn, but he hadn't made an appearance as of yet, not since a few days after our move. We had no idea when he might return, we never did, and this was work that couldn't wait.

We drove over and parked by him. Nev got out of the car first to talk to him, asking a few questions about why he was there, bad luck was the answer he gave. He was a friendly, well-spoken man, slightly embarrassed by his circumstances, but cheerfully hopeful that things might, in the end, work out for him.

We made him an offer, he'd work for us to get the apartment repairs completed and in exchange, we'd allow him to live in one of the empty apartments, we'd share our meals with him, along with a little bit of cash to sweeten the deal. He gratefully accepted. We loaded up his lawn chair and tool box while he placed his backpack in the car, which was the sum total of all of his worldly possessions and came home with us.

We showed him around and gave him the list of things that needed to be done. While going over everything he would nod frequently, saying "Yep", "No problem", and "Easy enough" to everything on the list, then set immediately to work on the irrigation system. The following day he disappeared and we decided when he hadn't returned in a few hours that we'd lost him. A little disappointed, but still happy he'd gotten at least one thing crossed off the list.

We were mistaken. He returned, standing at our

doorstep later in the evening, with two others behind him. He introduced them to us and explained they'd work for just a place to stay. Even going so far as to have them show us the food they had in their backpacks, reassuring us we wouldn't have to feed them, just let them work for a place to live. Surprised, we accepted with a bit of hesitation, but overall happy that soon things would be done.

They quickly cleaned up the entire outside, spruced up the courtyard and trimmed up the palm trees, they laid down grass seed and swept the outside front porches, even washing all the accumulated grime from the outside walls. Once they finished with the outside, they began working on each of the apartments, quickly checking off items from the seemingly endless list of repairs, eventually moving on to the manager's apartment I'd been struggling to get cleaned out by myself.

By the end of the month, everything on the list was crossed off. Their last act was to help me pack up everything from the upstairs apartment and move it down into the now clean and decent smelling lower one. Once I was completely settled in, I made dinner for everyone, which I'd done on many other occasions during the month to show my appreciation for their hard work. All of us, including Nev, sat down around our small table for dinner. The conversation was lively. Each of these men were entertaining, with many amusing stories to share and at the end of the meal, Nev pulled aside our original handyman and paid him the remaining balance we had agreed on.

The following afternoon I wandered over to the apartment where they'd been living in to say hi, but it was dark. I tried knocking on the door, but there wasn't answer, turning the knob, the door opened to a completely empty apartment. Sometime during the night, they had packed up and left without a word to anyone. We never saw any of them again.

Now that the complex had gotten a makeover the units started to quickly fill up, which pleased the owner greatly. While most of the tenants gave us no problems a few added some interesting moments to life. One of the tenants who predated our arrived was behind on the rent for the past several months. when I recommended evicting her unless she paid but the owner balked. Giving several lame excuses as to why she should stay, eventually ending the conversation by insisting she stay. As I came to find out, she was his out of town girlfriend, giving me endless problems knowing she was almost completely immune to any consequences because of it.

Another long term resident gave us some great outdoor theater one day when the Native American council came to remove her children and return them to the reservation. She had eight kids stuffed into a small one-bedroom apartment, an arrangement I'd never been happy with. She was also a holdover from the previous manager, she had a lease, and the owner was content to let her stay as long as she paid the rent on time each month. She was a drunk, but since the kids were all clean, fairly well taken care of and mostly kept to themselves I let it go without saying much. But it seemed the Reservation agreed with my assessment of the situation and had come to remove those children who belonged to the local tribe.

Oh, how she had screamed, but there was little to be done about it. The police would not interfere with a tribal matter. Nor could she prove she could provide a better home than the reservation would. She tried to barricade the doors to keep them from entering, but eventually, she relented, allowing them in. The fathers of her various children were there, and after gathering up their offspring, they left without a word.


And so life went. I got bigger with each passing day, but still tiny by pregnant standards. And once, even got stuck laying on the floor for six hours while I waited for Nev to return home from work. It was not my proudest pregnant moment. I'd become awkwardly pregnant, fondly missing the pool at our previous apartment, and thought stretching out on the floor might relieve some of the back pain I'd been having. I was sadly mistaken. Instead of finding any relief, I found instead, I could not sit up without my back seizing up, leaving me immobilized. With the TV just out of reach, I was forced to watch six hours of horrid programming while waiting for my husband to come rescue me, hoping all the while that someone might stop by just to visit. No such luck.

Nev had also begun to act moderately odd since moving into the complex. Nothing I could exactly put my finger on, so I set it aside, blaming it on hormones and pregnancy. There was a touch of distance, a distraction I couldn't quite place, and he began acting more assertive, allowing me to make fewer decisions about things. He consulted me less and demanded more, but for each of these things, I found an excuse for his behavior. He was nervous about becoming a father, work was getting to him, and on went my list of reasons for his actions, while I smiled and told everyone that things were great.

As my due date approached, he started questioning what kind of parents we would be. Perhaps it would have been better for us to have waited to have a baby, not seeming to realize that without this baby our lives would have taken an entirely different course that did not end with us getting married. I would have instead been a single college student, starting my freshman classes at the University, using the full scholarship I'd earned before graduating. But again, I brushed it off to nerves.

Until I came home one day and there were two strangers sitting at my kitchen table with a pile of paperwork in front of them. Giving Nev a questioning look, I sat down at the table with them. They pushed a piece of paper in front of me and asked me to sign without any explanation while Nev kept saying "Sign, it's for the best for everyone."

Feeling panicky, I scanned the paper, looking around the table as I did so. The strangers were earnest while Nev was nervous. I knew something was very wrong with this entire situation. They were adoption papers, giving away my rights to the baby.

Standing up suddenly, I shouted at Nev, "What the hell is this?"

Nervously fiddling with a pen, he said, "This is for the best for everyone. Just sign the papers and we can have another baby later when we are in a better position to have one."

"Are you out of your mind?" I shot back. "How could you do this without even talking to me about it first?"

Like a broken record, he kept insisting, "This is for the best." While looking at the other two for support.

In soft, soothing voices the two in turns gave me a spiel about the benefits of putting my baby up for adoption. How happy I could make a desperate couple. How I could be paid compensation as a thank you from the newly made parents. How I was young and could have other children later. All the while trying to push the papers towards me to sign, noticing

Nev had already done so.

I grabbed up the papers and for a brief moment, I saw triumph on all of their faces, to be quickly dashed as I tore them up and threw them in the trash. "Out!" I yelled as I pointed at the door, "Get out of my house and don't ever come back!" Knowing there was nothing more that could be done, they quickly gathered their things and exited without another word.

Turning on Nev as soon as they were gone, I announced, "Leave or stay, I don't care which, but this baby is staying with or without you." Without giving him a chance to respond, I stormed into our bedroom and slammed the door.

He left the apartment and was gone for several hours. I did not know where he went, but he came home full of apologies, swearing he would never do anything like that again. I forgave him, again, finding excuses I could live with for his behavior. Marriage was hard work after all and we all make mistakes. And for a while, he was loving, kind, caring and attentive. In other words, the perfect husband, and life, once again, settled back into normalcy.

He made other mistakes along the way while we waited for the baby to arrive. His parents sent us money as a baby gift, which he instead used to buy parts for his car. His parents never forgave him for it, and I was distinctly unhappy as well. I'd planned on using it to get everything we needed, crib, clothes and all the accessories that go with having a small bundle of joy, and now there was no money for any of it.

Once again, he was contrite and apologetic for his behavior, and once again I made excuses for him. I was hurt, I was upset, and I was mad at the irresponsibility of his actions yet again. And yet, I once again forgave him. Setting a pattern that was never broken for the rest of our relationship.

## IT'LL FEEL BETTER WHEN IT QUITS HURTING 235

 ## Look! I have Boobs now!!!

After having my first child, something miraculous happened. I had, for the first time in my life, actual boobs. Before becoming pregnant, I weighed all of 92 pounds, and I kid you not, my bra size was Almost-A. Having actual cleavage was a novelty I can't even begin to describe. I was enamored by the size of my breasts, I'd gone from an A to a D-cup literally overnight, and to me, it was amazing.

So thrilled I was with my new tatas, I went out shortly after coming home from the hospital and bought a few new shirts to showcase them. I had the body of a woman now, with boobs and hips and everything, and it was wonderful. So wonderful, I wanted to share it with everyone I met.

After assaulting Doug for days with demands that he look at my boobs, he decided what I needed was to get out of the house and out among some people. Loading me and the baby into his car he took us to Metro Mall in Phoenix. It was one of the largest in the area and a place we often went, whether we had money or not, just to get out and wander around. There was even an honest-to-god Arabian looking castle on the grounds that was an arcade, complete with go-carts and mini-golf.

In we wandered, into this place filled with people, me in front in a low-cut shirt, and Doug trailing behind holding the baby. Happy to be out of the house, at first, I just slowly strolled through. But, the deeper we moved into the mall, the urge grew for me to share my newly acquired breasts with onlookers. I'd already been getting side, sneaky glances, size D boobs with a 24-inch waist did bring some attention after all. But what I really wanted was outright appreciation, and those side glances were simply not doing it for me.

Walking up to the first guy I noticed giving me that sly glance, I grabbed him by the shoulders and demanded, "Look at my boobs! Aren't they wonderful?!"

With a look of sheer panic, and looking everywhere but at my boobs, his eyes fell on Doug, ever faithfully behind me holding the baby. Nodding at him reassuringly, he said, "Just tell her they're nice and she'll leave you alone."

Googley-eyed, he looked back at me and mumbled, "Yeah, ummm, they're, uh real nice."

Shaking him slightly, "No! Look at them! I have boobs now," with a big grin on my face, truly enjoying this moment.

Deliberately now looking, not knowing how else to get out of this bizarre situation, he said, "Yep, those are some nice boobs there," bolting away as soon as I let him go.

Getting my compliment, I scanned the crowd looking for my next victim. And so we went, up and down the mall, accosting every man who gave me that sly glance at my boobs. I would run up to them, demanding they tell me how amazing they were. And each time, they would look helplessly back at Doug, who would shrug and gesture to them encouragingly to just tell me what I wanted to hear.

I left a trail of male devastation that day in the mall. All men like to look at a woman's breasts, but they are not used to one of those women not only giving an encouraging look back when they do, but forcefully coming up to them and demanding recognition for them. Stutteringly, awkwardly, painfully, they each somehow managed to drag out some half-coherent compliment before bolting away in fear of what had just happened to them.

It was a beautiful day in my memory, and I'm sure many of them walked away with a "You'll never believe what happened!" story to share with their friends later, probably to be laughed at during the telling. At the end of the day, I went home content, happily smiling the whole way with memories of compliments of my fabulous cleavage rolling through my head.

 ## An Inconvenient Baby

Even though our little group was broken up and scattered throughout the Phoenix area, we still kept in touch and visited each other often when time allowed. But, it was never the same. We were rarely able to all get together, and after many of the things Nev had done, his presence was not always as warmly welcomed. While mine was still actively encouraged, causing tensions between us.

Richard and Lisa broke up, but Nev and I continued our friendship with her. Often inviting her over for dinner, or spending time with her family and daughter on the weekends. She was a frequent visitor to our home, randomly stopping by whenever she had some free time. Sometimes spending the night if we stayed up late watching a movie.

If I began to notice anything odd about her behavior at times, I brushed it off. Once finding one of her earrings in my bed, then excused it by saying it must have fallen off on the way to our bathroom, which you had to walk through our room to reach.

After the birth of my son, she spent more time with us. Cooking meals so I could sleep and keeping me company during the day while Nev slept. I enjoyed her company, and we got along well. And having a baby can be isolating, I was no longer able to just pick up and go as I'd been able to before. It was a hard adjustment to make. Having a friend who understood what it was like to be a parent and I could talk to about it made the adjustment easier.

Tensions were growing between Nev and I as well. I think he was jealous of the time I spent on keeping the new human alive and cared for, time that I'd previously spent on him. He took only a passing interest in our son, holding him on occasion, but, for the most part, ignoring his presence.

Falling to asleep early on the couch one evening while holding my son, Lisa told me not to worry about dinner, she'd take care of everything, and I gratefully drifted off knowing she would. Some dark time later I woke up. After putting my son to bed, I headed for my room and the bed that awaited me there.

As I quietly made my way to my room I heard something from behind the door. I assumed it was Nev, restlessly moving in his sleep. It was the weekend and he'd probably gone to bed not long after the dinner I slept through. Opening the door, all of my illusions were shattered as I saw the two of them wrapped in an embrace, highlighted by the light coming in through the window.

For a long moment, none of us moved as we stared silently at each other. Then in a sudden, violent movement Nev threw Lisa away from him and scrambled to his feet, "Aw shit!" he said, looking down at her, "You weren't supposed to see that."

Yeah, no shit.

I continued to stand there, not saying a word, while the two of them tried to find some excuse for what they had done.

Lisa, now wrapped up in a blanket pleaded, "I'm so sorry, I didn't mean for you to find out." Yeah, I didn't suppose she did want me to find out what was going on, that was true enough.

I wasn't sure what to say, so I said nothing. Turning around, I walked back into the living room and laid back down on the couch. I was tired. I had too many conflicting emotions and I knew I couldn't sort through them all as tired as I was.

They both came into the living room a short time later. Now, both dressed, and tried to get me to talk to them, but I ignored them both. I just wanted to sleep. I didn't want to answer their questions or listen to their excuses. The nothingness of sleep was all I wanted. Eventually, they realized I wouldn't respond, and they left me alone. Where they went or what they did, I didn't know and I did not care. Tomorrow was soon enough for their excuses.

Morning inevitably came rolling around, no matter how much I wished it wasn't so. I sat up on the couch and stared at the wall until my son woke up and needed me. Taking care of his needs distracted me from my own problems and I was grateful for it.

Nev and Lisa were moving around towards the back of the apartment but were keeping their distance, and that's how I preferred it for the moment. I was surprised she hadn't

# IT'LL FEEL BETTER WHEN IT QUITS HURTING 239

left during the night, but in another way, I wasn't. I knew she wanted to plead her side of the story, and you can't do that if you're not around to give it or back each other's story if you're not together.

I was hurt, not by their cheating, but by their lying. If either of them had come to me before this we could have talked about it. There was no need for them to sneak around behind my back, to lie to me. Arrangements could have been made to resolve the situation that wouldn't have resulted in the hurtful way it had.

I'd always treated Nev with honesty, from the very beginning of our relationship. I didn't sneak around behind his back, was always upfront about my expectations from him and always tried to treat him fairly.

Doubts that had already begun were now looming large in my thoughts. Could I trust him again, not only in this, but with anything? Could I put my faith in him, after all, he had done in the last few months? If he was lying to me now, what would our relationship be in five years or ten?

His distance of late, how he'd gone to the adoption agency behind my back, using the baby's money for his car, and a very dark moment between the two of us a week after I'd gotten home from the hospital that left me hurt and crying, and him apologetic and full of excuses for his behavior. All of these things ran through my brain as I tried to figure out, what was a marriage worth?

Eventually, I knew I had to go and talk to them, I couldn't put it off much longer. After rocking my son back to sleep and putting him in his crib, I went to confront the two of them.

They were sitting together talking on the futon in our bedroom. They stopped as soon as they saw me standing in the doorway, waiting for me to say something.

"We need to talk." taking a seat on the edge of my bed.

At first, the two of them continued to watch me without saying a word. I wasn't outwardly angry, nor was I crying or giving them any other indication of how I felt. I let them shift around uncomfortably on the couch for a while, as I sat quietly looking at them.

I began with Nev, looking him in the eye, "Why didn't you come to me and talk to me about how you were feeling?" Without waiting for him to respond, I looked directly at Lisa, "And you were supposed to be my best friend, how could you go behind my back like this?"

Both of them looked embarrassed, and Nev sheepishly said, "You've been busy with the new baby, we didn't want to hurt you, but I was feeling lonely and Lisa was here for me when you couldn't be."

"No, this wasn't my fault," I told him. "You could have come to me and we could have talked about it. You could have told me you wanted to have sex with Lisa since I can't for another couple of weeks yet. We could have worked this out honestly, you both choose to lie to me instead."

The excuses poured out of both of them and justifications for their actions, putting off any true responsibility for their choices. And in the end, apologies from both of them, that went on endlessly as they tried to soothe not only me but their own consciences. During it all, I thought to myself, what is a marriage worth? I could walk away, I could leave them both to each other. I could take my son and begin again, without either of them. What was a marriage worth?

In the end, I forgave them both, not for their sakes, but mine. I did not want to be my parents, to walk away when things became difficult. To continually start new lives, starting over every few years when things became hard. I told myself that all marriages were hard work, and every relationship had its bad moments. I made a commitment to this man and I was determined to see it through to the end, come what may.

A month later, Lisa arrived on our doorstep with an announcement. I hadn't seen much of her since that fateful night, and while I'd forgiven her, we were no longer close friends. Sitting at our table with Nev and me, she fidgeted nervously, not looking at either of us.

"I'm pregnant." looking down at her hands, "About two months along."

"Oh," said Nev, looking at her hard, "who's the father?"

She gave him a brief glance, then shrugged her shoulders, "No one you know," looking back up at him, then slowly to me, "I just thought you guys would like to know. I wanted you to hear it from me rather than someone else."

Uh huh, I knew damned good and well who the father of that baby was. So did they, but if this was how they wanted to play it, I was willing to play along. "Well," I said, "congratulations then."

# IT'LL FEEL BETTER WHEN IT QUITS HURTING

Nev, giving her another hard look, echoed me, "Yeah, congratulations."

She left shortly after that, leaving Nev and me to look at each other across the table. Eventually, he said, "Well, whoever it is I hope they are happy together. God knows I don't want another kid." Getting up from the table, he went outside to work on his car, leaving me sitting at the table without another word.

Nev's indifference to her situation, combined with the friendship I'd once had with her, caused me to once again include her in my life. I felt pity for her. She was going to have to go through this all alone. She had few friends, and now that she was pregnant, Nev wanted nothing to do with her.

I started checking up on her, stopping by randomly when I had time and we began to rekindle our broken friendship. As she got bigger, the more depressed she became, she was alone in all of this, and we both knew it. She never once mentioned Nev, even trying to avoid him by only coming over when she knew he would be at work or asleep. I do not know if she ever went to him about the obvious paternity of her baby, but if she did, neither of them ever mentioned it and she strenuously avoided talking about it.

A month before her due date, I volunteered to go into the delivery room with her so she would not need to go alone. I went to the birthing classes, which I thought were redundant since she already had one child and I just recently had one, but if I was to be allowed into the delivery room we both had to go.

On the big day, I rushed to meet her at the hospital, leaving Nev at home with our son. He wasn't happy but didn't attempt to stop me, either. He tried to actively discourage me from all of this, but I felt if he would not step up, I needed to.

I arrived at the hospital, quickly locating her room, just barely making it before she delivered the baby, a healthy baby girl. Standing beside her, they placed the tiny human into my arms minutes after she entered the world and held her briefly before handing her over to her mother. I didn't feel love for this infant, but I did feel a certain amount of responsibility.

My husband helped create this life, but washed his hands of it. I had the same choice but found that I couldn't. This baby was not responsible for the actions of her parents, and shouldn't be punished for their choices. She was the only innocent among them.

I watched over this child as best as I could for many years, once taking custody of her for two weeks when things got very bad for Lisa. I raised her with my own sons, and while I was not always pleased with Lisa's actions, or Nev's for that matter, I never held it against the baby. Not once did Nev ever look at his daughter, nor acknowledge her existence. Not even during her two-week stay with us, which was impressive, in a certain blind fashion.

There was only one indication ever given to the paternity of this child. Lisa gave her the female version of my son's name. I was not pleased with this, but I never said anything to her about it. She hadn't discussed names with me, and until she put it on the birth certificate, called her nothing but "the baby". I knew why she had done it, but it did not make me happy. Then again, many things during this time made me unhappy, it was just one more thing to add the ever growing list.

 ## Locking Myself In

Eventually, we gave up the manager position at our previous apartment and moved into a small gated complex in a nicer area of Phoenix. It had 16-units, a pool in the center with all the apartments facing the center courtyard. Each of the apartments had two floors, a great room, kitchen, half bath downstairs and two bedrooms and a full bath upstairs. The downstairs had large glass panes for the whole front of the great room looking out on the courtyard, and the upstairs had small balconies that you could walk out on, but no windows anywhere that you could open. It was a big, spacious apartment, with lots of sunlight, built of cinder block so it stayed cool for the most part, and a pool not 10 steps from my doorway I could use any time of the day or night. I thought it was perfect the minute we walked through the doors.

My first move in Phoenix took 20 minutes and one small Toyota truck. This, my fourth move since arriving in Phoenix, took the better part of the day, and 3 truckloads to haul from our last apartment. Mostly it was furniture, which we had slowly acquired over the last two years. Including the leftovers we were given from my very first apartment by Yo. But the bulk of our new furniture was for the baby and all the other things that go with having a small child. For something so damned small, they do take up a lot of space.

Nev, Richard, and Doug all helped pack and load everything, splitting into three teams with one packing at one end, two loading and unloading, and me at the new apartment putting things away as they came in. By the time the last load was dropped off it was time for Nev to go to work and the other two to get home for bed since they worked daylight hours and needed to be up early the next day. After a full day and a flurry of activity, by 10:00 pm I was alone except for my son in the apartment. The phone wouldn't be turned on for another couple of days, and even having a phone was a recent luxury. I wasn't even used to having one in the house for the most part and gave it very little thought.

I set up my son's room first earlier in the day, and when he began to get cranky, I laid him down for a nap. We were night people. Nev had worked nothing but nights since he arrived in Phoenix, and I adjusted our schedule to accommodate, shifting our "days" and "nights" accordingly. Knowing my son would only be asleep for a few hours, I decided to use the time to get as much unpacked and put away before I made him his "lunch".

Digging into the boxes, I set up the kitchen first. I started next in the great room. When I started to run out of room to move with the stacks of boxes piling up by the door, I decided it was time to stop and take them all out to the dumpster before I continued. Breaking them down and piling them up beside the door until I had quite an impressive stack waiting to be taken out. Stepping up to the door with an armful of boxes, I turned the knob on the door, and nothing. The deadbolt was engaged. Laughing a bit at myself, even though I couldn't remember setting the deadbolt, I flipped the catch, and... nothing. The bolt wouldn't move, the catch was in the open position, but the bolt was still firmly in place.

I tried moving it back and forth a few more times, with the same amount of luck, none. Sitting down on the couch and I stared at the door. The phone wasn't turned on so I couldn't call the apartment manager. No windows opened at all on the first floor so I couldn't go out that way. And, while I could go to the second floor, there wasn't any way to get down from there and jumping from a second story balcony onto concrete didn't have much appeal. Not to mention, once I got down that way, I'd have no way back into the apartment until help arrived, and I didn't want to leave my son alone in case he woke up.

Glancing at the clock, and noting that it was close to midnight, I walked over to the windows to see if any of my neighbor's apartments were lit up. Of the 16 units, I could only clearly see about half of them. But, I did notice a few lights on here and there. If I could get someone's attention, maybe they could send for help.

Going upstairs to the balcony, I sat down at the edge, dangling my feet between the posts and started calling out, "Can someone help me?" Projecting my voice, not yelling, I didn't want to alarm anyone, I just wanted to gain their attention. I continued this for about a half hour, getting no response from anyone. Unsure what to do next, I thought maybe I could put a note on one of the windows next to the door. When Nev came home he would see it and get help. That decided, I started to get up when I saw flashlights at the front tunnel entrance. Maybe one of my neighbor's was coming home late and I could get their attention.

Calling out yet again, "Hey, can you help me?"

Flashlights whirling in my direction, I saw two figures edge around the corner and flash their lights up at me. I couldn't make out much but shapes at this time, but valiantly called out again, "Can you help me?"

Moving the lights up and down the apartment, one of them finally spoke, "This is the police ma'am, are you in trouble?"

At his query, I couldn't help but laugh as I answered, "Yeah, you could say that. I'm locked in."

Silence reigned for about 30 seconds as they processed this information, then one of them called out, "Excuse me, ma'am? How exactly are you locked *in*?"

I'm sure they thought this was some kind of really bad blond joke in the making. Locking yourself out. Yeah, sure, that's something that can happen to anyone. But locking yourself *in*? Oh, that was a whole different kind of strange.

"Um, yeah," I replied, "The deadbolt seems to be broken. I tried turning the switch about a half dozen times, but it refuses to budge. The windows on the first floor don't open, and I didn't feel like jumping from the second to get out. So, I decided to see if I could get someone's attention from up here."

Mulling over this information, the second one says, "Is there anyone else in the house? Are you being held against your will?"

"Just my 10-month-old son and only by a door," I replied.

Going up to the door, one of the officers started turning the knob on the door, pushing on it at the same time. I heard them discuss me in low tones, then, stepping back where I could see them again, called out, "Ma'am, can you come down here and try the door from your side?"

"Sure," I said, "Just give me a minute to get down there." Pulling myself up I went back down the stairs and flipped the switch on the deadbolt again. Hearing me, they tried the door with no more luck than I'd had.

"Can you flip it a few more times?" One of them asked.

"As many times as you want me to," and flipping it a few more times, with no better results.

"Um, Ma'am... do you have a key for this door?"

"Yeah, I do, I'll take it back upstairs and drop it to you, just give me a sec." Digging through all the stuff on the table, I found my keys and headed back upstairs. When I emerged from the house I called out and dropped the keys down to the waiting officer.

Hearing them fumbling with the keys, they finally found the right one and tried once again to open the door. And once again, the lock refused to budge. Stymied at this point, they walked back out from under the balcony and said, "We have a few tools in the squad car, sit tight and we'll be right back."

Sure, I thought to myself, where else am I going to go at this point? But calling down I said instead, "Okay, thanks." and settled in to wait for their return.

About 10 minutes went by before they returned, carrying a small black bag of some sort, disappearing again under the balcony. Seeing them go under, I decided to head back downstairs to watch what they were doing. Peeking through my window, I saw them standing before my door, heads bowed together, picking through an assortment of silver objects, barely seen in the flashlight. After some discussion and pointing, they seemed to settle on two items, and while one held the light, the other began working on the door.

I heard metal grating on metal, but couldn't really see what they were doing. The second officer holding the light was in my way, so I went back to the couch to wait. Several minutes went by, punctuated by soft cursing, and finally! the door swung open. Jumping up from the couch, I clapped my hands and went to the door to thank them.

They were both still staring at the door while playing with the lock. Which, after opening for them had snapped back into its extended position. They could push it back and set the lock, but as soon as they let go, back open it would pop.

One of them, looking over at me, asked, "Do you have duct tape or something similar to that around here," while eyeing all the boxes and random mess from the move.

"Um, maybe somewhere." Looking around, "We just moved in today and I was just starting to get things unpacked when this happened."

"Okay," said the second officer, "I think we may have something in the squad car, I'll be right back."

Leaving me and the first officer alone, staring at each other, I finally said, "Hey, uh, thanks for helping me out. I'm glad you happened by."

"Oh no," shaking his head, "one of your neighbors called in saying someone was in distress and may be hurt and asked us to check it out."

"Oh wow," blushing a bit, "I wasn't trying to scare anyone. I was just hoping someone was awake and could call the apartment manager for me." Looking over to where the phone was to be, I said, "The phone doesn't get turned on for a few more days and I didn't have any way to call out."

"Well, I'm just glad it wasn't anything bad," chuckling to himself, "and this will be an interesting story to share when we get back to the station."

Yeah, thanks, good to see I could be your entertainment for the night, but said out loud, "Well, I appreciate your help."

About that time the second officer came back holding a large roll of duct tape, and after pushing in the bolt, again, began to tape it. Putting one strip on it and stepping back, he watched the bolt strain and then spring open once again. Shaking his head, he pushed it back in and then using ever longer strips began to cover the entire area, until he could no longer see the bolt pushing back.

Stepping back from his handiwork, he motioned to the other officer and said, "I'll go outside and you stay in here and close the door. We'll see if this works."

Following deeds to words, he stepped out, shutting the door behind him. Waiting a few minutes he opened the door again. It stuck a bit with all the duct tape wrapped around the lock, but it did open. Packing up their tools the first officer looked over at me and said, "We'll take all of this back to the car, go ahead and shut the door. We'll come back after we get this all put away, and check to make sure the door can still be opened."

"Not a problem officer," I said, "and thanks again for all of your help. I'll call the manager in the morning and get this whole thing fixed so you don't have to come back again."

Shutting the door behind them, I went back to the couch to wait for their return, listening for the sounds of breaking duct tape that never came. When the officers returned, they tried the door a few more times, declared it good and went on their way, still chuckling at my situation.

Sighing to myself and thinking, I must be the only person in the world to ever lock themselves in. I shut the door, sticking my tongue out at it for good measure as I flipped the bottom lock. With a sigh, I returned to my unpacking while I waited for morning to get the damned thing fixed.

 ## A Shot in the Ass

By happy happenstance, both Nev and Doug's 21st birthday's were within days of each other, and the three of us decided to go out together and make a night of it. Since I was still underage, I offered to be the designated driver for the evening. Leaving the guys able to drink as much as they wanted, without any worries. I made all the arrangements with one of the neighbors to watch our son overnight, and we were all free to enjoy our night out.

None of us were "bar" people since none of us had been old enough to legally drink up till this point. Most of the drinking, if we drank at all, had taken place at someone's house so we were not familiar with any of the local bars. Picking a likely area near downtown Phoenix, we began to bar-hop. Each place we stopped the guys were offered a free drink for this occasion, and after about a dozen such stops they were well on their way towards utter oblivion.

Our last stop of the night was a kind of a lounge bar, complete with piano music and gaudy decorations. Sitting down next to another group of two couples, we began to talk back and forth, laughing and exchanging small stories, while the guys continued to steadily drink. By the time last call rolled around, neither of them were able to stand up on their own, much less walk, as they teetered on the edge of disaster in their chairs.

Looking on hopelessly at the two of them, I had no idea how I was going to get them to the car, much less back into the apartment all by myself. I stood there looking at them, shaking my head, and chewing on my lip watching them wobble, when the people we'd been talking to at the next table noticed my distress.

"Lisa, do you need some help?" one of the guys asked.

"Umm... yeah, that would be great," I sighed as I looked at them, "but how I'm going to get them in the house after we get home, I have absolutely no idea." Giving into a small laugh at the situation, "I'll probably just leave them in the car to sleep it off."

"Hey, would you like to come home with us until they sleep it off?" The woman standing next to the first guy asked, "We have a big house, we're all roommates." Pointing to the entire group sitting next to us, "We even have a spare room and a fold out couch if you're interested."

Not seeing any better options as I watched Nev slowly sink to the floor from his chair, I agreed.

I stood back while the guys first picked up Nev, and I walked them to our car once they were out the door. Going back again for Doug, they carried him to their car. One of the women came up to me as they were sliding Doug into the backseat saying, "They'll take him and I'll ride with you so I can give you directions, if that's okay."

I couldn't think of any reason to object to the arrangement at that point, and agreed, thanking them all for their help as I climbed into my car. Nev, snoring in the backseat, didn't even move as we started up the car and headed off.

Their house was less than a mile from the lounge, but a little hard to find. Tucked snugly back in one of the many small sub-neighborhoods that consisted of curving roads and cul-de-sacs. But, it was an actual house, not an apartment complex, and as stated, a big one. Pulling into the driveway behind the other car, I watched them drag Doug from the car and disappear inside the house with him. Getting out, I waited beside my car for them to come back out for Nev. After a few minutes they reappeared and repeated the process with Nev and I trailed behind them as they struggled to get him in the house.

It was a big spacious house with vaulted ceilings, a fireplace in the living room, and very well lived in. Bits of clutter and clothes scattered around everywhere, not dirty, but it was well on its way to hoarder levels. In the center of the living room there was, as I had been told, a fold out couch, already unfolded and waiting for Nev. I watched them dump Nev's limp body onto the bed and after he was settled, I walked over to cover him up. Standing over him, wondering what to do next, I began hearing sounds of distress from Doug. Followed the sounds, I came to the room they had put him in.

Poor drunk Doug was half leaning out of an un-baffled waterbed, looking miserable and green. Laying there while

# IT'LL FEEL BETTER WHEN IT QUITS HURTING

holding on to the side of the bed looking for all the world like a shipwreck victim clinging to a log for dear life. Every movement made waves, gently rolling his body in an endless cycle of pure misery. Looking up at me in distress as I walked in, he moaned, "Lisa, you've got to help me, the world won't stop moving!"

Laughing at his wretchedness, because I'm a good friend, I walked over to the side of the bed and sat down on the frame next to him. "It's okay sweetie, you're just drunk in a waterbed, you'll be alright." Stroking his hair as I spoke to him in soothing tones to quiet him.

"No," he moaned, "I'm not going to be alright, make it stop! Make it stop!"

Gently pushing him onto his back, I admonished, "Just lay here quietly and the world will stop, it's going to be fine." But pushing him onto his back made him aware of the ceiling fan above his head. With the bed moving in a rippling motion from foot to head and back again, and the ceiling fan going in fast circles above his head, it only reinforced in his head that the world was spinning out of control, the light shade of green, taking on a decidedly darker color.

"Oh god," he gurgled, "I'm going to die!" Hitting the bed with his fist, making the waves go, not only head to foot but now side to side as well.

Sitting next to him trying to calm him, one of the guys came to the doorway and leaned in to check on things. Disappearing after a quick glance to reappear a few minutes later with a bucket and a big glass of water, handing them to me with a grin. "I think he's going to need this." Shaking his head and chuckling to himself he walked back out of the room, leaving us alone for the time being.

"It's going to be okay sweetie," smoothing back the hair from his head, "just close your eyes and it will be all better in the morning, I promise."

"Nooooooo...." he whimpered, "it's never going to be okay, I'm dying."

Quietly laughing at him, "No, you're not dying, you're just very, very drunk. You're going to be okay. Just try and get some sleep."

His words were becoming increasingly hard to understand, mumbled something like "How can I sleep?" as he drifted off.

Sitting beside him a few more minutes to make sure he

was soundly asleep, I placed the bucket next to the bed and the glass of water on the nightstand. That done, I turned off all the lights except for a small table lamp next to the bed before leaving the room. I figured if he woke up in the dark, he'd have no idea where he was or where anything was and light would be helpful to him.

Wandering out of the room, I went back to check on Nev who was still passed out cold. He hadn't even moved as far as I could tell from when he was first put there. Not really tired, and unsure of what to do now that they were taken care of, I followed the sounds of voices. A few doorways down I came across the rest of the people in the house sitting in a bedroom not far from the room they had put Doug in. Seeing me in the doorway they smiled and waved me in to join them.

I was feeling a bit uncomfortable, now that the guys had been taken care of and it dawned on me that I was in a house full of strangers I knew very little about. They had been helpful, but it was an awkward situation. As I sat down in a chair near the door, they picked up on the conversation I'd walked in on. Doing their best to include me in the conversation, while trying to ease my discomfort. They asked all the standard getting to know you questions, how long had I been married, did I have any kids, how long had I lived in Phoenix, and I answered, getting into the flow of conversation and asking some of my own as well.

Passing a bottle around the room, continuing the party atmosphere from earlier, they started sharing stories and telling on each other much to each others amusement, and sometimes embarrassment, when this happened.

"Hey," said one of the guys to the other, "do you remember the time you cheated on her," pointing to the woman next to him with a wicked grin.

"Forget?" he exclaimed, "How could I forget that!" With a big laugh, he looked my way, and with a wink related this story to me. I could tell by the way everyone settled in to listen, this was a favorite group story, and from the way they acted, probably one told often as well.

"Men can be stupid, you know," looking at me and when I nodded he went on, "and like all men, I can be very stupid. A few years back, I was feeling kind of bored with my lady love here," smiling over at her, taking her hand in his, "and I decided that sleeping with another woman was just what I needed to spice things up in my life."

# IT'LL FEEL BETTER WHEN IT QUITS HURTING

With an eye-roll, his lady love punched him in the ribs, then motioned for him to continue his story.

"So, one night while she was out working late, I pick up some woman in the bar, and stupidly brought her back here thinking I had hours before anyone would be home." He paused right there, I think for dramatic effect, then went on, "I was wrong."

Patting the bed he was sitting on, he continued, "So here I was, naked as the day I was born. And I was into it. Not paying any attention to anything but giving her all I had, when the door opened."

His lady love next to him interjected with, "And I was not happy with what I saw!"

"No, no she wasn't!" Shaking his head and laughing, "But anyway, I'm banging away with this chick when I heard the door slam open, and I froze like a deer in the headlights. And there she stood, pissed as all hell, and grabs that shotgun," pointing to a gun next to the door I hadn't noticed before, "and shot me in the ass!!!"

Now, everyone in the group, except me, was rolling with laughter. I wasn't sure what to say, and not wanting to be left out, I kind of laughed with them. I mean it was a funny image after all, but damn! Wiping tears from his eyes and shaking his head, "It felt like my ass was on fire! The woman under me, she starts bucking like a bronco trying to get away. Scratching at my back, and flaying this way and that, and me just laying there afraid to move. And I have to tell you if you've ever been shot in the ass, getting moving in any direction hurts like a bitch. So there we are, my lady love holding a shotgun, me on this woman with my ass full of buckshot, and her trying like a wildcat to get the hell out of here. It was a helluva moment."

Taking his lady love's hands in his, he looked her in the eyes as he finished his story, "And that was the first, last and only time I ever cheated on her. I'll never do it, again."

Taking his face in both of her hands, "Damn straight you won't, cuz next time I won't aim for your ass!"

He then looks at me and says, "Moral of the story, never cheat on a jealous woman who owns a gun, especially in her own bed." All of them were sharing a laugh at this much-favored story, nudging and nodding to each other, enjoying the retelling of his misery and stupidity.

Sitting by the doorway in a houseful of strangers,

watching all of them laugh, all I could think of was, what the hell had I gotten us into?

Shortly after that story, I decided it was time for me to go back to Nev, and maybe even get some sleep. They all wished me a good night and to sleep well, I nodded and thanked them, but still felt a little out of sorts after the story. I laid down next to Nev, but I can't say that I slept well. But, no one came into the living room, and we made it through the night, and without a single gunshot being issued.

The next morning was a bit confusing for the guys. Doug had slowly emerged from the room he'd been put in, giving a wary glance around until he saw me sitting in the living room, and quickly hurried over to my side as soon as he spotted me. They only had spotty recollections of most of the evening after the third bar, and the lounge was a complete blank. Listening to my recounting of the night before, confused and horridly hungover, their looks of confusion were priceless as I related to them the evening's events and why we had been taken home by strangers.

While I was explaining everything to them, our hosts came into the living room slash dining area with breakfast for everyone and invited us to sit down and eat. I ate much better than the guys did, their meal was mostly coffee, water and a bit of toast. I don't think they were feeling very well, and still a bit green from the excesses of the night before. During the meal, our hosts told other stories and gave both the guys a bit of teasing as they described in detail the drunken state that brought them into their house. Nev and Doug both bore the conversation with the same fortitude of a last meal before execution, doggedly attempting to settle their maligned bellies. Before long, the food consumed, and the conversation dwindling down, the guys started making gestures to exit the house. Smiling with understanding, our hosts wished us well, and we went on our way.

I do believe they may have been the nicest psychotically insane people I have ever met in all my life.

## Right Name, Wrong Number

Once we had a phone, I started to reconnect with my old friends from home. About once a week I'd make a call to one of my friends and we'd talk for a little while. Not for long, because I couldn't afford much in long distance fees, but it was nice to hear from them now and again. And they, in turn, would call me a few times a month, and so it went back and forth. Some, I couldn't track down at all after so long a gap in time, but a few like Ginny & Michael, and my high school sweetheart David, I heard from fairly consistently.

One night after Nev had gone to work, the phone rang. Picking it up, I heard, "Hi Lisa, it's David, I just got back in town and wanted to call you."

Smiling to myself, I replied, "Oh hey David, how you been? How was your trip?"

"Oh, not too bad," came his response, "you know how it is, good to get away, better to get back home."

Laughing while agreeing with him, I settled in next to the phone to talk. After about 15 minutes of small talk, I noticed the conversation was getting a little wonky around the edges. Some of the things he was saying just didn't make sense, and he was beginning to sound a bit confused himself as our conversation meandered around. Despite the confusion, we continued dauntlessly on, up until he said, "Well, you know I've been working on that big engineering job down at (can't remember where now)" when I stopped him.

"Engineering job?" Completely confused now. My David was going to school to become a paramedic, and he had never done any engineering, much less been in charge of a big project of any kind.

"Uh, yeah," came his equally confused response, "we talked about it at dinner the last time I was in town, remember?"

Okay, this was getting weird. David, while he'd come out to visit some months ago, hadn't been back since then. And, we definitely had not gone out to dinner to talk about an engineering project while he was in town. "Uhhhhh..." pausing again, "I'm not sure you're my David."

Silence on the other side of the phone, then I heard him clear his voice and say, "You're not Lisa from (again can't remember the name of the company)?"

"Nope." starting to laugh now, this was actually pretty funny.

"Huh," came the response, "how about that?! So basically, we've just spent the last half hour talking on the phone to the wrong people?!" Starting to laugh as well.

"So it would appear." Really beginning to laugh now, and David joined me in appreciating the absurdity of the situation.

"You have a nice voice," he then said, "I thought you sounded a bit different, but I contributed it to a combination of bad connection and me being tired."

"Same here," I said, "you sound a lot like my David though, I really thought you were him."

Still chuckling a bit to himself, "So Lisa, nice to meet you, I'm David. What's a nice girl like you doing on a phone call like this?"

"Well," getting into the absurdity of the situation replied, "you never know when you might meet a mysterious stranger when picking up random phone calls in the middle of the night."

And so we went, bantering back and forth, making each other laugh, for several more hours. I think both of us were bored. We'd already invested a goodly amount of time talking before we found out it was the wrong person, and with the jokes and the laughter, we continued our ridiculous conversation for half the night. With the first faint light of daylight peeking through the windows, I could hear him beginning to yawn and wind down. He had actually just flown back into town when he thought he was calling his friend Lisa to tell her about the job, and now he was about to fall asleep on the phone talking to me.

"Well sweetie," I said after I heard another yawn from his side of the phone, "you should probably be going to bed. It was really fun talking to you."

"And you as well," pausing before he continued, he asked, "would you mind if I called you again? I have to say, this has been the most entertaining conversation I've had with anyone in a while."

Startled, but pleased by the compliment, I agreed, "I would like that. I'm awake most nights, and after my husband goes to work I'm pretty much free to talk whenever."

"Well, I have to head out back to the job site again on Monday morning, but when I get back into town, maybe I can give you a call."

"Yeah, I'd like that. You have a good rest of what's left of the night sweetie, and give me a call whenever."

"You too," stifling another yawn, "Good-night."

"Night," I replied and hung up the phone.

And you know what? He did call back that next week. We never met in person, nor did we exchange last names. I never knew when he would call, it was all completely random. Nor did I ever ask for his number. I have no idea what he even looked like, or where in the Phoenix area he lived. We could have walked by each other a hundred times and never known it in our real lives. Instead, we talked about books, art, politics, movies and favorite places to visit, all the things that interested us outside the grind of everyday living. Very little personal information was exchanged beyond the basics. He knew I was married, and that I had two sons. I knew he was single and worked long hours and had little time to socialize outside of work. There was an almost magical spell about our conversations, this anonymous person on the other end of the line, who nonetheless, cared and listened.

 ## Selling Death Over the Phone

In my life, I have held a lot of weird jobs, jobs my guidance counselor back in high school had never even hinted at as a way to make money. Some have paid well, others not so much, and somehow I have managed to obtain employment in many of them. I have worked for the psychic network, ran a porn site, made door knob coverings, I was a secret shopper and a host of other just odd things you can (legally) do for money.

This one was a phone soliciting job. Not a great job, but the pay was decent if the product odd. My job was to cold call people to set up appointments for prearranged funeral packages. This is not something most people want to talk about to begin with, and some get downright hostile when there is any mention of their own mortality. But there were enough people out there with some foresight to make it profitable for the company. I was paid an hourly wage, got a bonus for each appointment made, and another bigger bonus if a sale was made. In a good week, I could make some decent money, on a bad week, I'd make enough to pay for my gas to work and a babysitter for my son.

Five days a week I would sit down at a phone in a large room with dozens of other people and make calls all day long. It was a boring job for the most part, with long lines of numbers who never answered, and others that, when they found out who I was, would become irate. But, there was a small number of people would listen, and of those few, a couple would make an appointment, and a smaller number after that actually bought what we were selling.

Telemarketing is both boring and somewhat stressful. Management had their contests to try to break up the boredom with small giveaways to keep us happy. But we also had what we referred to as our "favorite number list". This could be anything from someone's funny answering machine, up to our favorite crazy lady. Someone stumbled across her shortly after I started working there, and at least once a day,

# IT'LL FEEL BETTER WHEN IT QUITS HURTING 259

someone from our department would call her. Believe me when I say she didn't mind. Honestly, I'm not sure she was even aware of who we were, she never once gave us a chance to say anything during the entire phone call.

Each and every time this is what would happen. Dialing her number she would always answer, and without waiting for a single word from us, she would go into some diatribe about, well, just about anything. Her kids, her grandkids, her great-grandkids, family members, politician's, people on the TV, her neighbors, it was never the same and all delivered the same rapid-fire speech. And then when she was done, she would stop and say, "Well, that's all I have to say." and hang up the phone.

She described cheating husbands, alcoholics, illnesses and surgeries in the family, the state of the country, the activities of her neighbor's and what she had for dinner, all in a single stream of consciousness spewing of words. We had no idea who any of these people were, where she lived or anything else, but it was a wonder to behold each and every time. I think she may have liked us calling her, and didn't care who it was as long as she was able to have her say before we hung up. I think if we had called her a dozen times a day she probably would have done the same, without fail each time. Not that we ever did.

But for me, my one shining moment of "damn!" came after a long day of no answers. It happens sometimes. You'll be sitting there, calling number after number for hours on end, and get nothing but answering machines or ringtones. You begin to get lulled into the tedium of it, dial number, wait for it to ring, no answer, hang up, dial number... well, you get the idea. After an entire day of this, my mind began to wander and my eyes idly fell on the name of one of our cemetery's listed on a sheet of paper by my side called Green Acres. I began to softly sing to myself the intro to an old TV comedy called, of course, Green Acres.

So there I am, on the phone singing, "*Green acres is the place to be, farm living is the life for me...*" completely oblivious to the phone still cradled against my ear. My eyes, drifting around the room as I waited for it to be the end of the day when I realized, there was no longer any dial tone. No ringing in my ear, nothing but silence, as I reach the end of my little ditty. When the last note ended, I heard someone on the other end of the phone say, "Thanks for the serenade, but was there something I could help you with?"

Oh damn. Trying to rally, I started with, "Hi, my name is..." well damn.

"I'm with...." damn.

"I'm calling about..." damn, damn, damn. "Uh, I'll tell you what, you have a nice day and we'll try this again another time."

Hearing his laughter on the other end of the phone, he replied, "Well, alrighty, you have a good day." and hung up the phone.

Looking once again at the clock, I had an hour yet to go. It was already a very long day, and he was my only pick up of the entire day. Well, damn.

 ## The Second is Coming

When we found out I was pregnant again so soon after our first son, Nev was greatly displeased. I was almost five months along before I discovered it, much to the shock of both of us. I hadn't gained any weight, and I was still nursing my first son, so all the other indicators of pregnancy weren't noticeable. I'd gone to the doctor's because I wasn't feeling well, I was more tired than usual and was having trouble keeping food down. I assumed my ulcer was acting up or something similar, and after a long round of tests that all came back negative, the doctor ran a pregnancy test. I almost fainted when he gave me the results.

Running other tests they found that my iron was low, very low. Bordering on you could die low. There were other complications as well, most foods made me sick, and I felt like I was always on the verge of fainting most days both from lack of food and low iron. Simple things became more complicated as I struggled to find the energy to accomplish almost any task. I tried to sleep more, napping whenever my son did, but it was never enough.

Nev became increasingly hostile to the idea of yet another child coming to take more of my attention away from him. He didn't want to talk about it, nor did he want to make any plans for the baby's arrival. Instead, he chose to ignore my growing belly and pretending it didn't exist. He refused to go to any of my doctor appointments, nor even look at the ultrasound photos that were taken. The only time he acknowledged my pregnancy was in the presence of other people, then he would smile and tell people about his new, expanding the family, giving them the impression he was a happy family man.

When I was seven months along, my mother, fourth step-father, and sister came out to Phoenix to visit. It was a trip that was already been planned before I found out about the impending baby, so for my mother, this became a bonus trip. When they arrived, they had lists of plans for things we were going to do while they were in town. Not taking into account how tired this pregnancy had made me, nor giving me a choice of joining in.

For a solid week I was stuffed repeatedly into the backseat of a compact car with my sister and my son as we traveled the countryside. We drove up mountains, went to tourist attractions, shopped at malls, stopped at roadside stands, and on one memorable day, we went to the zoo.

I didn't want to go to the zoo. It was July in Phoenix, which can translate to "You have now reached the ninth level of hell" hot. What I wanted was to take a nap, in the air-conditioned comfort of my home, while my husband, son and the rest of my family left me alone, but that's not what I got. After pushing, cajoling and nagging for most of the morning, my mother was able to persuade me, yet again, to be stuffed into the back of that tiny car.

Hot, tired, sick and miserable I was led unwillingly into the zoo. Despondently, I slowly followed them from attraction to attraction, feeling worse with every step. My feet began to swell, as my head began to ache with the heat. Reaching the center of the zoo, I was reaching my limit when I spotted a fountain. Picking a spot in a shaded area, I gratefully sat down, took off my shoes, and put my feet in the water. Sweet relief was immediate.

Here, I decided, was where I was going to stay for the rest of the day. The rest of the family could wander around and get heat-stroke for all I cared, I had found my spot and here I would take my stand (or seat as the case may be). Relishing the cool water, I wiggled my toes at the fish that swam by, content for the first time all day. Sitting there, a shadow stretched across the water in front of me, then spoke "Ma'am, you're not allowed to put your feet in the water. You're going to have to move along."

Slowly shifting my weight towards the person behind me, allowing him to see my bulging belly for the first time, I gave him a level stare, and coldly replied, "Really?"

Staring now at my middle, he began to nervously shift from foot to foot, giving me a shrug, "Yes ma'am. You're going to have to move."

"No," I told him flatly and turned my back on him.

"Umm... ma'am," his voice now rising a few octaves as he asked, unsure of his authority in this matter, "It's park regulations."

Turning around to face him once more, and beyond caring what "park regulations" were at this point, I simply looked at him for the longest time as he continued to shuffle his feet uncomfortably under my scrutiny. "I see," I said, turning away from him to look back on the wonderful, cooling water. "I don't care."

Looking around now for any type of support, and failing to find it, he tried one last time, "Ma'am, I'm sorry but this fountain is just for looks. You're not supposed to get in the water. There are signs up all around here saying so."

Keeping my back turned to him, I said, "I'm not moving. There is nothing you can do short of picking me up and removing me from this spot that will get me to move. But if you want to," at this point I turned around, grinning maliciously at him, "you're welcome to try."

Putting his hands up in front of him, he slowly began to back up, shaking his head in the negative. Something in my smile, my stance or my voice triggered a fear response in him and he was trying now to get away from the entire situation. "No, no, no..." taking a few more steps away from me, "I'll just leave you alone, ma'am. Sorry to have bothered you." Retreating quickly to some other part of the park, probably as far away as his ego would let him.

After my little exchange with the zoo police, my Mother walked up and said it was time to move on to explore the rest of the park. Giving her the same look I had given security, I shook my head and told her no. I had found my spot, and I was not leaving, period. I was hot, miserable, sick and tired, and all I wanted at that moment was to sit there with my feet in the cool water and do nothing. They could go on and explore the park and when they were ready to leave, they could come back here for me. And there I stayed for the rest of the day.

Less than a week after my family left, I went into labor. Awakened by a sudden pain in the middle of the night, I bolted straight up in bed. But, after a few moments, the pain subsided and I settled back into bed thinking it was just a cramp. I'd been pushing myself too much lately and my family's visit had taken a lot out of me. Beginning to drift off, I decided I needed to take it easy in the morning. On the verge of sleep, I felt yet another bolt of pain run through me, causing me to suck in my breath with the urgency of it.

Sitting up and grabbing the clock off the headboard, I fought to hold off panic. I couldn't be in labor yet, it was too early. Much too early. I wasn't due until September, Labor Day to be exact (a date that secretly pleased me when told my due date). Sitting in the dark next to Nev, who was still sleeping soundly, I tried to convince myself it must be Braxton-Hicks. It couldn't be anything more than false labor. Yes, that had to be it. Working myself up to the conviction I was right when another pain came, less than five minutes after the last, stronger than before.

Now in a panic, I reached over to Nev and began to shake him awake. "Nev! Nev!" Shaking him some more as he mumbled something incomprehensible, "The baby's coming!" Giving him yet another shake I yelled "Nev, damn it, wake up!"

Rolling over and looking at me, he mumbled, "It's just your imagination, go back to sleep." Promptly rolling back over again.

Feeling yet another pain build up, I tried shaking him once more, "No Nev, it's not! The baby is coming. Now!" Beginning to cry as panic took hold of me.

Not even rolling over, this time, he mumbled, "Leave me the fuck alone and go back to sleep."

Suffering through another contraction, I debated what I should do. I couldn't drive myself, not with the contractions as close as they were now. I didn't even know if I could make it to my hospital that was almost a 45-minute drive from where I lived. My first son had come in 42 minutes after the first real contraction and would have arrived sooner if there hadn't been complications. But I did know I couldn't just sit there any longer and hope the contractions went away, this was happening now, like it or not.

Pulling myself out of the waterbed, I crawled down the stairs, unsure if I could stand at the moment on my own and afraid to try. Reaching the bottom of the stairs, I half pulled myself up into a walking crouch, and somehow managed to make it out the door, heading straight for one of my neighbor's apartment. PJ lived two apartments down from me, she had a set of twin boys and we'd become good friends since I moved into the complex. She was a bouncer by trade, and she scared the crap out of Nev quite a bit. He never said anything, but he was never happy when she was around, keeping to himself whenever she was near and rarely saying

# IT'LL FEEL BETTER WHEN IT QUITS HURTING 265

anything to her.

Banging on her apartment door, I started shouting for her to please come out and help me. Two contractions later, the door opened and I saw her sleepily looking down at me with a questioning look. "The baby. It's coming and I can't get Nev awake."

Instantly coming fully awake, she jumped to my side and led me into her apartment and gently lowered me to the couch. "Have you called your doctor yet?"

Shaking my head, she ran to her kitchen and brought me her phone. "Call him and let him know you're on your way." Stopping and giving me a hard stare, she flatly stated, "I'll be back shortly with Nev," and was out the door before I could say anything else.

Dialing the number for my doctor, I waited for him to answer. Crying with pain and panic, I was almost hysterical by the time he answered. Quickly explaining what was going on, he directed me to a small community hospital less than a mile from my house. Telling me he would meet me there, he also said he would call the hospital on my behalf, alerting them to my arrival.

While I was making my phone call, PJ had gone over to my house and very unceremoniously dumped Nev from our bed. In a scene she later described to me in vivid detail, she had marched over and went straight up to our room where she found him fast asleep. Calling to him from the doorway, and receiving no response, she walked over to his side of the bed, grabbed him by the hair, dragging him out of the covers and out onto the floor. Standing over him, hands on her hips, she informed him that I was indeed in labor and he was to get his lazy, worthless ass up, dressed and out the door by the time she counted to 5.

Staring up at her, naked as the day he was born. At first, he didn't move.

Tapping her foot, she counted "One...." holding up one finger, she took a step towards him.

He scrambled up and ran over to where he had dropped his clothes earlier in the evening.

Protesting as he dressed, she counted "Two...." and he shut up and began to move faster.

On "Three..." he was moving towards the door, and by "Four..." had reached our front door with her close behind.

Running now, he reached her apartment and skidded to a

halt in front of me. "Are you ready to go," he asked.

Nodding my head, unaware at this time what had happened, I gladly took his helping hand to get off the couch, leaning on him for support as we made our way out the door. Looking over at PJ as we left, she nodded and said, "I'll get your son, don't worry about him, he'll be fine."

Grateful for her help, I thanked her as we left. Walking to the car I told Nev of the change of plans for the hospital. He nodded, then quickly moved to the driver's side and started the car.

Arriving at the hospital entrance, I saw a few people already standing outside the door with a wheelchair, waiting for my arrival. This was considered a tier-three hospital, more of a clinic that ran 24-hours, than an actual hospital.

They had a maternity ward, but only for low-risk patients, and not for many of those. For my entire stay there, I was the only person on that floor.

Swooping into action as soon as the car pulled to a stop, they were at my door and helping me into the wheelchair before I could even say a word. Thinking to myself, wouldn't it have been funny if they had gotten the wrong person in their zeal for getting me up to the labor ward? It's funny what goes through your head in times of stress, and between contractions, it gave me a small giggle. Looking at me oddly, I just shook my head, waving my giggles away, not in the mood to explain my irrational behavior.

Rushing me into the labor room, they had me stripped and on the bed in record time. Hooking me up to machines to check on my progress, asking me questions about when it started and a few other things, while they waited for my doctor, hoping that he would arrive before the baby did. It was a close call. In total, I was in labor for less than two hours, one hour and 42 minutes to be exact. I was already much too far along in my labor for them to stop it, there was nothing to be done now except to let nature take its course.

Arriving just moments before my son entered the world, my doctor ran in, hands still dripping as they hurriedly put a gown on him, tying the last of the strings as he sat down before me. Giving me one quick look, he said, "Okay Lisa, this is it, the next big push should be it."

In a moment of panic, I started shaking my head, for whatever irrational reason, I became convinced my baby would die if he didn't have a name. We had just briefly begun discussing names before I went into labor, thinking there was plenty of time to decide. I was wrong. Reaching up to grab Nev's hand, I pleaded, "He has to have a name. I won't have the baby until he has a name."

"What are you talking about?" We'll pick one later."

"No," I cried, "he has to have a name, right now! Help me pick one!" I was now straining not to push, I was determined to have a name before I had a baby.

The entire room began to become concerned, trying to talk to me soothingly, they said the baby was coming now, it was okay. Digging in, I tried to relax my body, refusing to let the next contraction cause me to push. I was determined that a name was going to be given, end of discussion.

Becoming a bit frantic, Nev looked wildly around the room for help, receiving nothing but confused and worried looks in exchange. "What do you want to name him?"

"Brandon," was the first name that came to my lips, "What do you think of Brandon?"

Nodding vigorously, he said, "Good name. That's fine."

"Are you sure?" I asked, panting now with pain.

"Yes," he cried, "it's fine!"

I had Brandon less than a minute later. They laid him on my chest and I saw him for the first time. He looked like a blue plucked chicken. Putting my hand on his tiny head, I said, "Brandon," feeling his small, faint movements before they took him away.

Rushing around now, the whole room was a swirl of activity. They rushed him to an incubator, I heard a small, faint cry from him on occasion, but it was not the vigorous crying my oldest son had shared with the world after his birth. During this time, another doctor had arrived. A neonatal specialist called in by my doctor on his way to the hospital. Tubes were inserted, and he was hooked up to machines as they all worked to keep him alive. While they concentrated on him, I was left to myself for a few minutes. I told myself over and over again, he was going to be okay.

It would be almost two weeks before I was able to hold him again.

Within less than an hour, arrangements had been made to move him to a tier-one hospital across town. He needed more care than the hospital he had been born in could provide. I would not be moving with him, in a glitch of insurance bureaucracy, I was not considered high risk so they would not approve of my being moved with him. I had to watch them take my son away while I remained behind.

Once they had taken my son, I started making a few phone calls. I didn't want to tell everyone yet, not with everything so uncertain, but I did make a few phone calls to parents and a few close friends. Calling my mother first, as soon as she answered the phone I said, "You're a grandma."

"I know I'm a grandma," she responded. I waited quietly for my words to sink in, "You had the baby," she shouted

"About two hours ago," I informed her. "I told you I wasn't feeling well when you were here," thinking back on all those hours cramped in the backseat of that horrid little car.

"You were fine," dismissing my announcement. "How's the baby doing?"

"Better than expected, but not good." Then I went on to tell her about everything that had happened and what the doctors had said. I also told her not to start making any announcements yet. I couldn't bear the idea of receiving baby gifts if there was no baby. Unhappy, but agreeing with me, we got off the phone so I could continue my calls. Nev's mother was also unhappy about having to keep the news to herself until we knew how things would turn out, trying to persuade me to change my mind several times before I got off the phone with her, but I was insistent. No announcements, no gifts, nothing until we knew for sure he would survive. Everyone else was understanding, and supportive of my decision, asking me to keep them informed if anything changed.

Being the only person on the ward the nurses gave me a lot of attention. I appreciated all of their efforts, but my only focus was getting released from the hospital so I could be with my son. After the doctor came to check on me, I asked if there was any reason for me to remain, he said no, but that he couldn't recommend me leaving, and that I should stay at least another day in case there were any issues. But when pressed, he said as long as I could walk out on my own he could not stop me either.

Through voluntary check out, I left the hospital less than 10 hours after I had given birth. I could not stand the idea of not being near my son when I had no idea if he was going to live or not. I was given 50-50 odds for his survival. He had been born 2 1/2 months early, caused by gestational diabetes that went undetected due to a glitch at the lab when they had

## IT'LL FEEL BETTER WHEN IT QUITS HURTING

been testing for it the previous month. The new test results showed up the day I had him, too late to do any good. The good news was it had caused him to grow larger, faster than normal, weighing at birth 5 lbs, 6 oz, huge for a preemie. But, there were still many other problems stemming from his early birth, and so the doctors could not give me any promises he would survive.

With the help of friends and neighbors, I was able to spend most of my days and nights with him as I watched him struggle for life. They took turns watching and caring for my older son and helped with cooking and cleaning the apartment while I was away. During this time, Nev only came to see our son a few times, often just for a few minutes before picking me up to take me home again. But, each day, Brandon became a little better and a little stronger. It was touch and go for the first few days, but then he began to thrive. Within three weeks I was able to take him home.

Brandon required a lot of care. He slept a lot, couldn't eat much at a time and needed constant monitoring. It was a very difficult time, with a newborn and a toddler only 15 months apart. Nev did not help with any of the care, expecting dinner on time and my attention when he required it. He made no allowances for my exhaustion, the strain of a newborn or the demands of a toddler.

It was fortunate that my neighbors, seeing my initial distress, pitched in to help as they could, taking my older son outside to play with their children, bringing by food for several weeks, and helping me around the house as I learned to cope with this new situation.

Shortly after Brandon's release from the hospital, my mother and grandmother came out for a visit. They stayed for two weeks to help out as well.

With them there I could concentrate more on my newborn son. I was also able to get a bit more sleep since they could rock him and care for him for short periods of time between feedings so I could get some rest.

But, very shortly, I was on my own again. Everyone had their own lives to get back to and I couldn't make myself ask for any additional help. From the outside, whenever anyone was watching, Nev gave the impression of a dedicated father and husband. And, as help faded away, everyone assumed that he would be there, helping me out as they had seen so many times when stopping by to visit. All left assuming they were leaving me in his capable and loving hands.

## Until Death do we Part... Sorta

Life is interesting. It comes with no directions, there are few road signs to help you along your way and we all muddle along the best we can, hoping for the best. There are points along the journey that make us stop and look around, wondering just how the hell we got there, and more importantly, how the hell do you find the exit.

You learn to laugh at some of the places you've found yourself, happily willing to share your disasters with friends, as you recount your tales of stupidity. But for other tales, no amount of laughter can save you, and these are the stories no one wants to share with anyone. These are the alone places, the dark places where anything can hide, and like an ostrich, you hope like hell that you can put your head in the sand and it will pass you by. This is, where it got bad.

I cannot laugh about this part of my life, nor can I make light of these events. I did not know when I started this book if I would add this part of my life. There are no funny stories here and I don't know that I would want to try, even if I could. But here's the thing, this is the nexus point of my entire life, where every event prior to this constricted down like a funnel, and I came out the other side as the person I am now.

And I cannot even say now, so many years past this moment, that I would want to go back and change anything if I was offered the chance. Without it, I would not be the person I became because of it, and I like this person. So for a little while, just a few chapters I promise, I'll ask you to walk with me in the dark. There is a light at the end of this, and it's not the oncoming train, even if it feels like it at times. So, take my hand and we'll finish this part of the journey together...

 ## A Broken Vase

Many years ago, I was once described as a Ming vase held together with Elmer's glue. As apt a description as any for what I have become.

You have to understand, abuse is a slow process. It does not happen overnight, it is gradual and methodical, building upon itself layer after layer. With a bizarre combination of restraint mixed with ever increasing violence. They will eventually, given enough time, achieve complete and utter dominance. Often with very little resistance. Violence is not the goal of the abuser. It is the reward they give themselves for a job well done. The goal is the complete submission of will. All of this training takes time and dedication. It is a focusing of effort on another person, to bend and mold them into what the abuser considers their ideal. Like water falling onto a rock, it only takes time and persistence to cause a rock to split in half and break, people are the same.

All abusers seem to have an uncanny sense of who they can achieve their personal goal of complete subservience with, and my entire life had conditioned me to be the perfect candidate. I had learned passive resistant in times of stress, to be still in times of trouble, to accept the will of others when it was imposed on me. It had been of necessity, a survival skill that made me extremely vulnerable to the predatory.

I had almost no knowledge of what a healthy relationship looked like. Only what I experienced with my parents, and a vague understanding from media of what marriage was, and neither were ideal. In the beginning, there was no basis to resist what was being done. I believed it was simply part of being in a normal relationship, or at the very least, acceptable behavior from a spouse.

All you had to do was look around to see what kind of misinformation was out there, "Married with Children" was one of the most popular TV shows at the time. This was not a functional family, it was anything but. Daytime soaps and nighttime dramas all warp what is reasonable and rational within a relationship. Using them as a comparison, my relationship was not outside of the culturally accepted norm. Cheating, lying, and manipulation were all acceptable, even a bit of hitting and smacking in context was to be expected.

I had come from a broken home, all of my friends had as well. I had no idea what normal was supposed to be, and even the advice on marriage can be warped as a justification for abuse. Marriage is about compromise. It is about putting the other person's needs ahead of your own. It is a fine line between a healthy relationship and an abusive one. That line, without context, can be easily crossed without knowing it.

And, the mind itself is capable of amazing justifications, making the bizarre commonplace, in an attempt to save itself. As the abuse escalates, it is capable of stripping itself down, destroying the ego in the process. The mind, in a last ditch effort to survive even one more day, turns the abuser into the giver of salvation.

Every line crossed is camouflaged afterward with sweet words and actions, pushing that line even further back. Once the new baseline of behavior is set, the abuser is then able to push again and again, in a series of cycles of abuse, violence followed by regret coupled with contrition, and then granting absolution for their behavior. This all allows the abuser to continue on in slow steps forward without question.

In this way, you become an accomplice in your own demise. It causes you to remain silent instead of reaching out for help. Partly because you know this is all your fault, you've been told so, many times, that all of this is a result of your own inadequacies, and to make it stop all you have to do is be good. You hide the other person's actions to hide your own failures. It is, after all, not their fault, but your own.

In order not to hurt, you begin to shut down your own emotional responses. If you feel nothing, nothing can hurt you. You begin to identify only with the abuser's emotional reactions while having none of your own. Survival requires you to have empathy for their emotional state while completely suppressing your own. In the end, how you feel means nothing. Everything is built upon the abuser's state of being. Your life, literally, depends upon it.

As time goes on, you become less and less, while the abuser begins to loom larger than life. They are your lifeline, your only source of comfort, drying the tears they themselves caused, soothing the hurts, all the while promising salvation in compliance.

The abuser begins stripping you of your will and your soul, creating a hollow shell where a person once stood, leaving nothing but the desire to please the other person.

Isolation and dependence further distance you from reality, or from what is normal.

You push away friends and family to avoid having to admit your personal failure or to make excuses for the inexcusable.

What the abuser began, you now help maintain. Slowly you withdraw from anything, or from anyone, that does not please your other self, because you are no longer a separate individual. You are only an extension of your abuser.

The longer this goes on, the harder it is to break away. You have literally given everything to this person. Shame keeps you silent. Compliance makes you complicit in your own demise. Fear of the unknown keeps you still, because there may be worse demons out there that you know nothing about, and this one you, at least, know how to, sometimes, please and placate.

Starting slowly, like an avalanche at the top of the mountain, my marriage began its downward descent. It began with small, petty things, things that seemed stupid to fight over. Small decisions he began to make for me that I conceded to him because it didn't seem worth an argument.

He took over the bills with the justification that since he earned the money, he should be responsible for disbursing it.

He'd leave me with very little money at my disposal at any one time. Without money, independent movement or action becomes almost impossible and requires the other person's permission and agreement for the simplest of things: a soda, diapers for a baby, or gas to see a friend. All those small decisions can be controlled by the abuser when the abuser controls the money.

Our mailbox was in a bank of many, kept locked at the main entrance. He "lost" his key so he took mine, promising to have another made to replace the missing one, but never did. By doing this he could control what mail I saw. I later found out he had kept many letters from me, using it as a means to begin cutting me off from family, friends and even financial obligations, made unknowingly, in my name. A key seems like such a small thing. Too small to fight over and something eventually even forgotten, as patterns of behavior are set. So small, and yet, when taken with all the other actions, it is yet another way to gain control.

I have always been an avid reader, but one night during a fight he became enraged that I had been reading a book while waiting for him to return home. Instead of jumping immediately up to greet him as he walked through the door, I had wanted to finish the paragraph before getting up. He snatched the book up out of my hands, then gathering the rest of my collection up, threw them all in a box and locked them in our storage unit at the back of the apartment complex, for which he had the only key. Telling me I could get them back after I learned to prioritize better.

An action he justified by calling me selfish, informing me that I had negligently put my personal pleasures ahead of my responsibilities. I had been completely self-centered by continuing to read when I should have been making dinner as a good wife would have.

Imprinting on me that I was both self-serving and a bad wife. The books were taken, he said, not to punish me, but to teach me a lesson about responsibility and how to care for my family selflessly.

He slowly began to center my world on him, shifting my attention solely to his needs and wants, while I disregarded mine in an effort to keep the peace. Each time he pushed too hard, hurt me too much, causing me to consider leaving, he would cry, beg for my forgiveness, making promises he would never do anything like that again. During those times, there would be flowers, small gifts, nice dinners out and his undivided attention to making me happy, and I would relent. Forgiving him for all he had done.

He gradually began shifting the responsibility for his bad behavior onto me, with phrases like "If you didn't do these things I wouldn't have to lose my temper" or "I don't want to do these things to you, but you're making me do it" creating the belief that it was me, not him, who caused these terrible things to happen. That if only I could be a better wife, a better person, then everything would be okay and he would never do these things again.

As my world constricted, ever tightening around keeping him happy, I let go of everything else except for caring for my sons. Self-preservation made me an expert on his moods. Microscopic twitches became loud shouts to my awareness of him, causing me to jump to do anything to keep him from becoming violent. His initial rages he had before taken out on inanimate objects, then, slowly shifted toward me: a light slap to stop me; a shove to push me down, a smack on the ass to get me moving in a certain direction. Not enough to hurt me, at first, but to shock and to stop me.

It is the same method used to train a dog. When a dog does something wrong, you rub their nose in it, paddle it so it knows it has done something wrong, while speaking in a firm voice to help imprint the lesson. Do this often enough, mixing it with affection and you can train a dog, or a person, to be the perfect pet.

An abuser feels no more guilt than a dog owner does during this training, telling themselves, it is necessary, good even, to do so.

The cycle that had begun slowly began to pick up speed with the discovery of my second pregnancy. I did not realize I was pregnant until late into my fifth month. My attention, so focused on him, had not even noticed the changes within myself. He was livid that I had done this to him yet again, and began to take it out on me in ever escalating rages, the bigger I became, the more incensed he became.

He was careful to leave no marks for casual observation, but not once during this time did any person come forth and ask me, is everything okay? There was no hiding the bruises or marks from the doctor or nurses, but none ever inquired how they had come about.

Friends came tentatively forward, but never pushed when I brushed off their concerns.

I'd once been an outgoing, gregarious person, with a ready smile. But as I withdrew, I became silent, passive, an automaton who merely looked human.

As my friend's cautious inquiries and veiled offers of help were rebuffed, they withdrew and became helpless onlookers to my destruction. They knew something was wrong, but were hesitant to intrude where they might not be welcome. They feared if they pushed too hard, I would reject the limited contact I had left, leaving me completely alone.

After the birth of my second child, a son born too early and in need of a great amount of care, I broke completely. Whatever I had been before was gone. My world now centered on keeping Nev happy and my sons alive. They became hostages to my good behavior, everything I did was to ensure their continued survival in the increasingly hostile environment we all shared. Nev, at least, claimed to care about me, and in some way, I suppose he did. He had put a great deal of effort into shaping me into his perfect woman, but he had no such similar feelings for his sons. They were an inconvenience, only useful in keeping me compliant, and kept alive only for that reason.

There was no longer any resistance left in me. Whatever he asked for, whatever he demanded, I complied with without a fight. In some ways, I think this began to upset him even more than my previous passive resistance, for there no longer was any justification for his punishments. I only spoke when spoken to, would not move or take any action without his consent, I would sit for hours without a single thought, completely blank to my own sense of self.

I slept very little in my attempts to keep my sons safe and Nev happy. I was chronically tired, sleep deprivation added to my muddled thoughts and sluggish reactions. In my lethargic state, I became even more susceptible to his influence, too tired and beaten to struggle against him any longer.

My compliance escalated his abuse, seeking some fight, some small piece of resistance to feed his need to dominate and control. Tossing me around like a broken rag doll, groping for newer, more demeaning and cruel forms of torture to elicit any kind of response from me, becoming ever more infuriated at me for my lack of response.

Only my sons would bring me out of this state, their well-being the only thing that could move me to action. I modified their waking and sleeping schedules in an attempt to keep them from any interaction with their father. He still worked third shift, so I kept my sons awake all through the night, in the hopes that they would sleep during the daylight hours when he was home and awake.

I would often wake them while he slept, keeping them quietly distracted, so as not to disturb him, but also ensuring that they would again be sleeping when he awoke later in the evening. During those times, I would take them outside and we would go for walks, swim in the pool or visit with the neighbors. All the while doing my best to project the image of a happily devoted wife and mother to anyone I encountered during those times.

All things reach an ultimate breaking point, all cycles

have their peak. A point of no return when the rag doll is no longer fun to play with. There are no longer any boundaries to push against, no challenge to stimulate, when the object of so much attention is no longer diverting or worth the effort. A time comes, in all abusive relationships when you become completely worthless to the abuser, not because you resist, but because you comply.

At this point, there is only one of two choices: you either die at their hands, or you find the will to leave. I managed both.

 ## The Event Horizon

This is the singularity which the remainder of my life has been spun from. I will live, forever and always, on the event horizon of this moment. There is no escaping it, no amount of effort or will can ever take me from it. It is darkness and damnation, light and salvation, and was the beginning of both my destruction and my creation.

My compliance became a source of frustration for Nev. He had achieved his goal of utter domination, but the enjoyment that came from the struggle was gone, and it left him feeling unsatisfied. Nev had gotten what he had wished and worked for, but now that he had it, he no longer wanted it. Without the struggle, there was no excitement in the domination, no victory in forcing my submission. Eventually, this caused an unmatched fit of disgust and anger as Nev worked himself up into a towering rage at my lack of animation. But my submission at this point was complete. No amount of shaking, punching or humiliation could rouse even a spark of life from me, pushing him to new heights unparalleled in all of our time together.

Unable or unwilling to control himself any longer, he threw me to the ground and pounced on top of me. At first, contenting himself with slaps across my face while screaming at me. Then, finding no joy or reaction from me, he slipped his hands around my neck to bang my head against the floor.

In utter abandonment of self-control, his grip tightened, bringing more and more pressure to bear, as his thumbs dug in under my chin. As the world constricted down to a pinpoint I began to struggle for air, and for life. I clawed at his hands, twisting in an attempt to break his grip and get away. My mouth gaping open but no air entered through my compressed windpipe. I was dying, and I knew it.

As my vision dimmed and darkness reached up to embrace me, I saw his face at the end of that ever lengthening tunnel that held life on the other end. Filling my vision was the image of him smiling with sublime joy and satisfaction while looking down at me. My struggle to breathe had given him what he desired most, and he was in ecstasy with my response. With that last image forever seared into my mind, nothingness claimed me for its own.

My life did not flash before my eyes, no angels appeared, I experienced only a great nothing. My only last thought was that I had failed my sons. They would be left alone in the care of a monster, and their lives might end just as suddenly, and as uselessly, as mine in a very short time. And then the world faded to blackness.

Slowly, gradually, in pieces, I became aware of some dimly remembered pain and the faint rasp of ragged breathing. I became aware that I was aware. My sight, bit by torturous bit, began to brighten enough for me to make out vague shapes. The feeling of weight descended, making me conscious of the floor I laid on and the feel of the carpet against my body. Small things snapping into place, this was alive, the rasping noise was me breathing, the weight I felt was my body, I was a person and I was alive.

Guardedly, I examined these sensations. Gathering from my mind the thousands of shattered pieces that stretched endlessly through the chasm of my brain. I'd been hurt, and groping through my thoughts, I searched for what had caused it. After what seemed like forever, I found my last image of Nev so far above me. Slowly gathering the rest of the sequence of events that had left me as I was, piecemeal at first, then gaining momentum, the entirety of my life clicked into place.

I knew then who I was: Lisa. I knew what had caused my pain: Nev. Connections were made. I was a wife, he was my husband. I was married. I was a mother. I had two young sons. They slept unaware in the next room. Hopefully, safe for the time being. I died, and now, once again I lived. I was alive. This was alive and it was painfully glorious.

I saw movement and turned my head to follow it. In a shift too quick for me to follow, Nev loomed large above me, filling the entirety of my field of vision once again. Looking down at me as he straddled my body, he smiled, softly brushing the side of my cheek. Tenderly, he spoke to me, words that will forever be etched in my soul.

"I let you live. I don't know why, but I did. I want you to remember this. From this moment on, every breath you take is a gift from me. Whatever you do from now until the moment of your death, it is nothing more than a gift I have given to you. Remember that."

Then, just as suddenly, he stood up and walked out of the room, leaving me alone to dwell on what he'd said.

And he was right. Every breath I take, each moment I experience, every choice I have made from that time forward has been a gift from him. He granted me my life back when he could just as easily have taken it for good. In some obscene, sick way I do owe him my life, and I live forever perfectly balanced between resentment and gratitude for my life.

 ## Ten Boxes

Sitting alone in the dark, my sons still asleep in the next room, I went over my life and my options. My mother made it clear when I left Quincy I was on my own, calling her was not an option I cared to pursue. There was Doug, my dearest friend in Phoenix, but I did not believe staying in the area was an option either. It was too close to Nev and he would find me if I stayed in the city. Going through everyone in my mind, discarding anyone close and all of my family, I decided I would call Ginny and Michael. Michael was stationed in Oklahoma, close enough for traveling, far enough away, hopefully, to keep Nev from following me.

Waiting until I was sure Nev was good and gone for the night, I made the call. Half asleep, Ginny answered the phone, at first not recognizing my voice. My throat was raw and bruised, speaking hurt, but I forced the words out anyway. "Ginny, it's me, Lisa."

Instinctively knowing something wasn't right, I could hear her waking Michael as she spoke into the phone, "What's wrong?"

"I have to get out of here," tears beginning to run down my face, "it's bad, really bad." These were some of the hardest words I have ever spoken. To finally admit my marriage had failed, I had failed, and I had made this horrible mistake.

"How bad?" She asked.

Swallowing hard before answering, I whispered, "He tried to kill me tonight."

"Oh my god, Lisa! We knew something was wrong, but... hang on."

I could hear her speaking to Michael, "Mike, wake up! No, wake up now, dammit!" Turning once more to the phone she said to me, "Hang on honey, let me get him awake and we'll figure something out."

I sat on the floor of my room, listening to her on the other side of the phone waking Michael up. I felt empty inside, there was only the need to get away now. To save my sons, nothing else mattered. I didn't know what I was going to do after I got away. It didn't seem important at that moment, because, if I couldn't get away, nothing else would ever matter again.

Eventually, I heard some rustling on the other end of the phone line, and Michael spoke into the phone, "Are you okay?"

"No," I replied, "I'm not okay."

"What happened?"

I didn't want to talk about it, but I knew I had to. Slowly, with many hesitations, I told him what happened, the rage, how he had choked me, how I'd lost consciousness and his last hateful words before he left.

"Damn," he said to me, then a muffled conversation I couldn't hear to Ginny, putting his hand over the phone while he talked to her.

"Damn," he said again into the phone, "I can't come get you right now Lisa. I leave in the morning for a month in the field." Feeling my heart sink with those words, a month, I couldn't wait a month.

"Okay," beginning to cry again, "I understand, sorry to have bothered you guys."

"No!" He almost yelled into the phone, then, lowering his tone, "We'll figure this out, we are going to get you out of there. Let me make a few phone calls and we'll get back to you. How long until he comes back?"

I didn't need to ask who the "he" was that Michael was referring to. "I have about six hours before he gets home from work."

"How safe will you be if he gets home before we can figure something out?"

I had to think about this one. "I really don't know," I replied, "he could be just fine when he gets home and act like nothing happened at all, but I really don't know. He's more unpredictable now, more violent, anything could set him off or nothing at all could happen."

"Okay," then more muffled talking to Ginny, "hang tight and we'll get you out of there somehow."

"Thank you," barely able to speak, "I love you guys."

"We love you too, honey," his voice breaking a bit as well as he spoke, "we really do. Just hang on a little longer."

Hanging up the phone, I tried to figure out what I was

going to do now. It had become a waiting game, and I wasn't sure how long I had to wait before it was game over.

I could hear my sons stirring in the next room. I went to them and tended to their needs, they were a distraction and a focus to keep me steady. As I changed and dressed them, I thought about everything I needed to do, but I had to wait until I knew when I was leaving. I could leave no evidence for Nev to find if I was going to attempt to escape.

He had been very clear about the consequences of trying to leave him. He would kill the boys first so I would be forced to watch them die, and then he would kill me. He had said it, in a matter of fact way, that was far more chilling than if said during a rage, if he couldn't have me, no one could. He would end my life, and our sons, before he gave me up. I had to be careful. I believed him to the depths of my soul that he would do exactly as he said he would.

Waiting for the phone to ring while I watched the minutes tick down on the clock was horrid. I wanted to leave right this minute, but I didn't have a car or any cash. I was stuck unless someone came for me.

Late into the night, while I was dozing on the couch the phone rang, startling me awake. My heart was thumping as I jumped up to answer it. It was Michael.

"Okay," rushing his words to get them all out quickly, "I know you're not going to like this but I called your mom."

"What?!" Startled he would call her.

"I'm sorry Lisa, but I didn't know what else to do," he pleaded. "I have to leave in just a few hours, I made other calls, but everyone else was like me, they can't get away and we don't have enough money to put you on a plane to get you to any of us in a hurry. Your mom has both the means and the money. She was the only thing I could think of."

"What did she say?" Afraid my mother, even knowing the situation would leave me to my fate if it interfered with her schedule.

"She'll be calling you soon," he replied, "she said she had to make a few phone calls of her own, but she would call you back within the hour."

More waiting. But I had to accept that, I didn't have any other choice. "Okay, I can wait. Thanks, Michael, for everything. If I don't get a chance again to tell you, thanks for everything."

"Hey now," trying to soothe me, "it's going to be okay,

and you'll get the chance to tell me all sorts of things. Just hang on and we'll see you again, soon. I promise."

I talked to Ginny a few minutes before we hung up, hoping that it wasn't for the last time. Checking on the boys again, I sat down next to the phone to wait.

On the first ring, I snatched the phone up off its cradle, "Hello?"

"I'll be on my way to you in five days," my mother said, "I can't get a flight any faster than that. Can you hang on until I get there?"

Five days. Could I last five days? "I don't know, but I'll try."

"Why did you wait so long before telling anyone how bad it was," she demanded, "and why didn't you call me for help?"

"Because you told me when I left for Phoenix that I was on my own."

"Oh well..." clearing her throat, "I didn't mean it for something like this!"

"How was I to know that?!" I shot back at her.

"Because I'm your mother and you should have told me."

This wasn't getting us anywhere, and my throat hurt too much to argue over whether I should have told anyone before this, or if I should have called her first. "Okay, sorry."

"Just hang in there for a few more days," she told me. "Is there anywhere you can go if you have to if things get bad?"

"Maybe," I replied, thinking to myself, I might be able to stay with Doug and his boyfriend, or maybe Richard. If I had to, I could probably hide out with one of them for a few days, "if things get bad". A horrid understatement, things were already bad, "I might have a couple of places I could go to if I had to."

"Tell Nev I'm in town for business, he'll believe that. I've done it before." Before hanging up, she gave me all of her flight details, along with the rest of the arrangements she had made before calling me. Now all I could do was wait.

Five days. Somehow I had to make it five days. I had to Keep it together, not let him suspect anything and somehow make my mother's arrival seem like just another normal business trip that put her close enough for her to come see us.

I decided I needed to call Doug next. I hated calling him so late, it was well past 2 a.m. but I needed to do it before

Nev came home in just a few short hours. I didn't think I could hide out with him safely until my mother arrived, but I wanted the option just in case.

Sleepily, he answered the phone, "Hello?" came his muffled greeting.

"Doug, it's Lisa." I knew from my other phone calls that I didn't sound like myself, my voice was lower, rougher, coarser.

"What's wrong?" Immediately sounding awake.

"I have to leave. In five days my mom will be here to get me and the boys, but if I have to find a place to hide until she gets here, could you take us in?" I hated the idea of leaving Doug, of leaving this city I'd grown to love so much, but I had to go. Staying was no longer an option.

"What did Nev do?" I could hear the anger in his voice. He had known something was wrong for a long time, but this was the first time I ever hinted at how bad it was.

I told him the story, the parts, at least, I could share, not just how bad things had gotten tonight but everything. Crying often, my throat burning, I finally poured everything out, all the secrets I'd kept hidden, some worse than others, from him.

At the end, he said, "I can be there within the hour."

As much as I wanted him to come so I didn't have to face Nev alone, or even for him to come and take us away, I couldn't. Doug's would be one of the first places for him to look for me, I would only go there if there was no other choice. Carefully, I explained all of this to him, how much his friendship had meant to me over the years, but leaving now would only put all of us in more danger. To get away, I needed to get far away.

He wasn't happy and insisted on coming by in the afternoon to check on me. Something not unusual, if no longer as frequent as it had been in the past, and I agreed that would be alright.

I spent the rest of the night dozing lightly on and off while thinking of everything I would need to do before my mother arrived. I could not call and say my goodbyes to friends or neighbors. I couldn't in any way arouse Nev's suspicions that something was not right. I had to pretend everything was as it had been, that I was beaten and without any will of my own. I could not let him see the resentment in my eyes, or my resolve to get the boys and me away from him.

I could not pack or set things aside, he was observant, often noting anything out of place or moved without his consent. I would have to keep on as I had in the past, with no deviation of behavior to make him mistrustful.

Still fitfully dozing when Nev returned home, I opened my eyes to flowers. He held them out to me with a shy smile, sitting down next to me in bed, stroking my hair and telling me how beautiful I was and how lucky he was to have me in his life. He acted as if nothing had happened. Carefully not looking at the dark, accusing swollen bruises around my neck, he gently caressed my hair and shoulders.

He was more relaxed than I'd seen him in a long time, like some kind of demon had been exorcised from him. Bending down and kissing me on my nose, he looked into my eyes and said, "I love you."

"I... I love you too." Afraid to say anything else, and yet knowing I did love him, after all the pain and torment, somehow I did still love him. It made me sad, and angry, that the person I loved could hurt me so badly and partly because of my love, I had stayed when I should have left. It was love that had, at first, made me hopeful he wouldn't hurt me again, and then later helped trap me when it didn't.

All that week he was kind to me, solicitous to my perceived needs. Often, there were flowers in the mornings, and sometimes breakfast waiting for me when I awoke. He reacted happily to the news of my mother's arrival and made small talk about going out to dinner and taking her around to a few places while she was in town.

The contrast between his current behavior and what I endured just a few nights previous couldn't be reconciled. I began to doubt my decision to leave after a few days. Maybe he really had changed this time, maybe whatever had been driving him to act as he did, was finally gone in that last act of aggression.

I found myself wanting to tell him everything. How scared I'd been. How I was planning on leaving town, but if he'd finally put to rest that part of him, I would stay. Tell him how much I loved him and wanted to make things work.

But the same instincts that had been so carefully honed during the bad times, caused me to cautiously wait and watch. There were small hesitations before he smiled, a quick tightening around the eyes when he talked about my mother's visit. A slight downward pull to his lips when he said, "I love you." Small, so very small were these indicators, but there.

I wanted to ignore them. I wanted to go on pretending everything was as it should be. That we were happily married, with no dark secrets. But, the same survival instincts that had helped navigate me through the wreckage of our lives together couldn't be ignored now.

With misgivings, I awaited my mother's arrival. The dark bruises that covered my neck were faded to a sickly green by the end of those five days, but by no means gone. As my mother greeted me at the door, she darted a quick glance at them but said nothing, for which I was grateful with Nev watching us from the couch.

He had the night off and planned to spend it with us. He and my mother had never been close, there had always been a distance between the two of them and, this time was no different. My mother may have been a bit cooler, and Nev a bit more stiff, while each pretending they were thrilled to see each other. I only hoped my mother could keep her mouth closed and not say anything to get him suspicious of her visit.

It was an odd 24 hours. On the surface, there was light conversation, talk of the boys and how much they had grown. My mother's travels for business and what had brought her to our area for a few days. Nev was congenial, smiled often, told funny stories, and feigned interest in both the boys and my mother. Whenever either of them looked at me, I would smile, nodding at whatever was said, but mostly doing my best to fade into the background where no one would notice me.

The tension of waiting was wearing on me. I felt equally compelled to hurry up and leave as soon as possible while at the same time wanting to stay and pretend none of this was happening.

Eventually, it all came to an end when Nev left for work the following night. As soon as he was out the door my mother was a whirlwind of activity. She ran to her rental car and removed packing boxes and tape she had stored there before coming to the apartment the day before. Randomly grabbing items and throwing them in boxes until they were full, then immediately starting on another box. As she filled the boxes, I readied the boys for our departure.

As the boxes were filled, she took them out to the car and

# IT'LL FEEL BETTER WHEN IT QUITS HURTING

when it was full she would drive off to a 24-hour mailing shop. Returning to fill up yet more boxes until all ten had been filled and shipped. Her suspiciously light suitcases she insisted on bringing in herself, were opened to receive odds and ends of clothing and other necessities for the boys and me until the rest of our things arrived in Quincy.

As the last item was added and the suitcases zipped closed, I had both the boys dressed and waiting at the door. The entire process had taken less than two hours all told. I had fearfully worried the entire time that Nev would suddenly arrive for no good reason as he sometimes randomly did. But this time, thankfully, there was no sign of him.

I stood in the doorway and sadly looked around my home for the last time. There were few signs of my departure, only a few small empty spaces here and there. I saw how little impact my impending departure had caused, almost as if I had not existed there at all. In my bedroom upstairs, most of my clothes still hung undisturbed in the closet. The knickknacks and paintings that decorated my home still remained, untouched, as Nev had ordered them placed. Many treasured personal items were left behind in my mother's haste in packing without my supervision while I'd been caring for the boys. To be found out later as I unpacked the boxes, much to my sorrow. I felt tears beginning to form in my eyes as I said my last goodbyes to this part of my life forever.

Silently, with regret, I shut the door behind me.

 ## An Infomercial Changed my Life

I settled into my new life in bits and pieces. At first staying with my mother, a month later with my friend LeeAnn and her husband. After a few months, I moved into an apartment of my own.

In fits and starts, I tried to adapt to this new life as a single mother, as an individual, and not doing a very good job of it. I reconnected with a few of the friends who had stayed behind in Quincy. But I'd changed so dramatically that the close ties I'd once had with them, were now strained and stilted. And in my case, the phrase, "it's not you, it's me" was quite literally true.

During this time I worked at several different fast food places, enrolled in college, and tried to build a life for my sons, all the while groping endlessly to fit in.

I'd forgotten in my time with Nev, how to laugh, how to interact with people, how to make decisions on my own. Making a menu choice could make me break out into a cold sweat. I would often retreat into myself when there were large groups of people around, be they close family or in a public place. I continually scanned for exits when I went anywhere and positioned myself in any room with my back to the wall so I could watch every person and no one could sneak up on me.

I could barely tolerate physical contact. Forcing myself to accept hugs and other small physical gestures, but people could sense the reluctance no matter how hard I tried to hide it. It isolated me from the warm companionship that I'd had so easily before in my life and I missed it desperately.

I went to a counselor a few times, but found her almost completely useless. Now, I would have been diagnosed with post-traumatic stress disorder, PTSD, but back then they called it depression, anxiety, or battered woman's syndrome. I was told I should just forget about it, move on, go back to the familiar and try to pick my life up from where it was before the abuse had started. But I had changed, my world had changed too much to go back to how I'd been before. I didn't even know who that person was anymore.

Running into old friends often opened the barely healed scars, most conversations starting off with "What have you been up to?". I didn't want to talk about what had happened or what had brought me back to town, adding to my discomfort around old friends.

I spent most of my time alone or with my sons, continuing unconsciously the isolation that had once been imposed by Nev. I clung to habits that kept me moderately safe before but probably made me look like either an idiot or crazy to those around me. If I was to be completely honest, I was quite nuts at this point. Functional, but nuts.

I cried a lot. Missing my old life, missing Nev, and then hating myself for it. As hard as I was trying to get my life in order, it was just as quickly spiraling out of control as I sunk deeper into depression and self-loathing. I suffered from severe insomnia, often staying awake for days at a time, further adding to my mental distress.

During one of these bouts of insomnia, while lying awake on my couch staring at my small black & white TV, unable to sleep no matter how tired I felt, and resigned to yet another night of listless wakefulness. As the night went on, the programming turned to infomercials without me really paying attention to what was on. With only two channels to choose from, it really didn't matter anyway. Mostly, I just wanted the company of sound in the quiet of the night.

As I aimlessly watched, a bright, happy woman came on, staring straight out of the screen, talking about her fitness program and how great it was. She gleefully droned on for a while about the wonders of her program, then she paused. Looking straight at the camera, she said, "After my divorce, all I did was sit on my couch, cry, eat ice cream and plot my husband's death." Sitting up, she had my full attention. She could have been talking directly to me with those words, "And then one day, I decided I was either going to spend the rest of my life letting his memory control my life, making me miserable, or I could get up and do something about it." And she was right, I needed to get up and do something about it. I didn't want to sit miserable on my couch anymore, cry and plot Nev's death.

I don't know why this fitness-happy woman connected so much for me. Or why her words motivated me when everything else had left me unmoved. Maybe it was her cheerful smile as she talked about her husband's demise. Maybe it was her bright, confident attitude as she talked about changing her life for the better. Or maybe it was her gleeful happiness about how much she hated her ex. But, whatever it was, it changed my life.

In the middle of the night, I had an epiphany. I could spend the rest of my life miserable or I could do something about it. I didn't have to sit around waiting for time to heal all wounds. I didn't have to go back to being the person I used to be. I could change the course of my life instead of waiting for life to change me.

I didn't know exactly what do to, but I did know what I didn't want to do anymore. This was not the life I wanted, this was not the life I wanted for my sons. I needed to change. I couldn't go back to the person I was, that person was a stranger to me now, and I wasn't even sure if I liked the person I had been. I didn't know who I was going to be, yet, but I was not going to be as I had been before. I didn't want to be just another victim, living scared and hiding from the world for the rest of my life.

And so, I set out to change my life. Real change isn't easy, it's hard and it comes slowly, and it is done only with a great deal of effort. It is taken in small steps, done methodically, carefully and with a lot of mistakes made along the way. I realized during this time most people don't truly know who they are. I didn't when I began this process.

It's hard to know where to start. You can't just throw in all the pieces any which way and hope for the best. So I began by watching people, learning from them, using the skills I'd honed from years of watching and deciphering Nev's moods and mannerisms, then imitating traits I found useful or appealing. I went through my personality, figuring out the things I liked about myself and more importantly, what I didn't.

I started slipping on persona's like a shopaholic does clothes, looking for the perfect combination. It was a tedious process, and to outsiders, I probably resembled someone with a multiple personality disorder. It would have been funny if I'd had the time to notice in the beginning. Instead, I focused on forcing the changes I wanted to make, no matter how awkward it felt at the start. Faking it until I was making it.

I had to teach myself how to laugh and smile again, and then how to tell a good joke with feeling. I forced myself to feign relaxation around people and practiced spontaneous hugs and other forms of casual affection without cringing away. When scanning a room, I learned to do so in a natural way that wouldn't cause comment from those around me. While I would sometimes be teased about having eyes in the back of my head, I learned to laugh it off without arousing curiosity.

Not all the changes were internal. I began changing the way I held myself, taking on more masculine stances in the way I walked and carried myself. Talking more with my hands, making big gestures, looking at people directly, while trying to take up as much physical space as I could without being obvious about it. I wanted to give the impression that I had an open, gregarious personality, someone people would like to know without needing to look too far beyond the surface.

I cultivated traits I admired: honesty, loyalty, empathy, and fairness, then built around them an ethical code of conduct for dealing with people around me.

With time, I became the person I wanted to be, strong, confident, powerful. When I was told in all seriousness, "You are a force to be reckoned with" I knew I had finally achieved what I had set out to do. As each of these traits became natural, I knew I had finally made it, after all the years of faking it. It had taken me most of my life to become the person I am now, it was not easy, but it was worth it.

I did not sit in a corner waiting for life to end, but went out and lived. I made mistakes, some truly grand ones on occasion, but I learned from them and never let it stop me. I learned to love again, to laugh again, to be happy with myself, to accept what had happened. To accept the consequences of my actions, whether they were good or bad.

I choose to live my life with joy, not dwell in the negative, to embrace every experience that was offered to me. In my life, I have traveled, climbed pyramids, swam with dolphins, played in the ocean, drank with the Aussies and stared up at the stars from the middle of the ocean. I have eaten questionable food from street vendors in foreign countries, laughed with strangers, and made new friends from almost every part of the world, if only for a brief time. I have slow danced in a parking lot at midnight, sang loudly to music while shopping at a store, I have fearlessly gone out into the world with a smile on my face and a song in my heart without a moment of regret.

I have loved unconditionally, even recklessly, because each time it taught me something new, both about life and myself. I learned I can have an open heart, and even if it hurts at times, know that I will live through it. I often have a hard time expressing it, but it is there. Love for those around me and for those now far away, love big enough to include anyone who is worthy of it. Life is too short to be stingy.

I took the lessons I learned and have tried to use them to make the world a better place, not just for myself but for others. I realized that at some time in everyone's life they may need a second chance. A hand up when the world has pushed them down, and that I could be that person. I cannot change the world, but I can change the world for a single person, and I can hope that they will do the same later on.

And, I accept that I am and will always be, a broken vase held together with Elmer's glue. I am not perfect. I still have some interesting quirks and anomalies that set me apart. Some I work on, and some I have simply come to accept and work around. I am now, and will always be, a work in progress and I'm okay with that.

I am sometimes asked if I could go back and change what happened to me, would I do it? The answer is always no, which usually confuses the person. Why wouldn't you want to? My answer is, I would never want to live through what happened to me again, but to change that, would be to change everything about who I am. It would change every aspect of my life and I would not be the person I am now, and I like this person.

I know exactly who I am, the good, the bad and the indifferent. I am fully aware of why I am the way I am, I question and I reflect before I act, and take full responsibility for whatever consequences those actions caused. I am a force to be reckoned with, securely aware of both my strengths and weaknesses. And I do not know if I would be any of those things if it wasn't for what happened.

My mother taught me to love chaos, to embrace the joy of the moment and accept the oddity that is living. My father taught me to accept the universe as it is, not how I would wish it to be, and to never take it personally. Eula taught me to accept people as they were and to never hold their past against them, to take in those in need of help and to love them while they were with me. And Nev taught me that I am a survivor. That even the most terrible things can bring about something worth living for, something worth striving for, to be more than I had been before.

This is my life, for better or for worse, and I would not change a single line.

# IT'LL FEEL BETTER WHEN IT QUITS HURTING

## Epilogue

*God one day decided too many people were getting into heaven, so he went to St. Peter and said, "From now on, only the ones with a good story can get in."*

*Peter shrugged his shoulders and agreed. Turning to the next guy in line, he says, "What brings you here?"*

*The guy responds, "For months I was sure my wife was cheating on me, so today I went home early to catch her. When I opened the door I found her standing naked, but alone, in the kitchen. I searched and searched but found no one. After all the running around, I became so overheated, I went to the window for some air and found a guy hanging naked from the windowsill! I started beating on his hands, and screaming at him, causing him to fall. But somehow, he landed in the bushes below unharmed. In my rage, I ran to my refrigerator and threw it out the window at him, but the exertion caused me to have a heart attack and I died."*

*"Okay," said Peter, "go on in."*

*The next guy walks up and Peter says, "What's your story?"*

*He responds, "Every day at noon I exercise naked in my apartment, but today I got a little carried away and tripped out my window. I somehow managed to grab the windowsill of the apartment below me when this crazy man sticks his head out of the window and starts beating on my hands and screaming until I fell.*

*Luckily I landed in some bushes unhurt, but then a refrigerator fell on me and I died, and now here I am."*

*Peter, now chuckling to himself, waves him through. "Next!"*

*"How did you get here?" he asked.*

*Standing with his arms spread wide the guy says, "Okay, picture this...I'm naked, in a refrigerator...."*

That's who I want to be, the naked guy standing before St. Peter with this great tale to tell of how I got there. I want to tell him the story of my tragic life and have tears rolling down his face in laughter, shaking his head in stunned amazement, waving me in.

I want my life to be well lived, a roller coaster of ups and downs, screaming in fear and joy while it's happening. I want to laugh at myself and at the absurdity of life. I want to spread my arms wide and say "Okay, picture this," with a smile on my face while spinning a tale of some misadventure I have found myself in.

Over the years, I have wondered if Marvin tells the story of his lost pants and the girls that tormented him one night. Or if Brian thinks about the stranger who appeared on his doorstep, sent by his mother. I wonder if Shawn ever thinks about me and tells jokes at my expense. And if the Navy buddies ever share a beer and talk about the girls they met on the road on their way to start a new life.

I'd like to think somewhere in the world, I am part of their stories and they laugh about it as much as I do. I hope that I am.

I am grateful for the friends I've had over the years, some still in my life, others lost as the years have gone on. I hope someday they will find my books and smile when they read their stories and know I have never forgotten about them.

My life did not end up where I thought I would be when I was young and was asked what do you want to be when you grow up.

I know the answer now, when I grow up, I want to be happy. I still haven't grown up, but I have learned to be happy, and maybe someday I will figure out the rest. Until then, I will continue to stumble along, laughing at myself and at my mistakes. Learning from them and sharing them with others.

I have more stories to tell, none as dark as those told in this book, but I hope you will read them as well. And, I hope when you do, you can see me standing before you with a wicked smile on my face, giggling as I tell it, arms open wide...

**If you enjoyed this book, please consider taking a moment to leave a review on GoodReads.**

You can use this QR code to take you directly to the GoodReads page.

If you are being abused by your partner,
know there is nothing you have done or are doing
to cause the abuse.
It is solely the choice of the abuser to abuse.
It may seem impossible to escape your abuser,
change your circumstances,
or find the help you need, but it is possible.
However, you know your abuser best,
so think carefully through your situation
and circumstances and do what is
the best for you.

## You are not alone

If you are in immediate danger
please call 911

For anonymous, confidential help 24/7 call
The National Domestic Violence Hotline
1-800-779-7233(SAFE) or
1-800-787-3224(TTY)

Or you can visit NCADV
online at: http://www.ncadv.org/

## *Author's Note about the Title

The title for this book came from my Grandpa Bob, it was his favorite phrase. It could be considered the family motto if we had one, passed along for three generations now. And I doubt it will stop with my children since I've heard them utter this phrase multiple times to their friends.

When I was young it was applied to boo-boo's and the small scrapes that come from growing up and falling down often. Growing up it became the phrase I began to apply to my entire life. It may be the truest statement ever made because it will always feel better when it quits hurting. You may carry the scars of it, whether physical or emotional, but in time, all things heal, and eventually, the pain will fade away, and you'll realize, "I'm okay, I do feel better."

My Grandpa died in his early 60's of cancer, my two oldest were too young then to remember him now. And sadly, my youngest three never had the chance to get to know him. But his legacy and his words live on through all of us, his descendants, and now I pass them along to you. It will feel better when it quits hurting...

...I promise.

To my Dad,
And to the Xanax he took
that allowed us to have a relationship
that wasn't possible when I was growing up.
I'm glad we got to know each other.


And to
David Flentjie
You were my first love,
my co-conspirator in mischief,
& you changed the course of my life more than once.
I will miss you forever & always dear friend.

*You can be right,*

*or you can be in a relationship*

*and by god...
I'm gonna be right!*

## *I want to be the Madame of a House of Ill-Repute*

When I was twelve, my English teacher gave us the assignment to write about what we wanted to be when we grew up, as I'm sure many of you were given in high school. But of all the papers I wrote as a child, this is the one that stands out in my memory. I'm an adult now and a mother of five, I no longer have the paper I wrote from that far away time, but I do remember the title, and that for one perfect moment in my life I knew exactly what I wanted to be.

I didn't actually know per se what a Madame was, or what it meant to live that kind of life, but I did know it involved pretty dresses, expensive houses, and gentleman callers, not that I knew what a gentleman caller was either, other than someone who brought flowers and money. Since most of my knowledge of what a Madame was came from the endless Spaghetti Westerns my father watched on TV, it's easy to see how I formed a somewhat skewed view of what it really meant.

It was the most glamorous career I could think of at the age of twelve when the world felt awkward and so did I. Boys were mean, we were no longer young enough for the playground, but not old enough to date, and we all lived in a horrible never-never land of not quite. To be a Madame was to be the pinnacle of adulthood with all the glamour, power, beauty, and grace that can only be sustained in the mind of a child. Why would anyone want to do anything else, if a career such as this existed? Now that I am older I can look back at that childish image and smile, but at one time this was what I wanted to be more than anything else.

I am an adult now, and I didn't grow up to be a Madame of a house of ill-repute, in my life I most often resemble the ringleader in a madhouse of anarchy. But sometimes, I wistfully remember the longing for flowers, gentleman callers, and the enchantment I think all of us have had at one time or another, whatever your childhood ideal of adult life might have been.

My life did not turn out as I thought it would when I was young, nor did it even turn out as I had hoped when I was a young adult. I lived through my parents' divorce, and their subsequent ones after that. I lived through foster care and after moving out on my own, an abusive marriage. But, over the course of my life, I've learned many things, about myself, and about life, and I believe it made me a better person, for all the pain and confusion that came with the lessons.

I learned to laugh, to love and to live my life joyfully. I learned I am a survivor, and for all the mistakes I made along the way, every one of them was worth it in the end. My life is not glamorous, it is often messy, confusing and running just this side of chaos theory, with the occasional surprise thrown in. But, looking back on my life, I realize by and large it has been a helluva ride I wouldn't exchange for anything.

In this book, I am a bit more cynical, a bit meaner, and a lot happier than in my last. Within these pages are my stories of rebuilding my life after escaping an abusive relationship and my numerous disastrous attempts at finding love, yet even so, I've never let it stop me from trying one more time to get it right. I learned I could love unconditionally, even recklessly, and I learned I could have an open heart, and even if it hurts at times, know I will live through it.

This is, in the end, a love story. You will not find any knights in shining armor, heroic rescues, or even a happily ever after at the end. It's going to get messy and nothing will be wrapped up in a neat little bow. Instead, you'll find confusion, sacrifice, poor choices, and heartbreak, along with those moments of happiness, contentment, and joy that makes it all worth the risk. It's about raising children, going to work and going on vacations, and doing the household chores with someone you love (or don't). It's about small moments that build up into life changing events. It's about making mistakes and learning from them. It's about reaching out to another human being and hoping you'll find your soul mate when you do. This is my love story, but I think you may find a bit of your story here too somewhere within these pages.

So, take my hand and we can begin this journey together...

### *Hitting the Reset Button*

On a cold, blustery February day, I found myself back in my hometown, broke, broken, alone and confused. In a daring escape, like something out of an old war movie, my mother came to Phoenix and liberated me from my husband.

In the dead of night, we packed up ten boxes and two suitcases, slipping away quiet as death, to board a plane early the next morning.

In Phoenix, where I had lived for three years, it was warm. Warm enough, that just the day before, I went swimming in the pool outside our apartment with my two sons. Stepping off the plane in the Midwest, it was cold, snowing and miserable. My boys had never seen snow in their young lives, and they were not impressed, loudly crying their objections to the entire situation. Shivering and blue, my mother hustled us into the terminal, and after claiming our baggage, out to her awaiting car.

It was a system shock for my sons, and even for me. I'd grown up in the Midwest, but after so many years of dry, desert heat, I was no more adapted to the cold than they were. Huddled down in the car, shivering in my thin coat, my mother blasted the heater to try to make us comfortable. But for most of the two-hour drive back to Quincy, the boys cried with the unfamiliar feeling of cold, and I was too emotionally and physically exhausted to do much more than tremble in the front seat. Both from the cold, and fear of the unknown, staring back at me.

I had no idea what I was going to do with my life. My only thought had been to run away, to flee while there was still time. Now that I had successfully escaped my former life, I had no idea what to do with the rest of it. I was completely broke. I did not, literally, have a dime to my name. Nev had not allowed me to touch any of our money in over two years. I did not have access to any of our accounts, credit cards or even loose change, ensuring that if I wanted or needed anything, I had to ask his permission to do so.

I lost almost everything in my escape. Taking only a few items we managed to salvage before leaving, packed into the ten boxes my mother mailed before our flight, to arrive sometime later in the week. Along with a few other miscellaneous necessities, stuffed into two suitcases, and taken with us on our flight, most of the space taken up with items I would need for the boys, and almost no space left over for me.

It was daunting.

And I was scared.

I had no idea what I was going to do. How I was going to live. What to even do with myself. For three years I had gradually given up almost any kind of independent thought, and now, suddenly, I was going to have to go it completely alone. I was terrified. What if I messed up? What if I made the wrong choice? How was I going to support myself and my two sons? What was I going to do?

I had absolutely no idea.

Staring out the window, watching the snow fall, shivering with the cold, and fear, I closed my eyes and silently cried for my lost life. For the friends I left behind, for the loss of my marriage, for everything that was lost in my mad dash to get away.

Staying with my mother and her newest husband, I quickly realized I needed to find somewhere else to live. Moving away from her home when I was 15, it was hard being a child in her house again after so many years of being an adult. Not a well-functioning adult of late, but still, an adult. I needed a place where I could start becoming what I had lost after years of dependence and abuse. With my mother, I would always be her child and treated as such. As much as she loved me, and was trying to help me, it was the last thing I needed if I was to become a functional human being again.

Although many of my friends from high school moved on to other places after graduation, my friend LeeAnn and her husband had returned to Quincy before my arrival. The local university offered her a full scholarship to continue her education, and they happily moved back to town after accepting it. Initially staying in campus housing, they decided after a year of cramped living in the dorms, to try to find a new place off campus with more room for the two of them.

Sharing the news with me that they were looking for an apartment, they asked if I would like to join them. With barely a hesitation, I jumped at the chance to get out of my mother's house. Joining them in their search, we eventually found a two-bedroom apartment, not far from the university, at a price we could afford. Within two days of signing the lease, I moved from my mother's into a new sort of life.

I still didn't have a job and almost no hope of getting any support from Nev. I was still broke and dependent, but living with LeeAnn and Vern, at least, gave me a chance to try to figure out what to do with my life. Putting my life through the filter of reality, I knew my future was bleak if I did nothing. My education had stopped at graduating from high school, and Nev hadn't let me keep a job for any length of time while I lived in Phoenix, making my work history spotty at best, and a less than enticing employee for most employers. I needed to make changes to my life; I just didn't know where to begin, yet. But, moving in with LeeAnn gave me some breathing room to try, and that was more than I had before.

It was time to begin again.

## *To Suffer in Silence*

Returning to Quincy, I kept a low profile. While there was comfort in the familiar, with family and friends to support me, there was also Nev's family nearby. I didn't want him to know where I lived or want any contact with Nev, partly out of fear I would break down and go back to him. I knew I wasn't strong enough yet to confront him, not yet. Knowing that I asked my family and friends not to share with his family where I might be living or give them any information, for now.

Learning of my arrival from her son, almost as quickly as I stepped into town, Pat began contacting my family to advocate for her son and my return to Phoenix. At first, I objected to meeting with her, but after several months of persistent harassment, his mother finally managed to persuade me to change my mind. With a lot of misgivings, I conceded to her demands and agreed to meet with her in a public space.

Arriving alone, I found her sitting at a table, staring out the window. Pausing a moment, I glanced down at her, "Hello Pat."

Sliding into the booth, we faced each other in uncomfortable silence. We had never gotten along. During the entire length of my relationship with her son, never once, did she call me by name, always referring to me as "That Woman." Nev's parents came from money, while my parents were often poor when I was young, only occasionally middle class, and she saw me as an anchor to her son's life. I saw her as a mean, meddling bitch who, not once, had a nice thing to say about me or her grandsons in three years. We did not like each other, at all.

Gazing coldly at each other, she eventually asked, "How have you been?"

Shrugging my shoulders, "Okay, I guess."

"How long do you plan on staying in Quincy, keeping my grandsons away from their father before you return?"

I didn't know how to respond to that. I had no plans of going back, ever. Slowly, pausing often, I described the downward spiral of my marriage to her. About the abuse, the bruises, how Nev controlled every aspect of my life, from what I ate to how I dressed, never allowing me to have money or able to move around freely towards the end.

Watching me, not with concern or compassion, but with growing confusion, shaking her head often at my words. But she did, at least, allow me to continue without interruption. When at last I came to a stumbling halt, not sure what else to say, she locked eyes with me, "It is a woman's place to suffer in silence for her man."

"Huh?" Caught completely off-guard by her statement.

Sighing, as if trying to explain something to a difficult two-year-old, she began again, "It is only right that we suffer for our men. They are the head of the family, it is up to them to maintain discipline and order. If we, by being weak, need to be corrected by our husbands for our failures, that is their right."

In disbelief, I blurted out, "You're kidding me, right?"

"No."

I looked this woman over, as if for the first time. She was not uneducated, she had a Ph.D. She had been successful during her life, with a well-paying career, only recently retired. She was not poor, both she and her husband had made a respectable amount of money in their lifetimes. I had no idea what to say to her statements. They were jarring, rolling around, echoing in my head as I sat in stunned amazement, looking at her.

"I'm sorry Pat." Quietly sitting back in the booth to put as much physical space between us as I could without leaving the table. "I can't do that. If I go back, he will kill me. Maybe not right away, but it will happen. I will not suffer in silence for him, not anymore. I will not be going back. Ever."

"But you have to. He's your husband."

"Not for much longer." Sighing, I shook my head. Listening to her was like having cold water splashed on my face. I realized that for him, what he had done to me was normal, expected, and completely acceptable, he learned it at his mother's knee, so to speak. There was no saving him, or our relationship. All I could do at this point was to try to save myself.

Pushing myself up from the booth, I stared down at her, "I won't be going back. Don't ask me again. You can be a part of your grandsons' lives, but not unsupervised. If you want to see them, I will bring them to you, at a park or a public place, but you will not do to my sons what you allowed to be done to yours."

"You can't do that!" Pushing her way up from the booth to stand before me.

"Yes. I can. And I am." Turning to walk away, I glanced back at her one more time, still standing in front of the booth, "I'm sorry it has to be this way. Tell Nev when you talk to him next, I won't be coming back. Don't look for me. Don't try to contact me. It's over."

Pushing open the door, I stepped out into the sunlight. Looking up at the sky, I felt its warmth on my face, and a small weight lifted from my heart. And I realized, it was only now that I had honestly decided to leave Nev. It had not been back in Phoenix, scared for my life. Or on my return home. Or even as I, haltingly, began making plans for my life once I moved in with LeeAnn and Vern. But there, standing in the sunlight, I let go of all my secret hopes of salvaging my marriage and returning to my life back in Phoenix. With a lighter step, I went home, to truly begin my new life.

## *A Memory Returns*

"Lisa!" Turning to the sound of my name I saw a face, once dearly loved and never forgotten.

"Billy?" A little flustered at seeing him again after all these years. It was not a pretty breakup, leaving me devastated and changing the course of my life.

"Hey! It's good to see you." A huge grin plastered across his face as he jogged over to me. "How have you been?"

"Not too bad. I stopped by your Mom's a few months ago for a visit, letting her know I moved back to town. She said you were in Germany."

"Yeah, I'm only back on leave before they send me to Panama next." Reaching out to give me a hug, "She said you were back but didn't know where you were living now."

Stepping back away from his embrace, I looked him over. He looked good, fit and strong, and I felt the old pull towards him.

"I heard things didn't work out with Ali." Wanting to dig at him a bit. She was the reason for our break up all those years ago. I would never forget that phone call, how much it hurt, telling me he was ending our engagement, breaking the news badly that he had just gotten married an hour before because he had gotten her pregnant.

Looking uncomfortable, he stared down at his feet shuffling around on their own below him. Giving me a half shrug, "Yeah... I was stupid."

"Yes, you were."

"What about you and Nev? I heard you left him earlier this year and came back home."

Still not comfortable talking about Nev, I tensed, then replied, "It didn't work out."

Watching him cast about for something to say, he eventually asked, "You want to go out for dinner sometime with me?"

"I... uh," I wasn't sure what to say to that, equally torn between wanting to say yes, while simultaneously wanting to scream in his face to get away from me. It was a dilemma. So instead, I stood there like an idiot, staring down at my feet.

Gently reaching out, he lifted my chin and looking me in the eyes, "It's just dinner Lisa, not the end of the world. Say yes, and we'll go wherever you want."

Looking at him, seeing his smile that had always managed to convince me to agree to things I knew I shouldn't, I gave in to him and nodded my agreement.

Giving him my address, we set up a date only days away and started a whirlwind that lasted until he left for Panama three weeks later. Falling back into old patterns, he came by my house almost every day. We went out for lunches and dinners, drove around in his car and spent quiet time watching movies on my couch. We took the boys to the park, and he rolled around with them on the floor while I watched him, always with a smile on his face. We went out to his parent's house for dinner, and once, took a trip north to visit his ex-wife and two children. To my surprise, and maybe even hers, we got along and had a wonderful weekend together.

The last week of his visit was a sad/happy time. He came

over every day, stayed every night and talked for hours about our lives, our mistakes and how much he had missed me after all this time. But as time slipped by, Billy started to push for us to resume our relationship where we left off. He wanted us to get married as soon as I divorced Nev, and move down to Panama with him. And I wasn't ready. Not for the intensity of the relationship or to be married almost as quickly as I was divorced, and most definitely not to move to a foreign country surrounded by people I didn't know. Hell, I failed my Sophomore year of Spanish! After a year of classes, I couldn't say more than "please," "thank you," and ask for the time. I did not have the gift for languages that Billy did.

Even so, before he left, with my heart pounding and a sinking feeling in the pit of my stomach, I found myself agreeing to an engagement. I had many ambivalent feelings about it, but even after all of these years, I never stopped loving Billy and loved his family just as much. Maybe this was the second chance I was looking for, and just too afraid to realize it. Or last least, that's what I kept telling myself.

With Billy gone, I started spending more time with his family. Laura had never been happy with his marriage to Ali, and losing me as a daughter-in-law had been a large part of it. But with Billy and I back together, Laura and I could resume our interrupted relationship. Years before, I hadn't wanted to put Laura in an awkward situation between Billy and me, and so reluctantly, I distanced myself from his family. But now, with our renewed relationship, I was warmly welcomed back as part of the family. Something I'd very much missed.

Once Billy was settled in Panama, he began calling me once a week, but we were only able to talk for a few short minutes at a time. Wanting to share with me everything going on his life down there, he sent long letters arriving in my mailbox every few days filled with pictures and lists of things we would do together as soon as we got married. He told me of the beaches he'd been to, the people he'd met, and all the things he wanted to share with me as his excitement grew with each passing day. Everyone seemed happy about the situation, except me.

Because I knew, marrying Billy meant an end to all the things I'd been working towards, or at least, they would have to be put on hold. My plans to attend college in the fall, something I had dreamt of for so long, would once again have to wait. My independence, something I treasured even as I groped for it, would have to be set aside in the new reality of "we." Like mist slipping through my fingers, I was once again losing myself in someone else's life. My resentment grew with the realization of everything I would have to give up to be with him. I wasn't ready for this, any of it. I had barely begun to rebuild my life, and now I was being asked to give it all away. To lose me, yet again, to become a we.

I loved him. I had never stopped. But I wasn't ready. I wasn't ready to date again, much less go to the whole "until death do us part" section of a relationship. I still hadn't gotten the hang of ordering for myself from a menu or learning how to do all the thousands of small independent things adults do every day without thinking. I still constantly reminded myself not to flinch when touched, and most importantly, I had not yet learned to say "No."

Because I knew I said yes to Billy because I couldn't say no. Not to him, not to anyone. And that was not a good enough reason to get married. I may have loved him, and he may have loved me, but fear of saying no to someone wasn't a good enough reason to commit my life to him. But, I couldn't express it in words.

Becoming restless and beginning to dread his phone calls, I stopped smiling when the phone rang as my anxiety grew a little more every day. I didn't want to confront him with my fears, yet I knew I should. I waffled back and forth in an endless agony of indecision, unable, or unwilling, to stand up for myself against his enthusiasm. So instead, I took the coward's way out.

Picking a night I knew Billy would be calling; I brought someone else into my bed. Afterward, I stared up at the ceiling, knowing the phone would ring at any time. The guy next to me innocently unaware of the trouble he was about to cause, babbled on about something. I let the rhythm of his voice lull me without paying attention to the shape of his words as I waited.

When the phone rang, I reached out to answer it, hearing Billy's familiar voice. "Hey baby, how's it going?"

"I'm a little busy now. I have company." Hearing this, the poor innocent sap next to me asked, "Who are you talking to?"

Hearing his voice, from a thousand miles away, Billy

echoed, "Who's that?!"

"I brought a friend home, I was lonely," ignoring Sap.

"I see..." came his slow response, "anyone I know?"

Shaking my head in the dark, I quietly answered, "No."

"Lisa, is there something you want to tell me?" Feeling the floodgates of emotion open at his question, I couldn't, at first, say anything. I had tried telling him this since we first saw each other, I wasn't ready. I couldn't be ready. I needed more time, more space to get to know this new person I was becoming, I couldn't explore a new relationship with the old one still hanging around inside my head. I couldn't give myself to someone else when I didn't even know who I was yet.

But I couldn't speak any of those words. None of them. Instead, I said, "I slept with someone else tonight. I'm sorry."

"I see." Came his terse response. He didn't, but that was okay. "I guess I will talk to you later then." Hanging up the phone before I could say anything else.

With equal parts sadness and relief, I hung up the phone. Looking over at Sap, he asked, "Who was that?"

"No one, just my ex-boyfriend."

## *I just buy 'em a House*

Sitting outside the courthouse waiting to go in to finalize my divorce, Tom Petty's "*Yer so bad*" came on the radio, bringing a small smile to my face as I listened to the words while I screwed up my courage. With the last strains of the song playing, I squared my shoulders and prepared for my day in court.

A divorce is never easy. It's harder if you are 21 years old and escaping an abusive husband. Worse still is standing up in a room full of strangers and forced to speak words you never wanted to share, to justify the ending of a marriage that had lasted less than three years. Mercifully, my soon to be ex-husband was not there, and after only a brief consultation, the judge granted me my freedom.

Walking away from the courtroom my mother turned to me, and said, "I need a drink." And I couldn't have agreed with her more.

My mother chose a bar near the river, a favorite drinking spot of hers from years ago. It was an older one, perpetually dim even with the morning light shining brightly outside its

# IT'LL FEEL BETTER WHEN IT QUITS HURTING

windows. A smoky haven for the dedicated drinkers, third shift workers, and us.

Walking through the door, I immediately knew we looked out of place in this seedy establishment. As silent eyes watched over half empty glasses, following our progress as we bellied up to the bar, I could almost feel their vague resentment at our entrance. If my mother was aware of it, she dismissed their unspoken disapproval at our intrusion into their world and waved over the bartender to order.

Taking our drinks in hand, my mother turned to me and raised hers' in a half salute, and I returned it with a nod. Tasting the alcohol, with its slow, familiar burn as it went down, gradually beginning to ease the fears I had held in all morning. It was over, finally and completely over.

Staring down into my almost empty glass, I sighed as I watched the ice clink down in its newly uncovered state. As if drawn to that soft sound, the bartender returned, "Another?"

With an affirmative nod from both of us, we began round two.

By our third round, a warm camaraderie began to envelop my mother and me as the bar accepted us as one of their own.

One gentleman at the end of the bar had been telling stories to the amusement of those around him since we walked in the door. He wasn't too particular who his audience was, directing them at anyone who happened to be looking his way. Even our entrance had barely caused him to pause between stories. After a while though, our clothes and somber, if sloshed, demeanor attracted his attention.

"So," he drawled, "what brings the two of here to this fine establishment so early in the day?"

"Divorce." my mother answered.

"Ah," giving a vague wave at nothing, "condolences."

"No, no," pointing at me, "my daughter's, not mine."

"I'm going to guess your first then?" Nodding, I agreed. "Don't let it get to you," giving me a wink.

I shrugged, not sure what to say or how to express the equal parts devastation and delight I was experiencing. The alcohol had been slowly chipping away at the hard ball of tension that had settled into my stomach before going into court. And as my anxiety diminished, I felt the first faint stirring of a smile, briefly sharing it with our storyteller.

Moving down to sit closer to us, he and my mother began

exchanging stories, laughing as they did so. Looking over at me on occasion as they swapped stories, and buying each other rounds, they continued to talk. I had little to say, but I enjoyed the feeling of being included while drinking whatever they put before me.

Eventually, the stories shifted over to relationships, generally broken ones, were exchanged between the two of them, with random interjections by those sitting nearby. Happily married people aren't known for early day drinking in a bar, or if they are, they don't stay happily married for long.

Once more smiling at me, the happy storyteller said, "I'll tell you the secret of my happiness.

"Okay," Shrugging my agreement, willing to listen to whatever improbable tale he had to tell.

"I've been married three times," looking me straight in the eye and holding up three fingers above his head, then bring his hand down, slapped the bar for emphasis, "and it was getting damned expensive!"

"I can imagine so," agreeing with him completely.

"So now, whenever I get that marrying urge again, I start looking around the bar for someone completely wrong for me, and I just buy 'em a house!"

Shaking my head and chuckling at his unusual, if improbable, solution.

"No, no..." waving both of his hands in front of me, "it's a perfect solution, I end up in exactly the same position I would have, without all the drama of the in between parts, leaving me the time to sit miserably happy in the bar without interruption."

Giving me a wicked grin, he patted the bar stool beside him, "So, what kind of house would you like, dear lady?"

Shaking my head at his offer, but giving him my first truly genuine laugh in almost three years, I said, "A nice one."

*I hope you've enjoyed this preview of*
***Wine Comes in Six-Packs***
*To purchase a copy, please visit my website*

## A Little About Me

Lisa Orban was born in Galesburg, IL a long time ago on a hot summer day. Due to various shenanigans by the adults in her life, her time in Galesburg was short and the family moved to Quincy, IL where they settled down for a good long stay.

Things were rolling along for a while inside the confines of Quincy, and Lisa rolled with them. There were several divorces, marriages, different schools, friends lost & gained, and many, many moves throughout all this activity. Until, quite unexpectedly, Lisa found herself in foster care at 16, much to her surprise.

Upon turning 18, Lisa ran away as fast as she could to Phoenix, AZ where she lived for 3 years. Got married, had two sons, made many mistakes, and then eventually, ran for her life back to Quincy, where she still lives to this day.

Lisa went to college, earned an Associates in Psychology, raised her 5 kids, got married, and divorced, several times, bought a house and eventually settled down to live the life she always wanted, as the ringleader in a madhouse of anarchy. She now writes books, takes in human strays in need of help, travels, opened a publishing house, and pretty much does whatever she wants, and is quite happy about it.

She became an author in 2015 with her first book, It'll Feel Better when it Quits Hurting, and hasn't stopped since. If you'd like to learn more about Lisa's misadventures in living, visit her website, The Talking Book with Lisa Orban